JESÚS SOTO

IN CONVERSATION WITH / EN CONVERSACIÓN CON

ARIEL JIMÉNEZ

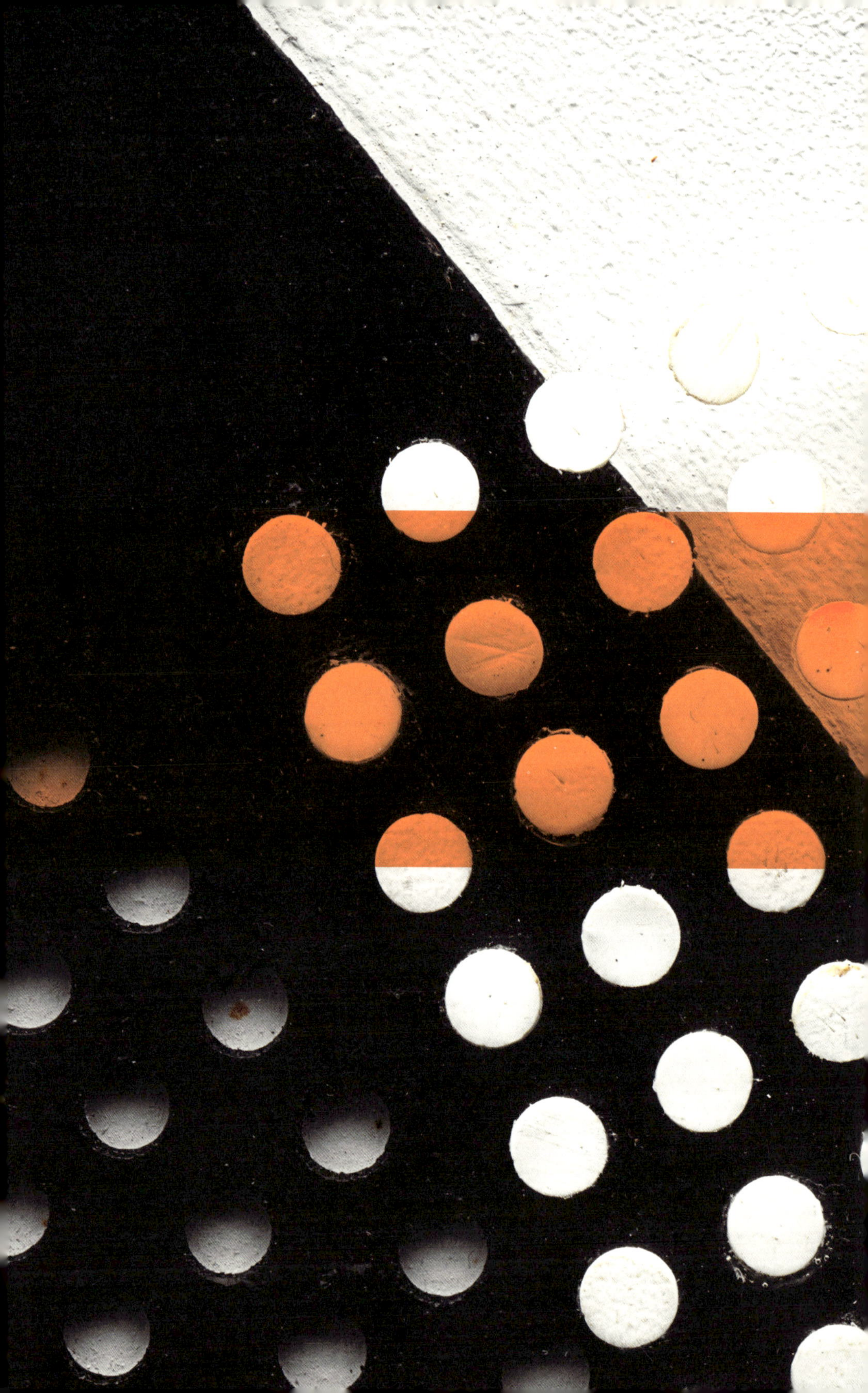

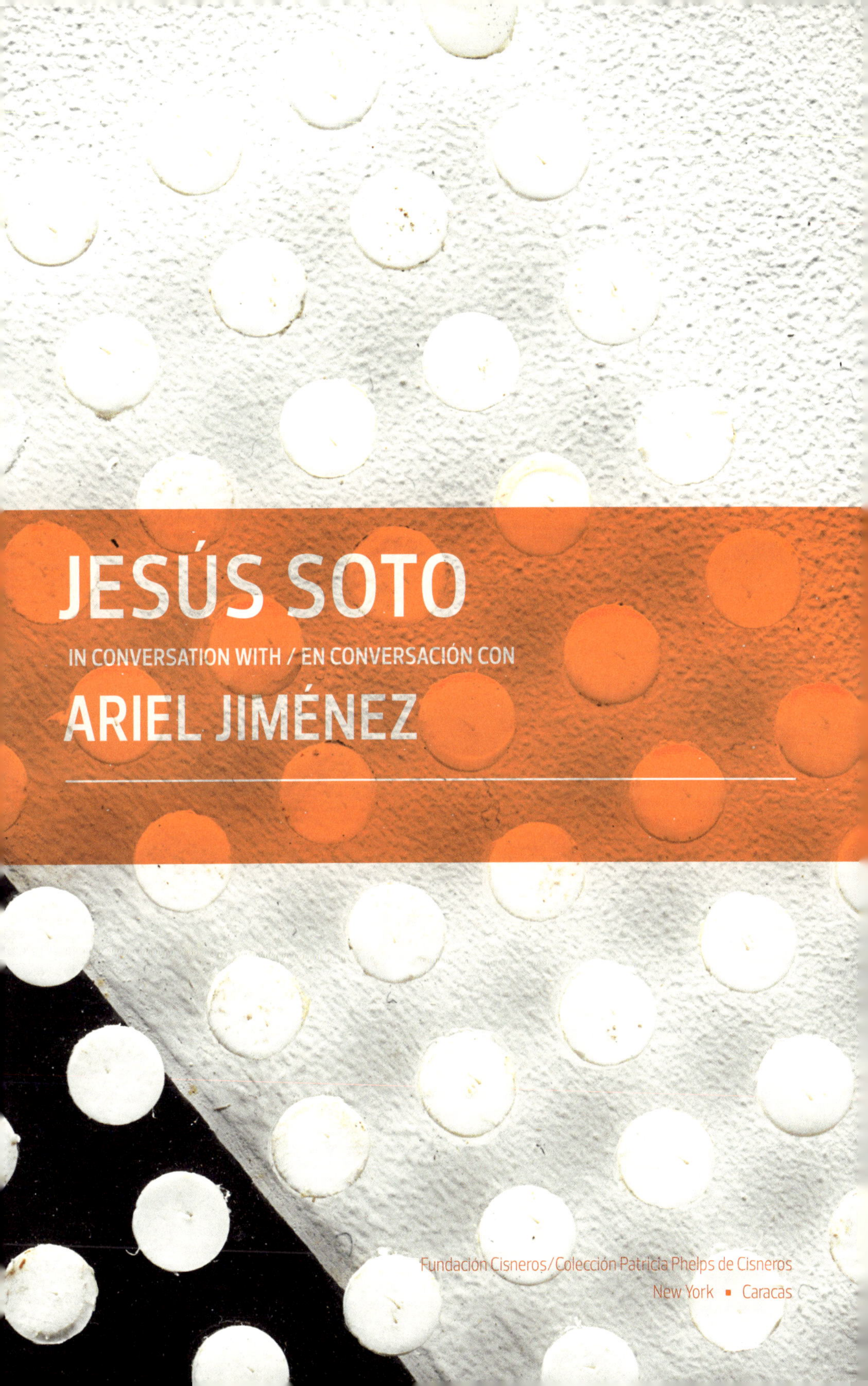

JESÚS SOTO

IN CONVERSATION WITH / EN CONVERSACIÓN CON

ARIEL JIMÉNEZ

Fundación Cisneros/Colección Patricia Phelps de Cisneros
New York ▪ Caracas

Fundación Cisneros
2 East 78th Street
New York, NY 10075
www.coleccioncisneros.org

Distribution in North America:
D.A.P. / Distributed Art Publishers
T 212.627.1999, F 212.627.9484
www.artbook.com

Distribution in Latin America and Spain:
Editorial RM
info@editorialrm.com
www.editorialrm.com

Library of Congress Cataloging-in-Publication Data
Jiménez, Ariel.
Jesús Soto in conversation with Ariel Jiménez = Jesús Soto en conversación con Ariel Jiménez.
p. cm.
In Spanish and English.
Based on the second ed. of "Conversaciones con Jesús Soto" by Ariel Jiménez published in 2005.
ISBN 978-0-9823544-6-9
1. Soto, Jesús Rafael, 1923–2005—Interviews. 2. Artists—Venezuela—Interviews. I. Soto, Jesús Rafael, 1923–2005. II. Jiménez, Ariel. Conversaciones con Jesús Soto. III. Title. IV. Title: Jesús Soto en conversación con Ariel Jiménez.
N6739.S65A35 2012
709.2--dc23 2011037625

Cover: *Penetrable,* 1990. Temporary installation at [Instalación temporal en el] Museum of Fine Arts Houston, 2005.
Title page: *Desplazamiento de un elemento luminoso* [*Displacement of a Luminous Element*], 1954 (detail).
Contents page: Jesús Soto in his apartment in Paris, 1997. © Ariel Jiménez

Series editor: Gabriel Pérez-Barreiro
Selection of artworks: Ariel Jiménez
Editors: Ileen Kohn Sosa, Donna Wingate [English], María Esther Pino [Spanish]
Translator: Kristina Cordero
Translator French excerpts: Ariel Jiménez
Proofreader: Beth Chapple
Designed by Zach Hooker
Color management by iocolor, Seattle
Produced by Marquand Books, Inc., Seattle
www.marquand.com
Printed and bound in China by C&C Offset Printing Co., Ltd.

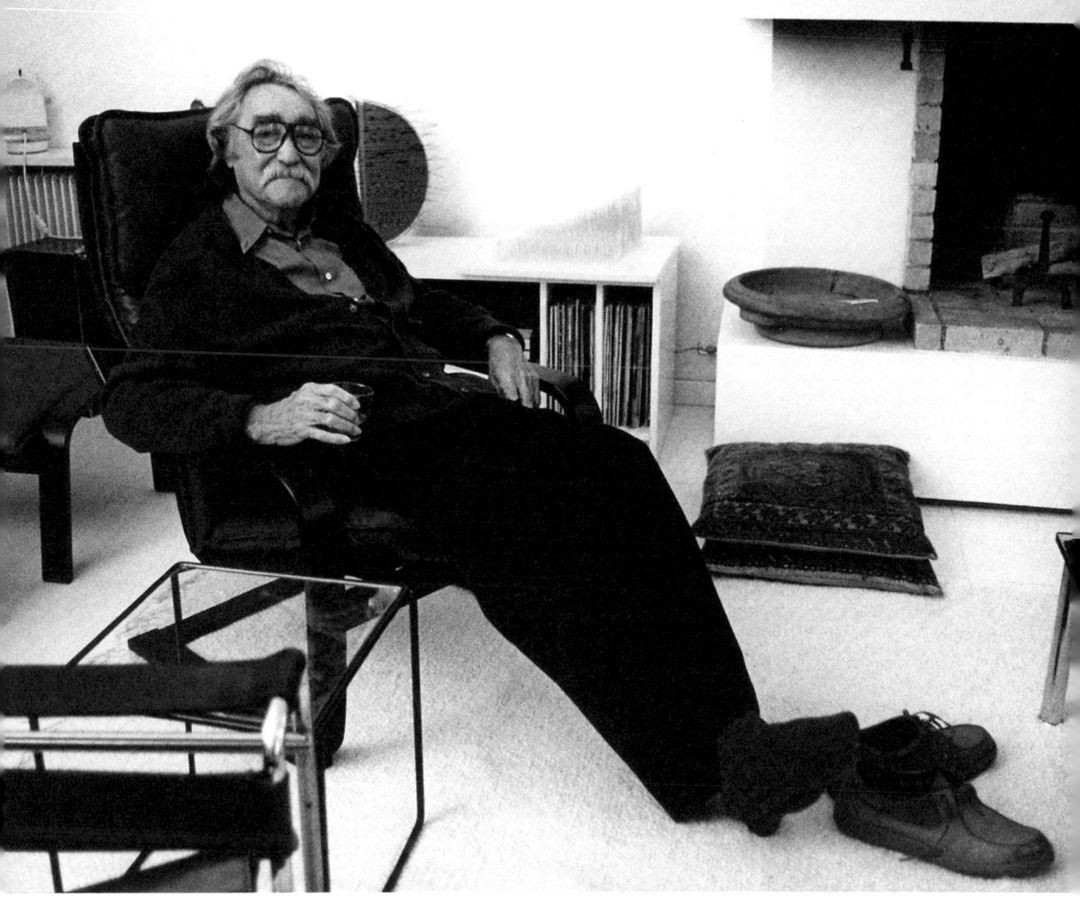

Contents

Índice

INTRODUCTION

In 2001 the Colección Patricia Phelps de Cisneros (CPPC) published the first version of *Conversaciones con Jesús Soto* by Ariel Jiménez in its *cuadernos* series. The book was considerably expanded for the second edition in 2005, which forms the basis for this current volume. The earlier two editions were published under the leadership of Rafael Romero, the first director of the CPPC and today Director Emeritus, and Peter Tinoco, former president of the Fundación Cisneros and today President Emeritus. Much has changed in the decade between the first publication and this one, not least the increasing international understanding of the contributions of Soto and other pioneering Latin American artists to the global history of art. The Colección Patricia Phelps de Cisneros has been both a witness and a co-author of this change, supporting exhibitions, loans, seminars, and publications with the mission of combating the stereotypes that have so long clouded the perception of Latin American art and culture; therefore, we are especially proud to be able to re-issue this important book to new audiences.

Conversaciones con Jesús Soto is a project of particular resonance for the Fundación Cisneros/Colección Patricia Phelps de Cisneros. A close friendship has existed between Soto and the Colección for many decades, and this manuscript provided the inspiration for the Conversaciones/Conversations series that is now the principal research and publication initiative of the CPPC. This re-edition constitutes the fourth volume of the series, after books dedicated to Carlos Cruz-Diez, Tomás Maldonado, and Jac Leirner. Jesús Soto was in many ways an emblematic artist for the CPPC; deeply Venezuelan in his origins from Ciudad Bolívar in the heartland of the country, his restless curiosity led him to Paris, and then back and forth between Venezuela and France, in a transit that made him arguably the most famous and visible Venezuelan artist in the global arena. Soto's lifelong research into form, vibration, and color took him to every continent, where he became for many an icon of an art that could be objective yet suggestive, scientific yet poetic. His example was also vital for many younger Latin American artists who were struggling to escape the folkloric prejudices associated with Latin America as a land of conflict and exoticism. Soto stood for a progressive and forward-looking model of a Latin America that could be in full and complete dialogue with the rest of the world, and his work and practice provided proof that such a thing could be possible. This shared belief was also the reason for the natural empathy between Soto

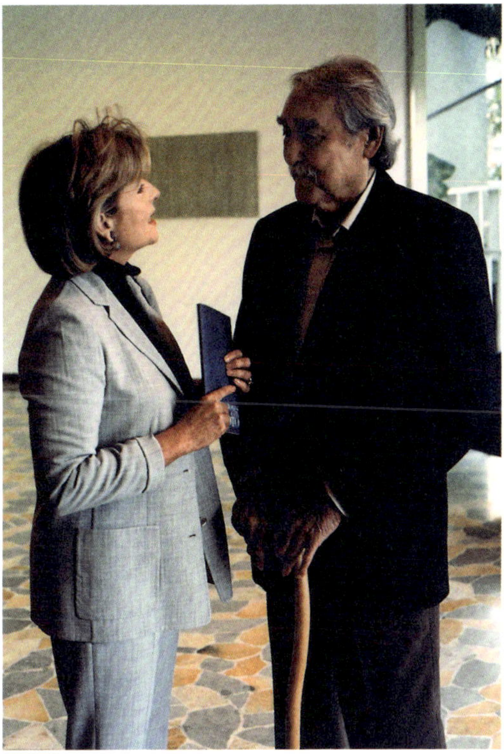

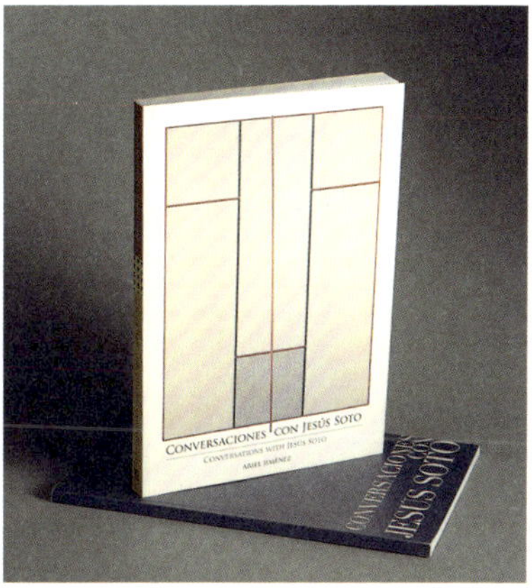

Above: First (2001) and second (2005) editions of *Conversaciones con Jesús Soto.*

At left: Patricia Phelps de Cisneros with Jesús Soto at the launch of *Conversaciones con Jesús Soto* February 6, 2002, in Caracas.

and the Cisneros family and Foundation during his lifetime, and a partnership of deep mutual respect and admiration.

Our thanks are due to Ariel Jiménez, Chief Curator of the CPPC, for his vision in carrying out this vital series of conversations, and his careful editing and assembly of the final manuscript. Jiménez and Soto met in 1977 and in the 1980s Jiménez worked as an assistant in the artist's studio in Paris, gaining an unprecedented perspective into both the philosophical and practical aspects of Soto's work. It was in 1995 that the two formally began these conversations, which continued with great intensity for many decades. Jiménez remains the international authority on Soto, and was the director of the Museo Jesús Soto in Ciudad Bolívar for the last years of Soto's life, a position he held simultaneously with his functions at the CPPC. The production of this edition was overseen by Ileen Kohn Sosa and Donna Wingate, who additionally revised the manuscript and translations with María Esther Pino and Kristina Cordero. We thank the professional team at Marquand Books for their great attention to detail and quality, and we especially thank the Sucesión Jesús Soto for their assistance in this project.

The testimony published here is by far the most complete and detailed account of Soto's work, and has provided scholars and researchers with invaluable information for many years. With growing interest in Soto's work, and in geometric and Kinetic art in general, we hope the publication of this volume will continue to inform and inspire an ever-growing audience for Soto's work and ideas.

Gabriel Pérez-Barreiro

Director, Colección Patricia Phelps de Cisneros

NOTE TO THE READER

For this third edition of *Conversations with Jesús Soto,* we have introduced a number of changes to enhance the reader's experience without altering the essence of the book that was published during the artist's life.

To start, we removed repetitive words, specifically those used inadvertently, which may be replaced without affecting the meaning of the text. Special care was taken to leave intact those terms that are of critical importance to Jesús Soto's way of thinking, as well as the descriptive terms that he used to describe concepts of space, time, matter, and energy.

Secondly, we relocated a question and its answer, placing them in a chronological sequence that was more consistent with the artist's processes. As a result, the positioning of certain images becomes more logical for the reader.

The only other modifications in this edition involve supporting materials, such as images and footnotes. To this end, we have included additional reproductions of Soto's works, and we reconceived the relationship between different works, as well as between the works and the text, with the intention of enriching the reading experience and the reader's understanding of Jesús Soto and his creative processes. Some footnotes were added, others were eliminated, and on occasion longer notes were included as part of the author's commentaries.

All in all, our goal with this edition was to provide those interested in Latin American art with a more complete and coherent version of the Soto conversations, and, therefore, a greater understanding of Jesús Soto's art and creative life.

Ariel Jiménez

JESÚS SOTO

IN CONVERSATION WITH

ARIEL JIMÉNEZ

The most beautiful experience we can have is the mysterious. It is the fundamental emotion that stands at the cradle of true art and true science. Whoever does not know it can no longer wonder, no longer marvel, is as good as dead, and his eyes are dimmed.

It appears to me that the most important function of art and science is to awaken this feeling among the receptive and keep it alive.

Albert Einstein
The World As I See It

GOING TO CARACAS

ARIEL JIMÉNEZ When thinking about what Ciudad Bolívar[1] must have been like in the 1920s—a small regional capital that was still dominated by the landscape, with no museums, no activities that could nurture the intellectual life of a young painter—one cannot help but recall Freud's description of artistic activity as a psychologically mysterious fact. How and through what path did your artistic vocation emerge, as a young man living in an environment where nothing seemed to encourage it? What idea of art could a young man have had in Ciudad Bolívar in the 1920s?

JESÚS SOTO When I started thinking about art and became concerned with creative problems, I really found very little—almost nothing—in Ciudad Bolívar. I knew of a theater that was destroyed during the rule of Juan Vicente Gómez.[2] I managed to see it when I was a child, when I was around four years old, but don't remember when it was destroyed. Interesting shows were produced there, for a center of that size. There were zarzuelas and recitals; there was something of a national and even an international movement there. At that time, Ciudad Bolívar was like a bridge between Europe and the interior of the country, mainly because of the exploitation of a variety of products that are no longer relevant in our market, like heron feathers, sarrapia trees, and rubber, which at the time were quite important. All those things passed through Ciudad Bolívar, the international port where people came to look for those products. I have always thought of Ciudad Bolívar as a kind of small Manaos,[3] where uncommon things happened. Artists would come directly from abroad without passing through Caracas. For them it was easier to arrive in Trinidad and travel by boat down the Orinoco [Fig. 1] than to go to Caracas, which was not connected by road [to Ciudad Bolívar], and by coastal ship it was a fifteen-day trip. I traveled in one of those ships; that's how I got to know all the little coastal towns between Ciudad Bolívar and the port of Maracaibo.[4]

1. Capital of the state of Bolívar, on the banks of the Orinoco River, in southeastern Venezuela.

2. Venezuelan dictator born in the state of Táchira in the Venezuelan Andes (1857–1935). He ruled the country between 1908 and 1935, created the first national road network, and started the industrial exploitation of oil.

3. A city located in the middle of the Amazon forest in northeastern Brazil, Manaos enjoyed considerable economic importance during the nineteenth century mainly as the result of its rubber production. It is primarily known for its famous Teatro Amazonas, where stars such as Caruso and Sarah Bernhardt performed.

4. Capital of the state of Zulia, at the northwestern tip of Venezuela, located on the shores of the lake of the same name.

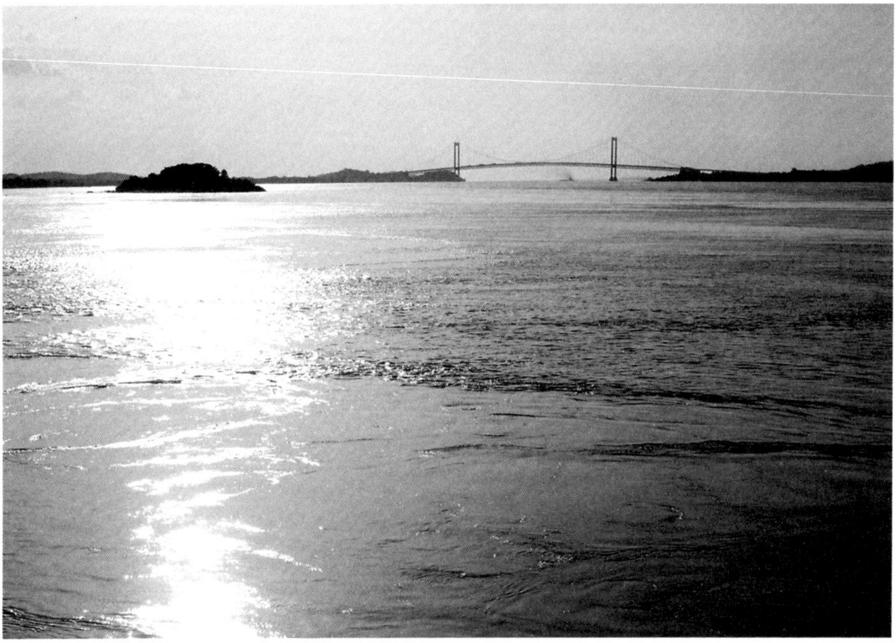

Fig. 1. Bridge over the Orinoco River, Ciudad Bolívar.

AJ Something similar happened with regional capitals like Puerto Cabello[5] and Maracaibo, which communicated with other countries somewhat independently from the Venezuelan capital.

JS They were regional centers that were quite independent of Caracas. In fact, young people from Ciudad Bolívar who couldn't study in Europe didn't go to Caracas; they would study at private schools in Trinidad. Many people studied there, until the roads were built between Caracas and Ciudad Bolívar . . .

Soto remembered the construction of the roads during the Gómez regime, which offered the possibility of sustained contact with the capital city for the first time.

That occurred after World War I. I was very young. An aunt of mine who lived with a military officer assigned to the garrison that oversaw the road construction took me to spend around fifteen days with her. That was how I was able

5. The most important port on the Venezuelan coast, because of the volume of cargo it processes and because it is the gateway to the country's north-central industrial zone. The port and the city of the same name are located on the gulf that is known as the *Golfo Triste*.

to visit the inmates at night. They allowed me because I was a child, and also because I was staying at the home of one of the bosses. There was a constable who slept there and took care of the inmates, and I wanted to meet him so the inmates showed him to me. I am talking about a place called La Canoa, located between El Tigre and Ciudad Bolívar. I later learned that another group of inmates was at work near Valle de la Pascua, in Palenque.[6]

AJ Without a doubt, your childhood memories are more intimately linked to the simple experiences of a child in the rural environment of Ciudad Bolívar than to those of a culturally rich life. That privileged interaction with nature, which Alejandro Otero[7] described as "contact with the elemental reality of the world,"[8] would lend you a curious kind of intensity, as did the limited reading that was then expanding your intellectual horizons.

JS One of the experiences that I recall most enthusiastically did not occur in Ciudad Bolívar, but at a house my aunt owned in the countryside, where I sometimes spent my vacations and where I lived for some time. While at my cousins' house, I had to work just as they all did. Everyone was assigned a job, and they made me be a messenger. Riding a donkey, I had to go from house to house, and I remember the awe I felt as I saw the vibration of the air through the reverberation of the sun upon the earth. It was something I never got tired of seeing, that vibrating mass floating in space and shining over the roads.

I also cannot forget the visual hallucinations I had once while I was ill; that happened at home. I had a very high fever—perhaps yellow fever, I don't know. All I know is that it made me perceive very strange things that were fascinating and gave me great pleasure—so much pleasure, in fact, that I didn't want to get better, because I wanted to keep seeing them. In these visions, I would be observing someone who would suddenly shrink all the way down to a tiny, luminous point. Then the point would grow back, and the original image was restored. I remember this as clearly as if it happened today.

6. The forced servitude of political prisoners was one of the cruelest practices of the Gómez dictatorship. Political prisoners were ordered to work, along with other inmates, on the construction of public works projects, specifically the network of national roadways for which construction began during the Gómez administration.

7. Alejandro Otero (1921–90). Venezuelan visual artist from the state of Bolívar. The progenitor of abstract painting in Venezuela and a founding member of the group known as "Los Disidentes" and its eponymous magazine, which was edited in Paris in 1950 by young Venezuelan artists and intellectuals. Major works include the series *Cafeteras* [*Coffeepots*] 1947–51; the *Coloritmos* [*Colorhythms*], 1955–60; and his civic sculptures, 1968–90.

8. Cited in Alexander López's chronology for the catalogue accompanying the exhibition *Alejandro Otero* at the Museo de Arte Contemporáneo de Caracas, 1985, 12.

Another experience I have never forgotten is the incredible skill of the Indians who fished with bow and arrow in the Orinoco. They didn't aim right at the fish, in a straight line; instead, they would shoot their arrows into the air, reaching the fish only after the arrow soared through the air in a curve. I found it incredible that they could hit their targets that way. Many other experiences like these would stay with me for the rest of my life, and of course, reading the few books I could find in Ciudad Bolívar also gave me some of my happiest childhood memories.

I specifically remember some Japanese stories that came from Chile. One tale was about a man who had been told that he would find the philosopher's stone on a beach, and that everything he touched with it would turn to gold. The man immediately started collecting all the stones he could find on the beach (there were thousands) and he would touch them with his iron ring. He did this with countless little stones, to no avail. Little by little his search began to lose momentum, until he practically gave up altogether, and when he did look he did it very automatically, surely convinced that he wouldn't find the stone. Then, one morning he got up and saw that his ring was made of gold, and understood that it had clearly been transformed by one of the stones he had collected and immediately thrown away, unwittingly. This was a story that affected me deeply because the man had found the philosopher's stone, but habit had prevented him from realizing it. He couldn't recognize it. The metamorphosis he had been waiting for had occurred by surprise, and he hadn't been able to see it.

Soto didn't want to miss the occasion of his own metamorphosis . . .

Another story was about a fisherman who, after diving into the sea one day, emerged to find himself facing a most incredible spectacle. His town had completely disappeared; nobody lived there anymore and the desolation of the place, the aging of the piled stones seemed to indicate that outside the water (where he thought he had been for just a few seconds), hundreds or perhaps thousands of years had gone by. The image of this man facing two radically different temporal coordinates just drove me wild, and would remain anchored in my memory.

He too, rightfully felt he was living between two radically different time coordinates; between the rich and prestigious recording of history in Europe and the passing of time unrecorded by history of his birthplace.

AJ Listening to these childhood stories—the reverberation of the sun on lonely roads, the hallucinations where people turned into light, the transmutation of matter and time— it is impossible not to think about what your mature work would be, completely devoted to the search for that "immaterial essence" of the universe. The theory of relativity, modern science, would then legitimize in the adult the experiences of the child in the timeless, historyless solitude of a rural childhood. But these were not the only readings that left a lasting impression in your mind. Pierre Arnauld, in the Jeu de Paume catalogue,[9] also mentions your experience reading Dante's *Divine Comedy*.

JS That's right, I read it when I was around twelve or thirteen. I climbed up a tree behind my house, alone, so that nobody would bother me or make fun of me. An aunt who had some books loaned it to me. I remember as if it were today, how unfair it seemed that Virgil remained in that sort of limbo, unable to enter Paradise because he hadn't been baptized. Above all, I remember the increasing anxiety I felt as Dante's encounter with God came closer and closer. My anxiety was very strange, very strong, and it came from my fear of the image that God might assume. . . .What would he be like? How would Dante see him? . . . The possibility of God having a figure, that he could resemble Michelangelo's bearded God, that threatening God who says, "You must do this because I feel like it," anguished me so deeply that even today, seventy years later, I remember it with absolute clarity. I also remember the great relief I experienced when I discovered that God was only light (in other words, energy), and that he had neither form nor a material body. That was a great relief. . . . Of course, my level of culture was extremely poor, but Dante wrote it so that humble people could understand it . . . and I understood it as a peasant would understand it.

Whenever Soto mentioned light, he hastened to specify that it was also energy. This is because as an adult, he would superimpose two possible interpretations: the religious one, derived from his childhood reading of Dante, in which light somehow manifests an ideal image of God, its purest sensible expression; and the scientific one, in which light is just an expression of energy, the source and the beginning of everything that exists. In both cases, light would become an explanatory and even legitimizing principle. Though he was not a religious man, both circumstances ascribe a transcendent value to light. Capturing it, somehow producing it through painting, and achieving its very real appearance in his work

9. Cited in the catalogue of the solo exhibition of Jesús Soto's work organized by the Galerie Nationale du Jeu de Paume, Paris, 1997, 35n.

would be, for the adult Soto, a visual goal and a double source of legitimacy, both metaphysical (the word religious bothers him) and historical.

AJ Your immediate concern was, nevertheless, painting: the possibility of giving and the need to give a visible shape to things, though your possibilities seemed dramatically limited from the technical perspective. What were your first contacts with the world of images, and what notion of painting could you have had then?

JS On the walls of my house I had some reproductions of Millet to look at, like *The Angelus* or one of those couples against the setting sun. There was even one of Murillo's Virgins. In Ciudad Bolívar not many people were interested in this type of thing, but in books I was able to see reproductions from the Renaissance as well as the work of the historical painters of Venezuela, which interested me quite a bit: Arturo Michelena,[10] Martín Tovar y Tovar,[11] Antonio Herrera Toro,[12] and the most modern of them, Tito Salas.[13] As a child I would copy and study them, but in black and white, you see, because I hadn't mastered the technique required for color. The first time I laid eyes on a palette and an easel was at nineteen, when I went to the Escuela de Artes Plásticas y Artes Aplicadas de Caracas [School of Visual and Applied Arts of Caracas].[14] Until then I had only seen them in magazines and in the movies.

AJ It isn't difficult to imagine the importance of films, that world of moving images, for a young man who aspired to be a painter and whose knowledge was limited to the few reproductions seen at his childhood home and in the books

10. Arturo Michelena (1863–98). Venezuelan academic painter whose work is among the most important collections of iconographic images of the nation's struggle for independence. One of his most notable paintings is *Miranda en la Carraca* [*Miranda in the Carraca Prison*], dated 1896.

11. Martín Tovar y Tovar (1827–1902). Academic painter and author who, along with Arturo Michelena, painted some of the most emblematic images of Venezuela's independence. His most significant work is, without a doubt, *Batalla de Carabobo* [*Battle of Carabobo*], commissioned by the Venezuelan government for the Elliptical Hall of the Federal Palace in 1888.

12. Antonio Herrera Toro (1857–1914). Another great Venezuelan academic painter who helped create the iconography of the country's independence. He worked for Tovar y Tovar on *Batalla de Carabobo,* and was director of the Fine Arts Academy of Caracas. Young artists protested his work as director, and founded the Círculo de Bellas Artes [Fine Arts Circle] in 1912.

13. Tito Salas (1887–1974). Venezuelan painter and creator of the most important and best-known collection of iconographic work on the life of Simón Bolívar. His most notable works include the collections at the Birthplace of Simón Bolívar and the National Pantheon.

14. The school was founded in 1835 as the Escuela de Dibujo [Drawing School] and then called the Academia de Bellas Artes [Fine Arts Academy] during the administration of Guzmán Blanco, before finally being named the Escuela de Artes Plásticas y Artes Aplicadas de Caracas [School of Visual and Applied Arts of Caracas] in 1936.

and magazines from Chile and Spain that made their way to you. From your experiences with the realm of movies you nevertheless remember, specifically, your circumstantial contact with color.

JS In those days, there were three movie theaters in operation: the América, the Mundial, and the Royal, all under the same ownership. When I was about sixteen I learned to draw letters well, so when the man who made the signs retired, I was given the job. I was a kid, and this was a true graduation, to have been given the only paid job in the city for a painter. I worked a lot during the day and at night I painted signs. Sometimes I had to paint them in the morning, because the man wouldn't know which movie was going to be playing, and he wouldn't tell me until 5 a.m. I would have to start them then so that they would be ready by 7 a.m. I developed such technique and speed that I don't understand how I was able to produce so many signs in such a short period of time. They were big signs measuring 1.5 meters. I would paint them and another person would take them away, placing them to the side.

I also had a friend who knew how to shade; at some point I saw some of his drawings that used this technique and asked him to teach me. This was marvelous for me, because it allowed me to achieve chiaroscuro with all its possible subtleties. I also went to the movies frequently, almost every night, taking advantage of the free tickets they gave me. There, I would meet some friends who would be waiting to see what I had done, and that was very stimulating. I kept on drawing and used the movie signs to do more than what they were asking of me. The owner would scold me, saying I wasted a lot of pigment and was wasting my time, too, when he only needed me to paint the signs. But deep down I think he appreciated it. In any event, it was an experience I used to learn how to handle color. We used powder pigments, very beautiful, mixed with a starch paste, and I learned how to mix colors with them. The funny thing is that the colors I used every day when I painted the signs—because they were the cheapest colors—are the same ones that I used and continue to use in my work. Back then I used cobalt blue a lot, perhaps a little bluer than the one I use now. There they called it navy blue. I also worked with black, white, green—that olive green you see in my *Vibraciones* [*Vibrations*]—and yellow, and especially brick red, which was the cheapest of them all. Those were the colors that were available for me to work with every day, and they may have become etched upon my retina. In any event, they are also the ones that work the best in my paintings.

AJ Given the scarcity of images that could nourish the appetite of a young painter, one could presume that the movies you saw in those years had a decisive impact on your later works. And yet you say that no movie had a distinct influence.

JS I retained all those movies as a big mass in which some images stand out for their imaginative rather than their discursive power. I don't remember any one that interested me because of its plot. I liked funny movies a lot. I truly loved Charlie Chaplin, though I had no idea that he was a genius, because he was never presented to me as such, but rather as an amusing man. His miming fascinated me. As a boy I went to the movies almost every day, not only when I worked there but later, too, and I saw many black and white movies—silent, of course—which are the ones I remember the best. There are even some I would like to see again, like the one with the black girl wearing two pigtails on her head. It is winter in the United States, and she is skiing. Suddenly she gets lost in the forest. She is frightened by all the noises she hears: the birds, the owls, and all the sounds of the forest. Then you see her skiing, looking for a way out, when she ends up in a cemetery. She is so frightened that when an owl hoots, she opens her mouth, sticks her tongue out and we see a heart painted on her tongue. . . . I don't know which movie that was or what it was called, but it left such a lasting impression on me that I've remembered it all my life. Things, images like that one, deeply affected me. The truth is, I never thought of movies as art; they were something else, an amusing spectacle, a simple distraction. I came to understand that films could achieve an artistic dimension when I got to Paris, and went to the Cinemathèque. In Venezuela people had already begun to talk about film from an artistic perspective, but deep down, I continued seeing them as an amusing spectacle and nothing more.

AJ Perhaps that's why your evocations of movies are more linked to the art-making experiences you had during your work as a sign maker, and the possibilities they gave you for your profession. The world of films opened a door to painting, both through your concrete experiences with pigment and the contacts it gave you.

JS That's right, because that was how I managed to get a scholarship to study at the School of Visual and Applied Arts of Caracas [Fig. 2]. I was so determined, so enthusiastic, that some of my friends began to talk about my potential until finally someone insisted that I apply for a scholarship. Since I didn't know anyone who could help me get one, some friends convinced the bishop of the city to agree to see me. I went, with all my doubts, to see him. I remember showing him some copies of nudes, and after he saw my work I think he decided that I had some talent. So he gave me a lovely recommendation, which I took to the secretary of state, who was indeed a man with an interest in culture. When I went to see him he said, "I think it's good that you want to study. But we don't have art scholarships. Come back tomorrow or the day after and I'll see what I can do." When I returned he said, "Look, Soto, the only thing I found is a scholarship for teachers, but it's not much, only ninety bolívars." It doesn't matter, I said to him. Give me that and I'll be happy, I'll figure out how to get by. "But first you will have to go see the president of the state (which is what state governors were then called), because he has to endorse it." The president of the state was a humanist, a historian; I always remembered his name though I had no idea how important he was. Many years later I found out who Mario Briceño Iragorry[15] was in Venezuela.

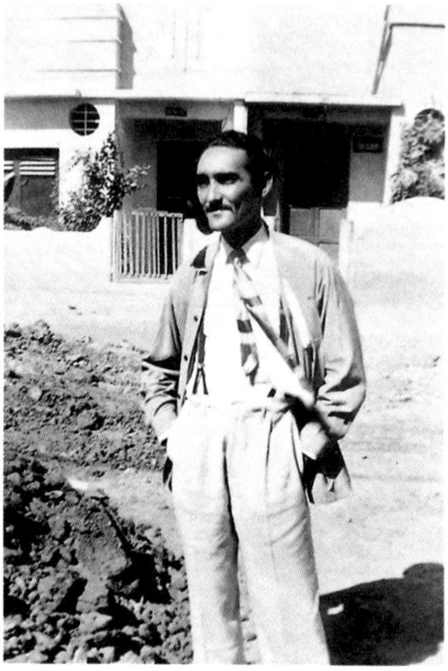

Fig. 2. Jesús Soto as a student in Caracas, c. 1943.

Just like so many other young people of his generation, Soto went to Caracas with the immense hunger to learn that is found among those people who have lived in the extreme cultural void of rural areas—a hunger that eclipses all other appetites, that becomes a sole, inevitable, and pressing need that guides a person's life in one direction, so that every last bit of energy is devoted to satisfying the need to see and understand that thing that, for some unknown reason, has captivated one's attention.

I arrived with my scholarship of ninety bolívars, determined to dedicate myself to art. But since the money wasn't enough I tried to earn a living by making tombstones, which I learned at the school workshops. With that, I made enough money to buy clothes and those basic things one needs. Then I found some cousins who were working as jewelers in Caracas, and they took me into

15. Mario Briceño Iragorry (1897–1958). Venezuelan historian, essayist, lawyer, and diplomat. Member of the Academies of History and Language. Among his many different activities, he was governor of the state of Bolívar from 1943 to 1944.

their house because they saw what a hard time I was having. I stayed with them until I finished my studies at the school. The important thing is that I was able to do it, to finish. During the day I studied at school, and at night I took teacher-training courses.

He arrived in Caracas with the few references he had from Ciudad Bolívar, determined to learn, his eyes wide open.

I was a great admirer of Venezuelan historical painters, and I think I came to Caracas with the intention of following their path, not so much as a historical painter but as a naturalist. All of that went straight out of my head when I first saw a still life by Georges Braque, which made a great impression on me although I didn't understand why. I saw it when I entered the school, probably the day I arrived. Of course, I had already seen reproductions of some modern works in the magazines I could find in Ciudad Bolívar. I also remember a book I won in a storytelling contest during primary school. A Spaniard sent by the Ministry of Education brought some books that were distributed as prizes during the contest, which I won for being a storyteller, and the prize I received was a book with some modern poetry and images, paintings that used a technique similar to that of Sorolla.[16]

AJ No doubt imbued with the Impressionist spirit . . .

JS Yes, though of an Impressionism in which the light was brown, not like French Impressionism, in which the light is silver. I also had the chance to collect some magazines from Chile that sparked my interest in that style of painting, but I wasn't sure of what I wanted to do. So when I went to Caracas, I arrived with the idea of creating paintings inspired by the Venezuelan classics, but also with the flavor that that modern poetry book had awakened in me. Of course, when I started at the School of Visual and Applied Arts of Caracas and saw Braque's still life on the easel, I felt a tremendous impact. I immediately began asking my classmates, particularly the more advanced ones, about the meaning and significance of that work and its creator. First I spoke with Alejandro Otero, who was also from my hometown, and he gave me a good explanation. Then I asked the teachers. . . . At first I was quite satisfied with their explanations, but

16. Joaquín Sorolla (1863–1923). Spanish realist and impressionist painter. His oeuvre captures the light of the Mediterranean and the popular customs of the Spanish people with a particular zest and in an often yellowish-reddish light.

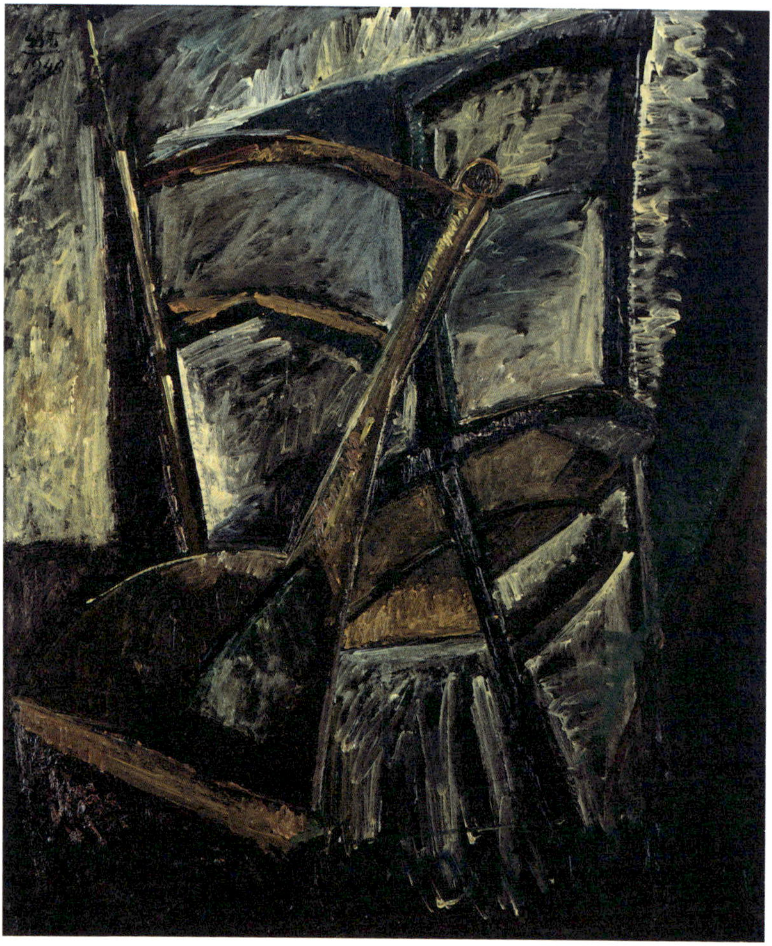

Fig. 3. *Sin título* [*Untitled*], 1948.

I immediately wanted to know more details about Cubism and the whole story of the fourth dimension. And so they told me that first I had to study a lot, that I wouldn't be able to understand it without the background. The important thing was that I wanted to understand it, because after that impact, my problem was to create work that went beyond what was already known [Fig. 3].

AJ For the students at the School, Cubism and the fourth dimension had become one of the main concerns of their intellectual education. Their manifest obscurity—clearly supported by the prestige of science—seemed to sum up the mystery of painting and the modern world that Soto wanted to understand. Was this the experience that led you to take an interest in science?

JS Well, maybe because they didn't give me good explanations and I wanted to know exactly why one painter was more important than another, when the two were similar. That concerned me, and when I arrived in Caracas, I wanted to understand why Cézanne, for example, was more important than other painters who seemed to me to be more effective. Then I understood that, to a certain degree, history itself clarified the evolution of painting through periods and situated artists in their places. That, in my opinion, was a scientific aspect. They immediately started talking to me about the fourth dimension, which undoubtedly sharpened my interest in science.

AJ In any case, this concern with time and with the organization of the painted surface, as you discovered in Cubism, is already evident in the pieces you created during your last years at the school and later on in Maracaibo [Figs. 3–4].

JS Of course, because I immediately understood the problem of time in Cézanne, as I understood it in Impressionism, when they told me that they painted light at different times of day to show how it was constantly changing. In this way, I was gathering a series of small elements about time, movement, and space, which later emerged and helped me understand. I was also interested in many things I saw in the magazines, particularly the Chilean ones, which showed reproductions by artists who painted in the style of Picasso in his Greek period, and I was fascinated by those images. All of this was preparing me to understand modern art. I was also very influenced by the concept of perspective in the Renaissance. The idea of creating a virtual space inside a kind of large cube seemed to me to be a wonderful invention, and when I discovered that in Cubism the Renaissance cube, that monocular perspective, transforms into a space that is multifocal—polyocular so to speak—it was a wonderful revolution for me. So when I encountered the Klee of the cities and the tightrope walker, where every house, every little cube responded to a different vanishing point, I was amazed by the possibility of apprehending that other notion of space.

For Soto, the visual arts became a field where he could search for answers to the unknowns that present themselves to every child who tries to understand time, matter, space, the finite, and the infinite. The works of artists already inscribed in the annals of history were examples of what had already been done and were clues to the path he needed to take. The School allowed him to investigate this world of history as he learned to see and create.

JS I started studying in 1942,[17] and I followed the same method as the older students, like Alejandro Otero. In my opinion, the most important thing was the nonrestrictive attitude of the teachers. They guided without imposing, and if someone had concerns like mine they gave him the freedom to research. When I started a canvas, a landscape for example, I would start by doing it more or less as I saw it, and then I would look for a synthetic way to do it. My landscape teacher, Rafael Ramón González,[18] said, "I'm going to let you do what you want, and you show it to me when you finish." Then we would discuss the work and he would tell me what he thought of it. Sometimes, looking at my landscapes, he would ask, "Don't you see the violets hidden in the shadows, don't you see the variety of tones hidden there? . . ." And I would include the violets and the tones that the teacher said, because he was the teacher, but the truth is I could never see those colors. I didn't understand Impressionism in Venezuela. I couldn't see those ranges of color in the landscape. I only came to understand it when I arrived in France and saw the European light, that silvery light of Monet's that I could verify in the landscape. By the second year I no longer had to wait for the teachers; I would choose any theme and bring it to them when I was done. And so I went to see them around every fifteen days, unless I thought I was creating a painting that was interesting. Then I would bring it to them immediately and they would give me their opinion. They never imposed a way to do things.

By the third or fourth year, we didn't speak with them as student to teacher but as colleagues, painter to painter. . . . This was wonderful for all the inquisitive students, because they didn't have to spend four of five years repeating and copying, learning techniques or problems that would be useless to them later on. However, students who wanted a strictly academic education were able to do that as well. More than a school in the academic sense of the word, it was a large collective workshop, a circle of artists. This was all enriched by a solid intellectual education, taking advantage of the experiences of the teachers who

17. Soto says he received his scholarship thanks to the support of Mario Briceño Iragorry in 1942, but Iragorry's biography states that he was governor of the state of Bolívar between 1943 and 1944. In all likelihood, Soto obtained his scholarship in 1943, certainly no earlier.

18. Rafael Ramón González (1894–1975). Significant Venezuelan landscape artist. He taught landscape art at the School of Visual and Applied Arts of Caracas. His work greatly contributed to making the Ávila Mountain a focal point of the Venezuelan landscape painting.

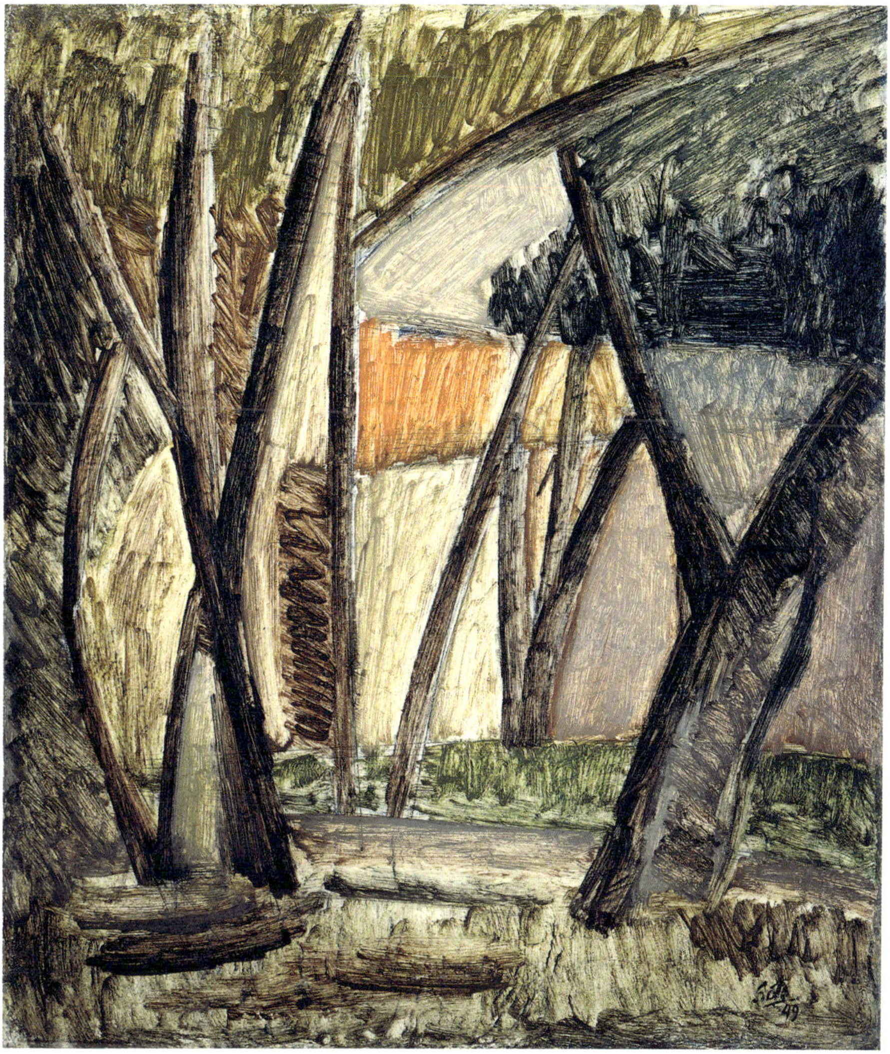

Fig. 4. *Sin título (paisaje)* [*Untitled (Landscape)*], 1949.

were able to travel, and of those who had read a lot, like the director of the school, Antonio Edmundo Monsanto.[19]

AJ Art comes from art; every work has a family tree to which it belongs as if in a family of forms, with its close and distant ancestors, broken branches, and descendants, in some cases. Did any of these have significant bearing on your education?

JS I think they all gave me the best of what they had. I've been talking about landscape, but there was also Marcos Castillo,[20] who taught me a great deal in the field of color. I also learned a lot from an artist who, unfortunately, is poorly remembered, Juan Vicente Fabbiani.[21] While Castillo taught me how to enrich every square centimeter of the canvas through color, Fabbiani taught me the meaning of synthesis, painting without insisting on the details. In that sense the education was quite varied and there was plenty to choose from.

AJ Alejandro Otero used to say that Héctor Poleo's[22] return from Mexico had a tremendous impact on his generation. He gave them a different way to approach landscapes, with all that very fine frottage that he took from Mexican Muralism, in particular that of Diego Rivera. Did this influence you in any way?

JS What really interested me and still continues to interest me about Héctor Poleo is his Surrealist period, although at that time he arrived with his muralist ideas and with works that I admired because they were well executed, but that was not the path I wanted to follow. Maybe it was because of how affected I was by Braque's still life, and the freedom I had sought through what few images I had seen in Ciudad Bolívar . . . something less thematic. I never did a thematic painting.

19. Antonio Edmundo Monsanto (1890–1948). A modest painter of very few works, he was a founding member of the Círculo de Bellas Artes [Fine Arts Circle] and Director of the School of Visual and Applied Arts of Caracas (1936–48). During this period he had a decisive influence upon the education of Venezuela's most important abstract artists.

20. Marcos Castillo (1897–1966). One of the main exponents of the so-called Caracas School, Castillo was considered one of its best colorists. He taught Jesús Soto and most of the abstract artists of the 1950s.

21. Juan Vicente Fabbiani (1910–89). A Venezuelan painter known primarily for his nudes, he taught at the School of Visual and Applied Arts of Caracas. His inclination toward formal synthesis had a significant influence upon the abstract artists of the 1950s.

22. Héctor Poleo (1918–89). Visual artist whose work, at first influenced by Mexican Muralism, left a deep impression upon young artists during the 1940s. During World War II, overwhelmed by the catastrophe, his painting approached Surrealism.

AJ Even so, like many Latin American artists, you had to take part in the discussions that attempted to explore the social function of the artist. Those debates about what was local and what was universal that were implicit in the ideas of Héctor Poleo and that would later become the focus of *Los Disidentes*[23] must have had some influence on your thinking.

JS Without a doubt. The group of Alejandro Otero, Pascual Navarro,[24] and others organized large meetings that the younger generation of students like Carlos Cruz-Diez,[25] Guevara Moreno,[26] and I participated in, and they had some impact upon me but at no point did they ever lead me to believe in the need to subordinate the artist's freedom to political problems. Our great concern was related to the need to decipher Cubism and the complexity of that whole issue of the fourth dimension. We couldn't understand it, but we sensed that it had a transcendent importance. I came to understand it much later, when I threw myself into an investigation of the movement in the 1950s: that was the fourth dimension we were looking for. I believe that time and our individual oeuvres have proven not only that most students decided to go the way of Post-impressionism, but that in Venezuela this path has brought better results than the Americanism influenced by Mexican Muralism.

AJ That has to do with the essential orientation of the country, both then and now: to modernize and leave underdevelopment behind. There are perhaps few countries where "the modern" is as prestigious as it is in Venezuela. And in addition, our pre-Columbian past is not as strong or as present as those of Mexico and Peru. Venezuela lives for the future.

JS Yes, but at that time politicians presented socialism as the only possible future, and in art, Socialist Realism. The political pressure forced people to take that path. Even so, I was never interested in that, and I was certainly never passionate about Russian Communism; I wasn't a believer, and Stalin terrified me.

23. *Los Disidentes* was an art collective and an art magazine, the latter edited in Paris in 1950 by Venezuelan artists and intellectuals such as Alejandro Otero, Mateo Manaure, Narciso Debourg, Perán Erminy, and J. R. Guillent Pérez, among others.

24. Pascual Navarro (1923–85) was a visual artist and founding member of the group *Los Disidentes* and its eponymous magazine, for which he wrote controversial articles about Venezuelan painting.

25. Carlos Cruz-Diez (1923). Venezuelan kinetic artist and classmate of Soto. His mature work focuses on the study of color and the attempt to present it as a physical reality, regardless of all representative or symbolic intent. It is for this reason that his best-known works are called *Fisicromías* [*Physichromies*].

26. Luis Guevara Moreno (1926–2010). Venezuelan painter and founding member of *Los Disidentes*. In the 1950s he created a considerable body of abstract work, which he would later abandon to focus on the human figure. He was part of the Madí movement.

I tried to participate, believe me, because the attraction and the intellectual pressure were very strong. So many intelligent people were involved in it that I thought I was wrong, but I was just never able to feel fully convinced, and I always defended the artist's independence from ideological principles. In Paris I would go to their meetings with my guitar because I wanted to support them, but I always told them that I couldn't do the same with painting, because I didn't understand that path. They, on the other hand, chastised me with unpleasant words, and I would tell them, "If I am a man of the people, whatever I do must come from the people and must be useful to them." But it was impossible, every time I said that they would accuse me of being a traitor to my class [Fig. 5].[27]

These types of things, little by little, turned me off. I would tell myself that perhaps they were right, but I didn't understand them and couldn't follow them. I never accepted the interference of politics in art, in literature or in songs. The image of a compromised artist always disturbed me. It was a way of seeking society's protection, which never happened with abstract art, which has never been protected by anyone. It has been attacked, or in the best of cases, tolerated, but there has never been a political regime or group that has seen it as what ought to be the art of the present or the future. However, (politically) committed art has had and continues to enjoy that protection. This doesn't mean that I criticize this type of situation—everyone has the right to his own attitude toward life. I still believe that art is more important than any kind of proselytizing position or ideological group. Ideologies end up becoming a load of prejudices, whereas the arts are a positive contribution to humanity. And if they don't seem important, they aren't bothering anyone.

AJ One pathetic case of this surrender to political ideologies, and the inevitable disenchantment they ultimately lead to, is that of the Russian artists at the beginning of the twentieth century. They believed that through artistic revolution they were fuelling a movement parallel to that of social revolution, and they naively imagined that the ruling classes would perceive this as such. Art, science, and the organized populace would carry out the great revolution that history demanded. However, they were rejected and shunned, reduced to silence and condemned, that is, if they didn't commit suicide. Today, while

27. It wasn't only great thinkers like Hegel and Marx that imposed the idea of a single history oriented toward a future liberation of humanity: during the first half of the twentieth century, a number of historic events (the Bolshevik revolution, followed by the Chinese and the Cuban Revolution) certainly suggested the possibility that humanity was inexorably heading toward that future, a future that was clearly identified with Communist societies.

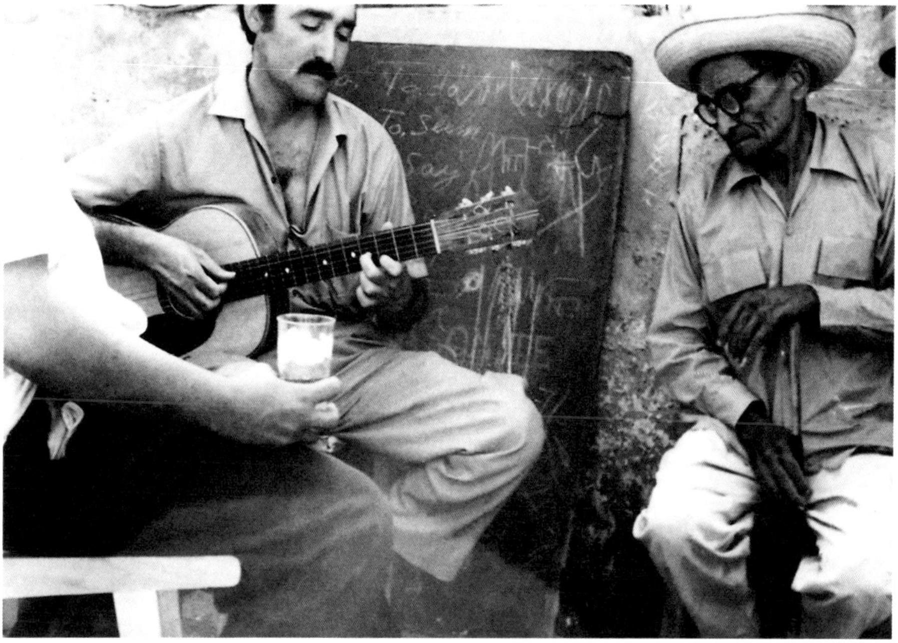

Fig. 5. Jesús Soto playing guitar with his uncle Pedro Soto, Ciudad Bolívar, 1961.

the political system that condemned them has ended as a colossal failure, their works remain among the most beautiful triumphs of the century.

JS You are talking about the most painful case, since the only art that was at the level of the ideals that mobilized Communism from 1917 to 1927 was the art that they created: Malevich, Tatlin, Mayakovsky, and the others. If you wanted to break away from all the historical and social parameters of the bourgeois world, you also had to break away from its artistic ideals. And yet the official art of Communism was the most traditional and conventional in history. What happens is that in any regime, art and science are always more advanced than politics. Politicians, even those of the most elevated hierarchies, never attain the visionary capacity of artists. Imagine what it must have meant for men of conviction, like Malevich, to have to repaint those conventional figures . . . a real tragedy. This proves that we must never put ourselves at the service of a partisan cause, whatever it may be. And if society doesn't consider artistic activity an immediate need, at least it should not condemn artists to ordinary life. Leave the artist alone, because in general he sees beyond what they see.

It remains true that modern artists, even when they were not trying to do anything but find solutions to the pictorial problems of their age, were always very aware of their social responsibility. By creating their art they believed that they were contributing to the creation of a new world order. We may find a clear example of this in Kazimir Malevich, whose totally abstract work was nonetheless thought of as yet one more battle among those being waged at the time against the already anachronistic past of humanity. For this reason he stated that "The October Revolution, destroying the foundations of the old State, has recognized, in part, those who are changing art. . . . Today we have the army of the new principle of economic life and we already have the artistic avant-gardes. The economic life of the new world has helped people advance. The creation of this new art has helped Suprematism to advance from the square."[28] *This was a battle against past forms that was to be waged in the virtual space of the canvas as well as in the collective life, and when Soto was faced with the responsibility of educating young artists in Maracaibo, he responded to the call. In 1947 he finished his studies and went to Maracaibo, where he assumed the position of director of the School of Fine Arts, where he tried to implement a new educational system that was open to the artistic practices of his time.*

JS I tried, of course, but I failed. While I was talking about Picasso, who was my greatest concern at the time, since I didn't know anything more advanced after Cubism, the rest of the teachers and students were interested in *pompier* painters.[29] I insisted that we should study Picasso and his generation, and even got the Ministry of Education to send me some reproductions, but I couldn't get anyone interested in them, so I left. The only people whose interest I managed to spark were two poets, César Rincón and Esnor Rivera. They were studying medicine, and as part of their studies they had to take drawing classes. So they approached the school looking for the teacher who taught that subject, and they saw the more or less Cubist pieces I was doing. It was amazing to them

28. Kazimir Malevich, *De Cézanne au suprématisme.* Lausanne, Switzerland: Ed. L'Age d'homme, 1974, 139–41.

29. Pejorative term used to characterize official and academic French art of the latter half of the nineteenth century. It is believed that the term refers to the similarity between the helmets or bascinets featured in many of these historical and mythological paintings and those used by French firemen. *Pompier* means "fireman" in French.

that this was being done in Venezuela, and they told me that they had read a lot about modern poetry and even about Cubism, and didn't think that in Venezuela there could be any interest in this type of painting. Then a Chilean journalist who settled in Maracaibo came and convinced them that Cubism was the manifestation of a decadent society and what was really important was Socialist Realism.

One essential fact made communication impossible between Soto and his colleagues, teachers, and students at the School of Fine Arts of Maracaibo. While they were interested in art that was already created, for its historical expression, Soto looked at those historical expressions for indications of what forms might emerge from them. For him, art was not a means of expression but a way of thinking, a way of responding to the questions posed by history. And if these questions were different, then the form of the art of his age would have to be different as well.

This conceptual opening "to the possible" is clearly what allowed him to assimilate the fortuitous experience that came about during a conversation in Maracaibo, an oral experience that would become a veritable guideline for his pictorial work: his first contact with the concept of Kazimir Malevich's White on White [Fig. 6].

JS It was a totally chance encounter. I was a friend of Lya Bermúdez[30] and her husband, and we always got together to talk. On one of those occasions a young woman appeared, a cousin of hers who had just returned from a trip to Europe and New York, and I asked her about what she had seen during her trip. She told me she had seen Picasso, which didn't excite her too much, although she thought she saw something in him. "But," she said, "when they showed me a white square with another white square on top, I thought they were going crazy. That's nothing, there's nothing to see there. . . ." She couldn't understand it, but for me it was a true revelation. From that moment on, that work became a source of inspiration: it was the most perfect, purest way to capture light on a canvas. When I got to Paris, I didn't even know the artist's name; that's why I say his contribution was of a conceptual nature. When I saw it for the first time, almost ten years later, the work didn't give me anything more than what I had imagined in Maracaibo. I managed to understand its importance and assimilate its content without having to see it.

30. Lya Bermúdez (1923). Venezuelan sculptor and painter. She was a friend and student of Soto's while he was director of the School of Fine Arts of Maracaibo (1947–50). In 1993 she opened the Centro de Arte de Maracaibo Lya Bermúdez (Lya Bermúdez Art Center of Maracaibo).

Fig. 6. Kazimir Malevich, *Suprematist Composition: White on White,* 1918.

This may be the very best example to show that much of what makes Soto's structures interesting is derived not from the optical illusions they set in motion, but from what they suggest or attempt to make visible: the dimension, as such, of the sublime, of everything that we can conceive but can neither see nor make someone see, to paraphrase Jean-François Lyotard.[31] *In this brief description of Malevich's* White on White, *Soto intuitively discovered a point of contact with his most intimate concerns, particularly with the classic example of the sublime described in the* Divine Comedy: *Dante's encounter with God, a God described precisely as circles of light upon light. Thus, having heard of this work was enough. The desire to go to Paris, that nerve center where Impressionism and Cubism had emerged and where undoubtedly a new art would emerge, became urgent.*

31. Jean-François Lyotard, *Le Postmoderne expliqué aux enfants.* Paris: Editions Galilée, 1986, 27.

JS I was looking for a scholarship, because with what I earned there, it would be impossible to save the money I would need to pay for the trip. That same year I got the scholarship and left for Paris. I went straight to Guevara Moreno's apartment and immediately got in touch with my friends from the School: Alejandro Otero, Pascual Navarro, Mateo Manaure,[32] Carlos González Bogen,[33] and Narciso Debourg.[34] With their help I started to get my life together; I found a small room that I shared with Lira Sosa.[35] Since he spoke French a little better than I did, we managed to get along with the lady who rented us the room and gave us food. I immediately had to start working by playing my guitar because the scholarship from Maracaibo was just enough to cover my housing expenses, and it was only going to last one year. But I got organized quickly, so I was not traumatized by the fact that I would lose the scholarship after a year. When they raised the rent on our small room, we moved into an attic. We found a small restaurant nearby where, incredible as it may seem, you could eat for the sum of a hundred francs of that period. It was full of Spaniards and very poor people. Some time after that, Alejandro Otero found me a small room where I lived for a while. The only problem was the bathroom installation of the apartment above: the drain was right in the middle of the room, and when the toilet got clogged, it would leak water into the middle of my room. Then, thanks to my income as a guitarist and with the help of my guitar teacher, Alexandre Lagoya,[36] I was able to move to a third-floor apartment in the Rue du Temple. There I got my life together; I married Hélène in 1952, and my children were born.[37]

AJ Your entire life was organized around the demands of painting. Besides the contact you had with your Venezuelan friends, in what directions were your interests oriented within the French cultural environment?

32. Mateo Manaure (1926). Venezuelan visual artist born in Uracoa in the state of Monagas. Founding member of the group *Los Disidentes* in 1950. In 1952 he participated in the art integration project led by architect Carlos Raúl Villanueva at the Universidad Central de Venezuela. In 1960, he abandoned abstract painting and returned to more nationalist themes.

33. Carlos González Bogen (1920–92). Venezuelan sculptor and painter. Founding member of *Los Disidentes.* During the 1950s he did a great deal of abstract work, which he then abandoned in 1966 to focus on themes with political content.

34. Narciso Debourg (1925). Venezuelan visual artist. Founding member of *Los Disidentes.* Since then he has cultivated a significant though not abundant oeuvre of abstract-geometric work.

35. José Lira Sosa (1930–95). Venezuelan Surrealist poet from the state of Monagas.

36. Alexandre Lagoya (1929–99). French guitarist. In 1950 he and his wife, guitarist Ida Presti, formed the Presti-Lagoya duet.

37. On April 5, 1952, Soto married Hélène de Robert, with whom he would have four children: Isabelle, Christophe, Anne, and Florence.

JS The first thing I did was ask my friends about the artistic activity of the city: the galleries they went to, the museums they knew, etc. I immediately became acquainted with the four or five galleries that exhibited the most interesting things, among them the Galerie Denise René.[38] With the same objective I went to the Musée d'Art Moderne de la Ville de Paris [Modern Art Museum of the City of Paris], but nothing was going on there, it was very mediocre. This was 1950, when I arrived in Paris. At the beginning of the following year Fernando Rísquez[39] and I went to Holland, where I finally saw Mondrian, who I knew only from reproductions, even though it had been the starting point for my first abstract experiences.

AJ For the majority of artists who experienced it, the transition toward abstraction involved a gradual pictorial process. This was true in the case of Kandinsky, Mondrian, and Theo van Doesburg at the turn of the century, and also of Otero in the late 1940s, starting with his *Cafeteras* [*Coffeepots*].[40] However, for you this process unfolded intellectually; in other words, not buttressed by practice, and it occurred over the course of a few months.

JS The thing is, I knew abstraction existed (don't forget, Otero exhibited his *Cafeteras* in Caracas before my trip to Paris), but I didn't know how one arrived at it. I was looking for abstraction, and my thinking was right, except it was thinking from 1910 to 1915, which meant extracting abstraction from Cubism, not inventing an abstraction. I wanted to eliminate the elements to find the true meaning of painting. Of course, I was reading a lot, because my quest was to find what had happened after Cubism. Aimée Battistini[41] helped me greatly in this. Among other things she showed me reflections on abstraction, Mondrian and then Malevich, whom I knew through the magazine *Art d'Aujourd'hui*. I wondered why and how these artists had reached that point. That's how I discovered

38. Important gallery founded in Paris by Denise René in 1945. It was one of the main spaces for abstract and Kinetic art in the 1950s, 1960s, and 1970s in France. In 1955, the first Kinetic art exhibition, *Le Mouvement*, was held there, featuring works by Soto, Yaacov Agam, Víctor Vasarely, Alexander Calder, Jean Tinguely, Marcel Duchamp, and Paul Bury, among others. In 1957, the gallery held the first exhibition of Mondrian in France.

39. Fernando Rísquez (1923). Important Venezuelan psychiatrist and president of the Liga Midicorum. Author of *Homeopatía y psiquiatría* [*Homeopathy and Psychiatry*], among other works.

40. *Las Cafeteras* [*Coffeepots*] was a pictorial series that Alejandro Otero created in Paris from 1947 to 1951. When it was exhibited at the Museo de Bellas Artes de Caracas in 1949, it caused a controversy. *Cafeteras* is a collection of works in which the artist slowly moved from representative painting to abstraction. It was the first manifestation of abstraction in Venezuela.

41. Aimée Battistini (1916–89). Venezuelan visual artist from Ciudad Bolívar, of Corsican origins. Living in Paris since 1928, she introduced the young Venezuelan founders of *Los Disidentes* to abstraction. Her support was also important with regard to introducing Soto to the world of abstraction.

Mondrian's trees and cathedrals, and then understood their evolution toward abstraction. That was when I told myself that, from that point forward, I had to go in that direction. Just as they had reached abstraction through Cubism, I had to start from abstraction in order to move forward. It was also clear to me that what I was doing at that time was not important, because that investigation had already been resolved. My problem was how to go beyond it. . . .

> *Otero also knew abstraction and nevertheless arrived at it gradually, following and experiencing for himself the process others had experienced before him, demonstrating through his practice the impossibility of any voluntary gesture. Soto, on the other hand, sought to detect the most advanced state of abstraction—for him the most significant movement of the twentieth century—in order to throw himself into the adventure of creating a body of work that could continue the tradition and move it forward. A linear concept of history guided his thought.*

From there, I put myself through a very conscious study discipline. Coming from an education in drawing, I forced myself to totally abandon representative drawing. It was like eating chickens with the feathers to quell the urge to eat them. Then I began studying the dilemma of abstraction, starting with the artist who, in my opinion, had gone the farthest down that path: Piet Mondrian [Fig. 7].[42] The first thing I tried was to make a dynamic situation out of his compositions, to take them out of their two-dimensionality. I understood that Mondrian had problems with two-dimensionality in the crossing of verticals and horizontals, where vibration occurred. So I told myself that if he had those types of problems, the path could not insist on two-dimensionality and I would have to take it to another dimension.

It was a relatively quick process. I started by making it dynamic with diagonals and curved lines, always on the plane [Fig. 8]. Later I realized, when I encountered the *Boogie-Woogie* paintings, that he had already tried to make them dynamic, to depart from two-dimensionality. When I discovered this, "the Mondrian problem" ceased to exist for me and another process started, this time through music and other artists, like László Moholy-Nagy.[43] He had

42. Jesús Soto and his colleagues attended courses and lectures at the *Atelier d'Art Abstrait,* created in Paris by Jean Dewasne and Edgar Pillet in 1950. The end-of-the-year program announced several lectures on Mondrian and Neoplasticism. The impact of these lectures must have been considerable, because between late 1950 and early 1951, both Otero and Soto went to Holland in search of the work of Piet Mondrian.

43. László Moholy-Nagy (1895–1946). Artist of Hungarian origins and author of a complex and varied body of work as a painter, sculptor, photographer, filmmaker, set designer, and graphic designer. Professor and theorist of the Bauhaus. His book *Vision in Motion,* published posthumously in 1947, had a great impact on Soto's work when the artist read it in 1953.

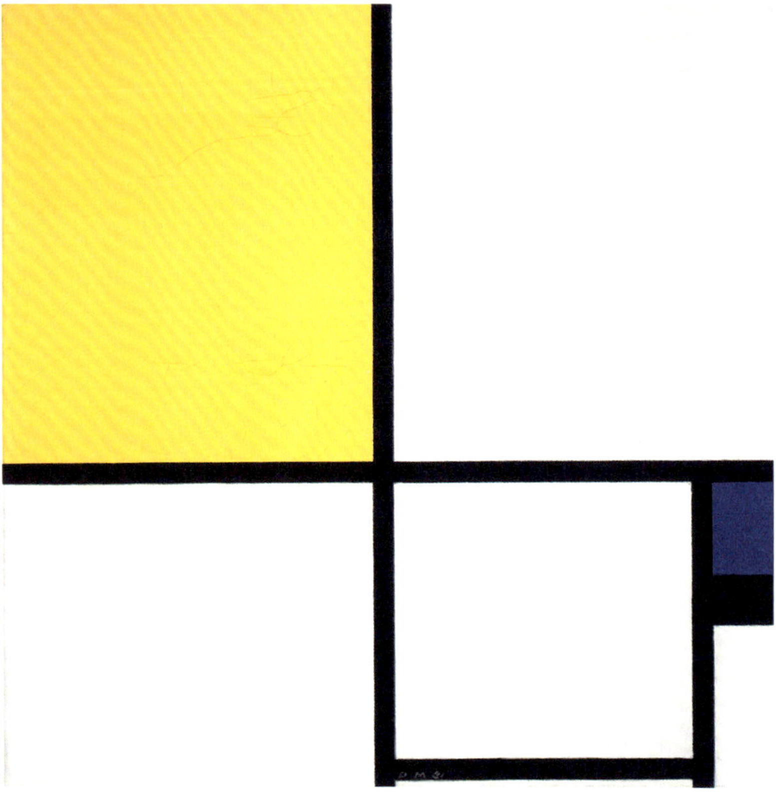

Fig. 7. Piet Mondrian, *Composition No. II, with Yellow and Blue,* 1931.

written an important book on movement, but it was in English, so I had to read it with a friend who translated it for me; every night we read a part of the book. That was how I came to understand what Moholy-Nagy was looking for in the idea of movement. After the series in which I attempted to make Mondrian dynamic, I made a series of works based on non-drawing concepts, like repetition and progression. I told myself that I could no longer continue to draw impulsively, or with that intuitive freedom of traditional drawing; I thought I had to find a way to work that opposed so-called sensitivity, that I had to change the script, and I found this in repetitive elements. One of the first works I did was a yellow repetition, *Repetición óptica nº 2* [*Optical Repetition No. 2*], of 1951 [Fig. 9]. I made several *Repeticiones*, but almost all of them were lost. This is one of the few that survived. It is a structure comprised of the repetition of diagonals that I confronted with verticals. Right away I did another one that interested me a lot more, because it was unbalanced. I remember that at the time Dr. Rísquez would come by my house a lot, and he would tell me that

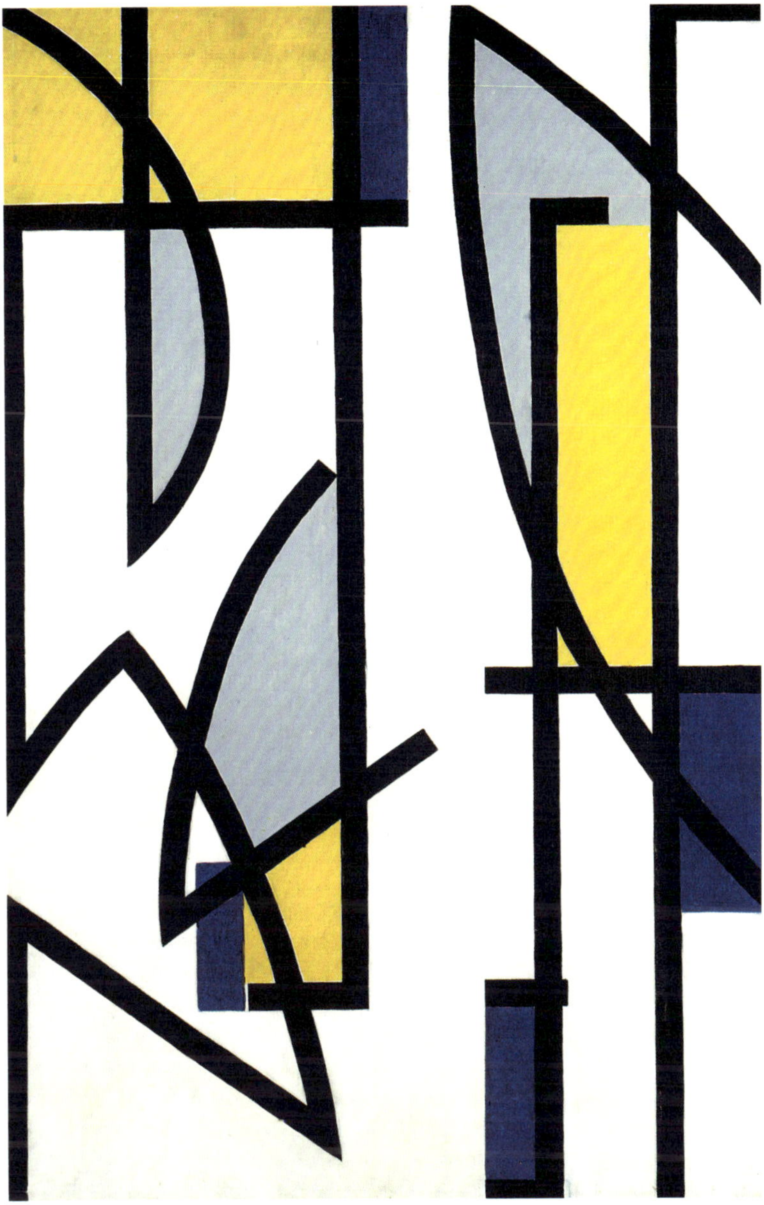

Fig. 8. *Composición dinámica* [*Dynamic Composition*], 1950–51.

that work suggested an ascending noise, something like the French "rr." That's why we called it "the work of the rrs," because it produced a sensation that was both visual and aural.[44]

The reflections of modern artists on the limitations of painting as a medium for representation evolved simultaneously with a growing interest in its inventive possibilities as well as its capacity to suggest realities that exist beyond the senses. To suggest the audible through painting, an art of vision, is one of these attempts to overcome its limitations.

I was searching for a vibratory state through repetition. I was interested in the problem of vibration and the study of light, which fascinated me in Velázquez, and that the Impressionists, whom I have always respected, studied very consciously. That's why when I went to Holland, what surprised me—besides Mondrian, of course—was the work of Vincent van Gogh and Johannes Vermeer. Van Gogh showed me that the darkness of his tones had nothing to do with being Dutch, and Vermeer surprised me with his eerie ability to express light, as if he had lived in the tropics, in a totally different place.

I specifically remember a landscape in which he depicted the city of Delft, a canvas I always remember along with *Las Meninas* and the great works that left their mark on me. It was almost luminous stained glass, with a luminosity no one else had achieved. Seurat tried it later on, and through other means, but didn't achieve it. This made me understand that whoever is interested in light paints it anywhere, even if he doesn't live in the tropics . . . and in the case of Armando Reverón[45] this is very clear. He painted it from memory. He didn't paint it because he lived in Venezuela but because he was interested in it, and he did it as Vermeer would have done it in Holland.

44. Soto is probably referring to *Repetición y progresión* [*Repetition and Progression*], of 1951.

45. Armando Reverón (1889–1954). One of the principal artists of the so-called Caracas School, and without a doubt the most potent and original Venezuelan landscape artist of the first half of the twentieth century. Works from his "white" and "sepia" periods (to use Alfredo Boulton's categorization) are among the most outstanding works of modern Latin American art.

Here we come across one of Soto's contradictions, which says a great deal about the conflicts that identify countless Latin American artists when they think about their historic reality. When he tried to ponder the light in Reverón's work, Soto believed there was no connection between the artist's work and the light of his tropical environment. It bothered him to think that Reverón had been able to paint the light of Venezuela. For him, Reverón only painted an idea of light, a universal concept, and he did this "as Vermeer would have done it in Holland." However, when he thought about Impressionism, Soto stated that he couldn't understand it in Venezuela because in the Venezuelan landscape he could not see the ranges of colors that he saw in Monet's works. He only understood it, he said, when he traveled to France and saw for himself that the silvery quality of the light in Monet was indeed that of the French landscape. Now, if Monet painted the light of France and made a universal work out of it, why couldn't a painter like Reverón do the same with the light of the tropics?

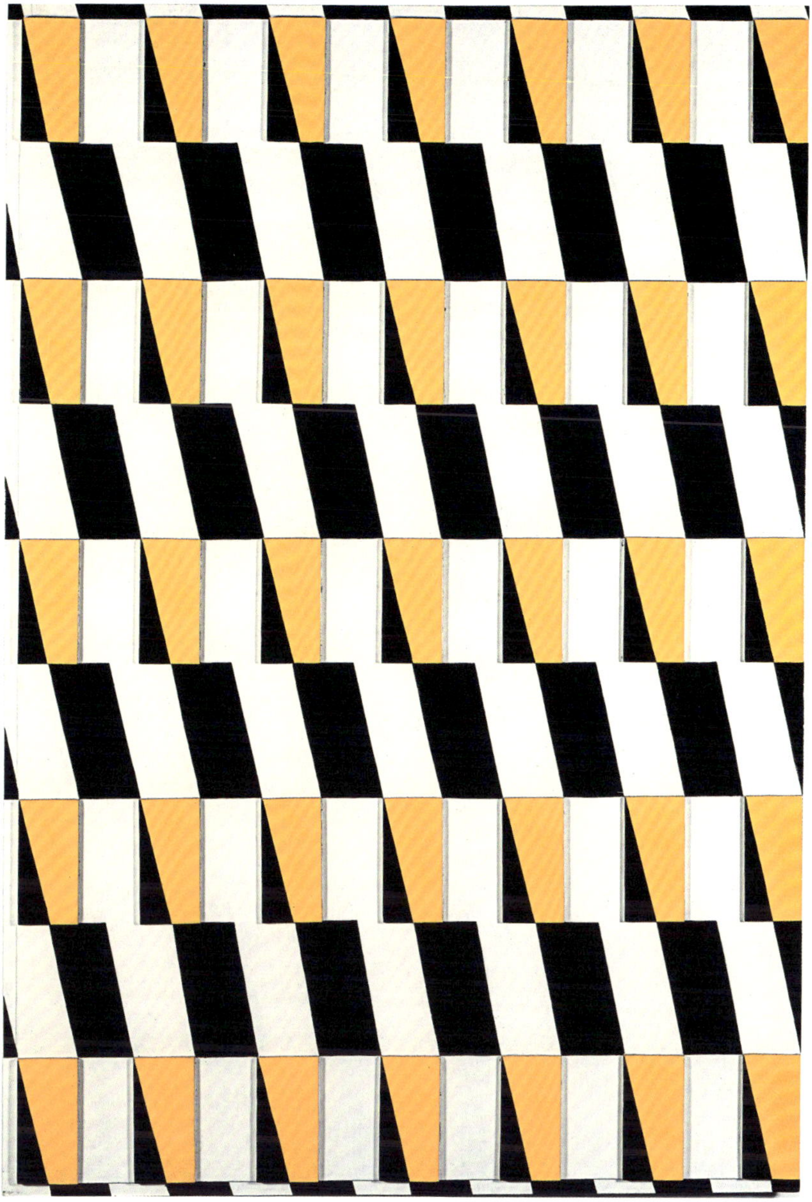

Fig. 9. *Repetición óptica N° 2* [*Optical Repetition No. 2*], 1951.

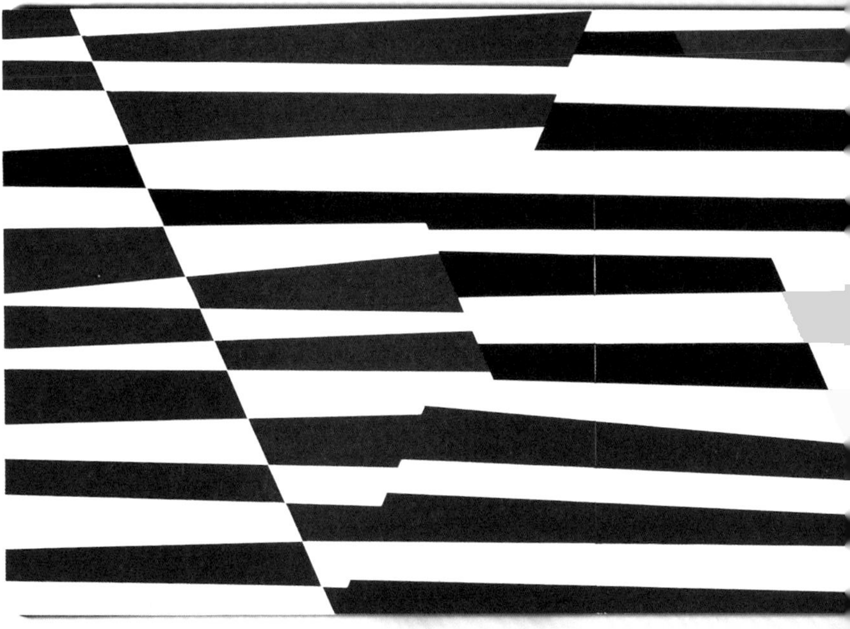

Fig. 10. *Muro óptico* [*Optical Wall*], 1951.

At that time, as I was saying, while I was interested in vibratory states, I was trying to break away from the essential codes of figurative art; that's why I wanted to do away with the notions of composition and balance, two of the great classical codes of representational painting. Among the things I tried to do are those first *Repeticiones* I mentioned, where the concept of composition no longer exists because it is an order that can be repeated ad infinitum, and where every segment is equal to the whole. The work was just the fragment of an infinite reality.

AJ That notion of the work as a fragment of the universe comes, precisely, from the Impressionists, where the painting seems to be composed through the viewfinder of a camera. No longer is it the creation of a self-sufficient totality, that order in which the composition, the shape of a body or a tree in the landscape, jibes with the discourse or theme being addressed. On the contrary, not only did the Impressionists paint fragments of space, they attempted to capture a fleeting moment in specific atmospheric conditions, with specific luminosity and color. This explains, in part, those human figures that are cut off at the edges, clearly indicating their continuity outside the boundaries of the canvas.

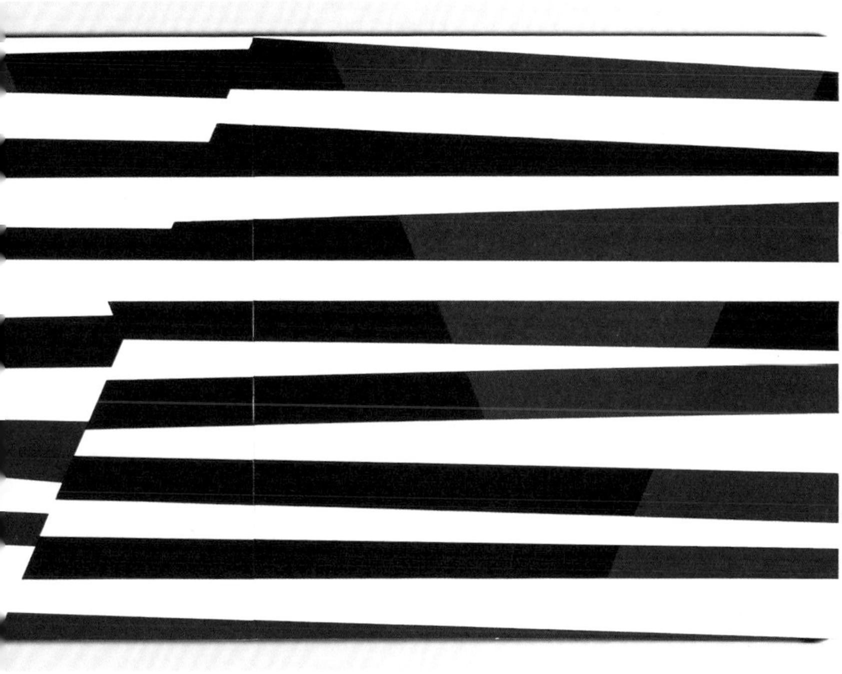

JS Of course, and that's why I love the Impressionists, because they cared primarily about light and its vibration as the essence of everything, and not about the object, the form, and the theme, as the academic artists did. In parallel with these *Repeticiones*, or perhaps even a bit earlier, I made a series of works where I looked for a structure similar to those I had observed in Cézanne while I was a student at the School of Visual and Applied Arts of Caracas. I don't know what his intention was in creating those works, but I could see that in some landscapes he started on the left with great density, and slowly liquefied everything toward the right. This method of proceeding stayed with me and I used it in a panel entitled *Muro óptico* [*Optical Wall*], from 1951 [Fig. 10].

AJ It was a search for the vibration of the Impressionists through Cézanne's compositional structure.

JS Not exactly through his compositional structure. In my paintings from that time there was no composition in the classic sense of the word, it was more like a progression of pictorial density from left to right.

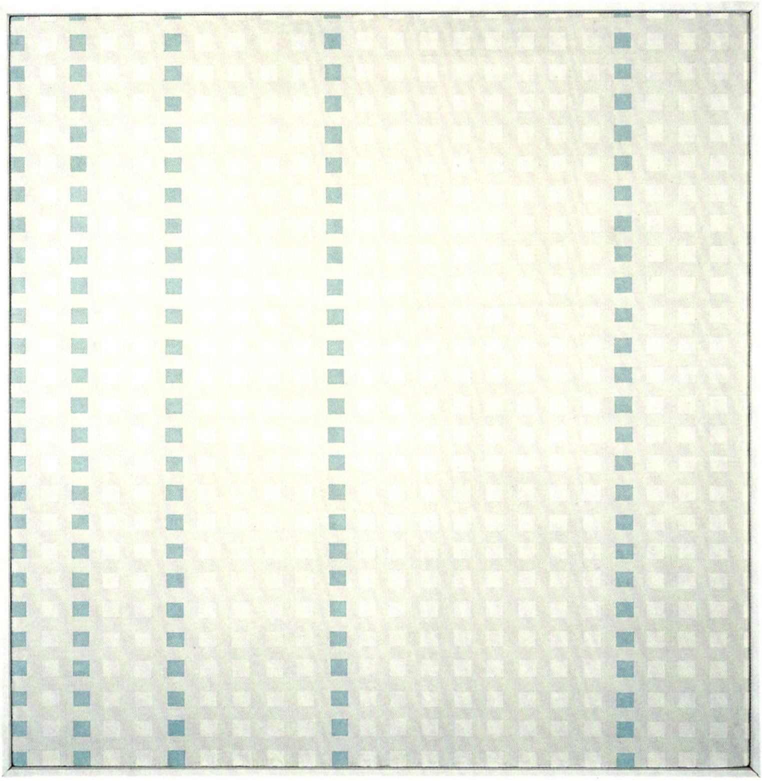

Fig. 11. *Sin título (Progresión)* [*Untitled (Progression)*], 1952.

AJ In any case, what matters is that this progression of density already suggested a new element: time, something that you formalized in the several *Progresiones* [*Progressions*] and *Repeticiones* you made in 1951 and 1952 [Fig. 11]. Immediately after these *Repeticiones* you made a work called *Rotación* [*Rotation*], in 1952, [Fig. 12] which seems to me to be key, not only because it was the beginning of your serial pieces that emerged directly from music, but also because it expressed, for the first time, a quality that would characterize your later work: the presence of a fixed element and a mobile element.

JS The idea was to make a moving square. . . . But how could I do it? How could I suggest the sensation of movement? First I thought of making a transparent square—as I had on other occasions—and turning it into something more abstract, because what interested me was the idea of the square. Then I decided to do it in white against an almost white background. In this way, besides using

Malevich's lesson, I was ascribing more importance to the superimposition of two luminous values than to the forms themselves. On the other hand, the square represented—and still represents for me—the most genuinely human form, in the sense that it is a pure creation of man. The square, and geometrical figures in general, are purely the invention of the human spirit, distinctly intellectual creations, and what particularly interests me about them is that they don't have a specific dimension. They are not limited by the relations of scale that exist between man and the various objects and beings in nature. A house, a tree, have more or less defined dimensions, they have a measurement, whereas a geometric shape can be infinitely small or infinitely large, it doesn't have measurable limitations and thus completely escapes the traditional anthropocentrism of Western art.

In Soto's interest in geometric figures and perfect volumes such as the cube, we find the pyramid and the sphere (those universal forms from which all other forms may be generated), a kind of Platonic dimension that Soto shares with the majority of abstract-geometric painters.[46]

For all these reasons I decided to use the square. Then, trying to make movement visible, I decided to repeat a series of squares on the surface, with a separation equal to the measurement of each square. Using a black line for one of its sides and making the line look as if it were moving around the square, I was able to suggest the idea that each one was turning clockwise around itself. Halfway through the work I realized I no longer needed the white square, and it was enough to make the black line turn. Always looking for greater abstraction, I thought of reducing the line to its two ends, indicating them with two dots that turned in the same direction. Finally, at the end, I wanted to represent all those dots and make a sort of summary of all their movements, and represented them as if it were an orthogonal projection onto the plane, which generated those continuous lines of dots.

AJ Speaking of this piece, Luis Enrique Pérez-Oramas[47] pointed out to me that if

46. Mondrian, of course, like all abstract-geometric artists in principle, ascribes a universal quality to these perfect forms. "The artist of the future will be able to begin from the universal, whereas the artist of today had to start from the natural (the individual)." Piet Mondrian, "The New Plastic in Painting," in *The New Art–The New Life: The Collected Writings of Piet Mondrian*, trans. and ed. Harry Holtzman and Martin S. James (Boston: G.K. Hall & Co., 1986), 62. Originally published in *De Stijl*, no. 11, September 1918, 127–34.

47. Luis Enrique Pérez-Oramas (1960). Venezuelan curator, essayist, and poet. Author of numerous texts on Modern European and Latin American art. Pérez-Oramas is currently the curator of Latin American art at the Museum of Modern Art, New York.

Fig. 12. *Rotación* [*Rotation*], 1952.

we follow the sequence of the lines that suggest the movement of the square, we find that the vertical step from one line of squares to the next occurs through a leap equivalent to two columns. That is, at the right edge two columns of squares are missing—they were not represented, which creates a virtual or invisible space that explains the leap that exists between one line of squares and the next.

JS That was a response to the notion of the open work, just as Umberto Eco mentions in his books, only I did it long before him. *Rotación* responds to that idea, that the work could be cut at any spot, or that it could continue indefinitely without my having to paint it.

AJ Yet, this is not exactly Umberto Eco's issue, because in *Rotación* two columns of squares were not represented; that is, they are more related to the unpainted lines of dots in the serial experiences like *Estudio para una serie* [*Study for a Series*] than to the *Repeticiones*, which are truly open works.[48]

JS Maybe, but what interested me at that moment was the intuition that it was not necessary to represent everything the work proposed, and that those situations could go on indefinitely in any direction. Now, *Rotación* had another function, to make the consequences of the series extend to the wall. It was a kind of reaction I had, the purpose of which was to give the supporting wall the same importance as the structures manufactured in my workshop.

AJ This is when you made the model with which you were going to participate in the architectural integration projects led by Carlos Raúl Villanueva[49] at the Universidad Central de Venezuela. It is a very peculiar work, because it seems to unite experiences from different periods. For example, it combines the problem of progression, which you had already worked on separately, with the theme of color and that of the rotation of small cubes [Fig. 13].

JS Yes, it is a mural that I wasn't able to carry out, in which I also tried to suggest the idea of a moving cube, like in *Rotación*. I added those color lines that expand to the left and to the right, in a progression without identifiable boundaries. But the interesting thing is that color already responded to a serial concern; it was already coded.

AJ And why weren't you able to make it?

JS Well, for political reasons, because of the opposition to the military dictatorship. My artist friends were telling me that we shouldn't cooperate with a

48. An "open work," according to Eco, is one that incorporates within its visual structure a certain tendency toward the incomplete and unstable, and above all, calls for the intervention of the spectator on various levels and to various degrees. This intervention by the spectator could be psychological or physical; the important thing is that the work does not present itself as a form that is completed and closed in on itself, but rather as a continuously open process. Thus, the open work tends to place the spectator at the active center of a network of inexhaustible relationships not necessarily oriented from the work. For further reading see Umberto Eco, *Opera aperta*. Milan: Ed. Bompiano, 1962.

49. Carlos Raúl Villanueva (1900–75). Venezuelan architect educated in France, indisputably the central figure of modern architecture in Venezuela. His most dense and influential work is the Universidad Central de Venezuela, built between 1944 and 1964 and declared a World Heritage Site by UNESCO in 2000. It was there that he undertook an ambitious project to integrate the arts, with the participation of artists such as Alexander Calder, Henri Laurens, Fernand Léger, Alejandro Otero, Anton Pevsner, Víctor Valera, Victor Vasarely, and Oswaldo Vigas, among others.

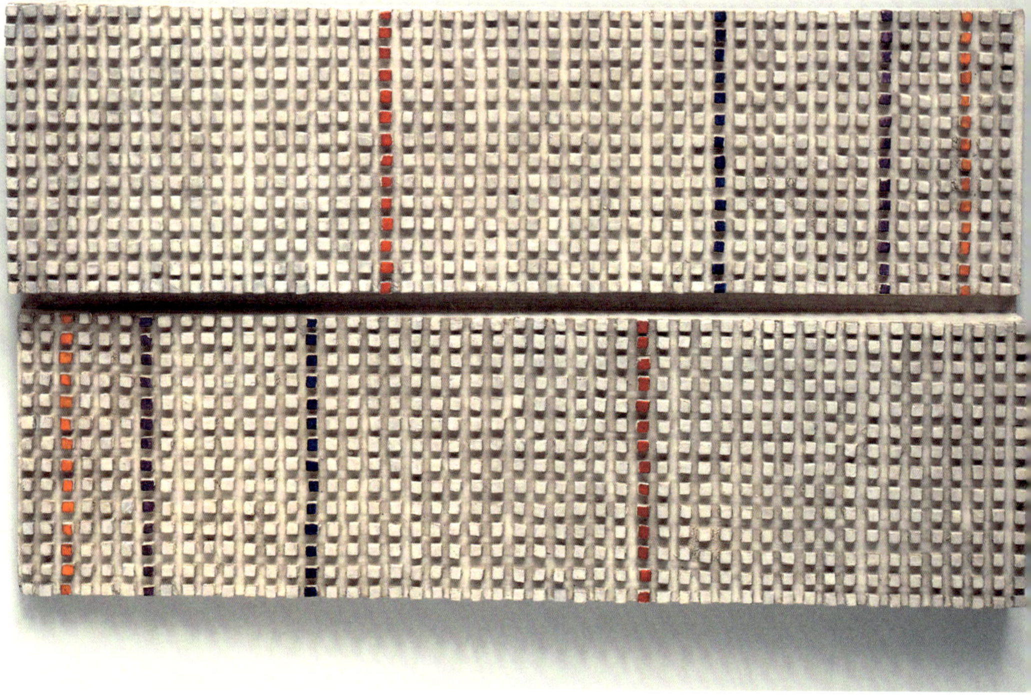

Fig. 13. *Sin título (Maqueta para mural Universidad Central de Venezuela)* [*Untitled (Maquette for a Mural at the Universidad Central de Venezuela)*], 1952–53.

military regime and I decided not to make it . . . but in the end, you know, they made theirs and the only one that wasn't made was mine.[50]

AJ Now, because of the fact that we are in front of a model, and also because the expression of movement *in* or *from* the painting produces many interesting ambiguities, I would like to know how you conceived both the apparent movement of these cubes and the expansion of the color lines. Was it something that occurred simultaneously in your imagination, or did it occur in stages? That is, should we imagine this piece as a space in which all the cubes are moving simultaneously, or does the movement go from one cube to the other, so that only one cube moves at a time? Suppose we wanted to animate them in a video, how would we do it?

50. Between 1952 and 1958, General Marcos Pérez Jiménez governed Venezuela in a dictatorial fashion, until a civil-military coup overthrew him on January 23, 1958.

JS No, I think that the objective was to do it like in *Rotación*: one square turned first, then the other, and so on . . . all those movements were supposed to suggest the idea of a cube rotating in space.

AJ If I'm not mistaken, these are the last pieces you made before going on to your serial experiences in the strict sense. You can already feel in them a great discipline; every line, every dot responds to a precise intent. What particularly interests me in your next pieces is that they express two qualities that I believe are fundamental to modern art. One is the relationship between music and visual art. Ever since Gauguin and later on Kandinsky and Klee, music has offered painters examples of what a nondescriptive pictorial creation can be. At the same time, painting offers music several creative possibilities, as we may note in the case of Pierre Boulez, who spoke, in 1950–51, of how he was influenced by some of Paul Klee's work. The second quality that interests me is the one that reflects the need to transcend the anthropocentric boundaries of the visual arts, attacking perspective, composition, and taste.

JS It's not exactly that Pierre Boulez awakened my interest in new musical structures. He got me interested above all in the concept of the musical revolution, through his idea of revolutionizing the art-sound phenomenon. At that time he composed *Le Marteau sans maître*, which has a structure that does not follow the traditional system of harmony. We had a good relationship, and he even invited me to work with the Stockhausen Festival in Germany. Unfortunately, I had already made a commitment to the Venezuelan Pavilion in Brussels, and I couldn't do both. This separated us, and we haven't seen each other since. I discovered the new musical structures, the twelve-tone system, and the serial experiments through a book by René Leibowitz.[51] He had been a disciple of Anton Webern and wrote a book on the twelve-tone system that I read and studied religiously, trying to understand the new musical systems and looking for a strategy to translate them to the visual arts.

When I understood serial music, I found a fabulous world where sound was not used as a function of taste; the assemblage of sound values was perfectly codified. Every musical value was a number, and using parameters whose measures did not correspond to the traditional ones, a totally different kind of

51. René Leibowitz (1913–72). French conductor, composer, and writer of Polish extraction. At the end of World War II, when Schoenberg's twelve-tone music was still largely unknown, Leibowitz began to teach this new musical language to a small group of musicians that included Pierre Boulez, Michel Philippot, Jean-Louis Martinet, and Serge Nigg. He is the author of *Introduction à la musique de douze sons* (Paris, 1949), which was Soto's starting point for the serial experiences he created between 1952 and 1953.

music could be produced. Following this example, I decided to codify pictorial elements and restrict myself to the use of eight colors. Every color had its corresponding number. I wanted to eliminate any subjectivity linked to personal taste, including my own. That's why I restricted myself to perfectly defined colors. It was not an olive green with reddish accents, nor a dark pink, colors that lend themselves to confusion, but the three primary colors, the three secondary colors, white, and black. (I later introduced ultraviolet, which was considered a sublime color. For this I prepared a relatively light violet, which I introduced into the series). White was number 1, yellow was 2, orange was 3, red was 4, green was 5, blue was 6, violet was 7, ultraviolet was 8, and finally, black was 9. After codifying them, I decided to perform a permutation, as is done with notes in serial music. I didn't make permutations of colors but rather of very simple numerical series: 4-1, 4-5, 3-7, and so on.

So you can imagine my surprise when, by starting from these basic elements and respecting the established permutations, I could produce a set of structures that functioned from the pictorial point of view.[52] In some of them, even, the dots started moving and vibrating in an Impressionist, almost Pointillist way. All those dots that descend vertically come from that study I did in *Rotación*, that is, a projection of the point into wherever there is space. Then I understood that I had encountered an amazing world, and that it was possible to codify pictorial elements as musicians had done with sound. I was still concerned with the problem of movement, and so I introduced some elements that, as in *Rotación*, sought to suggest the movement of an element in space. I did that in *Estudio para una serie* [*Study for a Series*], in 1952–53 [Fig. 14]. Sometimes between two series I would put a line of circles without color; just a mark I made with a hole-punch. I then would indicate a small line that seemed to rotate inside the circle. . . . Some above, others to the right, the next one down, so that the circle seemed to rotate clockwise. . . .

AJ I know that piece, but I don't recall having seen the marks you describe.

52. It is important to note that, based on the example that serial music offered him, Soto devised a strict codification method for color and form, so that its distribution across the space of the canvas did not respond to personal and discretionary criteria. In this sense, the established numerical structures were determined without knowing what the visual, pictorial result of such permutations would be. This was the reason for the surprise he says he felt upon discovering the final result. This was, in a way, a method of distancing that, of course, could only be effective for an instant. In *Estudio para una serie* [*Study for a Series*], for example, one of the permutated numbers corresponded to color, while the other corresponded to the number of lines of circles.

Fig. 14. *Estudio para una serie* [*Study for a Series*], 1952–53.

JS What happened was that one day I asked Mirtha, Carlos Cruz-Diez's wife, to restore it for an exhibition, and in repainting the white background, some of the marks were covered. If you look carefully you can still see them in several spots.

AJ The piece entitled *Pintura serial* [*Serial Painting*], of 1952–53, has been reproduced in all orientations. When you made it, did you want to give it a precise orientation [Fig. 15]?

JS When I made it, I envisioned it with the triangles oriented toward the right, maybe because of the direction in which we read in the Western world. But the truth is, that didn't matter to me at all; the large triangles only set the

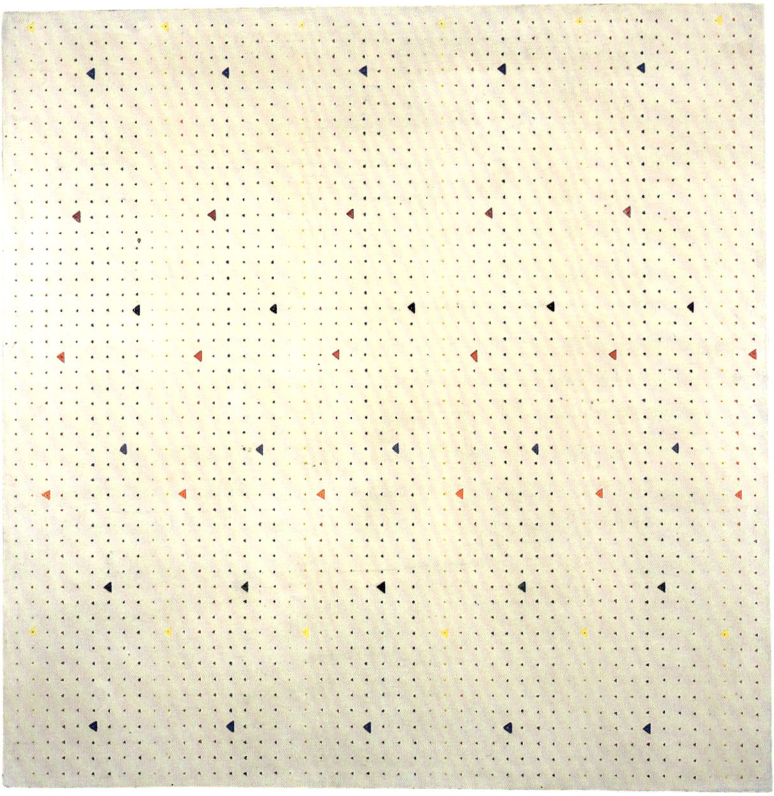

Fig. 15. *Pintura serial* [*Serial Painting*], 1952–53.

permutable evolution of the nine colors on its path.[53] These two works (*Pintura serial* and *Estudio para una serie*) don't have an above and a below, or horizontal, vertical, or diagonal positions. You can put them on the floor or on the ceiling, and their interpretation doesn't change even if we move around it. They could be oriented in any direction, but I needed to give reference points so that people could understand them. That's why I put the lines indicating movement, because if not, people wouldn't understand. I needed to explain that it worked like that. Maybe it has to do with my training as a teacher; don't forget, I studied education for over four years.

53. During our conversation, Soto stated that the large triangles were originally oriented toward the right. However, the indications written on the back of the painting—marking the upper part—would suggest that those triangles were oriented toward the left. This orientation and the fact that it coincides with a decrease in the material thickness of the paint seem, additionally, to agree with the desire to conceive what Soto calls "the immaterial essence of the universe."

AJ There are two curious facts about *Pintura serial*, as well: first, the material thickness of the painting decreases in the direction indicated by the large triangles, as if you wished to suggest that the evolution described there necessarily leads to its dematerialization. Second, each triangle—the large ones as well as the small—has a small hole in the middle. . . . What were you striving for, firstly, by reducing the thickness of the painting, and coinciding it with the direction suggested by the triangles? And what concern do the holes respond to?

JS You make a very interesting observation. It's true—if the theoretical evolution of the painting extends to the wall, the work would end at some point in time because it is immaterial. All of these elements were and continue to be essential to the evolution of my work. The holes have a more circumstantial origin. Back then, every time I sent a painting that was not well packed—by me, of course—and the work was damaged, it was easier for the exhibition organizers to run a white roller over the painting and repaint it rather than restore it. So I was careful to make sure that, at the very least, the roller wouldn't reach the small hole.[54]

AJ In your work from these years, there are two aspects that seem fundamental to me, and I would like to underscore them. One is the desire to transcend taste. At that time, as you have said on various different occasions, abstract art seemed to have reached its final consequences. You understand, however—and therein lies the importance of your reflections—that if you had continued down that road, where taste determined the construction of a work, your works would have only been a series of more or less beautiful variations in the style of Mondrian. Through the serial experiences, and above all through the almost total abandonment of traditional ideas of beauty, taste, and composition, you managed to find a new path. Proof that this attitude was not a personal whim but a necessity of the times is the impressive coincidence between what you were doing and what Pierre Boulez mentions, when talking about his piece entitled *Structures*, composed in 1951: "It was a test for me, what they call doubt, Cartesian doubt; question everything, make inheritance a blank slate and start over from zero, to see how writing could be reconstructed from a phenomenon

54. This curious restoration technique seems, more than anything, to indicate the very banal experimentation to which those pieces were subjected and, as such, what little respect people had for them. Today it would be simply unthinkable for the organizers of an exhibition to restore a work by repainting it.

that had annihilated individual invention."[55] The second aspect is the idea of breaking free from what you call the anthropocentrism that has characterized most of Western art. The fact that these works are structures with neither beginning nor end that can go on forever makes the works fragments of reality that, in principle, cannot be understood on a human scale.

JS Deep down, when I understood the problem of abstraction, I said to myself that it was absurd to continue with a formalism that didn't really break away from the structures used by figurative art of all periods, as many artists of the time were doing. That is precisely why the abstraction that people were working with in the late 1940s and early 1950s could not move forward. What was done was usually nothing more than a reinterpretation of the geometric structure used by the great Classical masters.

For example, I can tell you about one of the things that fascinated me during my studies at the School of Visual and Applied Arts of Caracas, when I discovered Giorgione's *Venus*. I thought that figure was something very special and that deep down it had nothing to do with being a nude. When I started drawing it, I found that the body of the *Venus* was made up of two ellipses that intertwined at the level of the womb; the first was formed by the torso and the position of her right arm, while the second was made evident through the peculiar position of her legs. I remember that later, when I was going to paint a landscape, I used the same structure to organize the fields. That was one of the most beautiful works I did in those years. Since then I have always said that art is structured in such a way that is not restricted to the imitation of natural forms, and that even during historical periods in which art seemed to have no other purpose, great artists used nature as a starting point from which they might create another reality, and that is the true meaning of art. The best example of what I'm talking about is found in the Renaissance.

So when I began to analyze abstraction in the early 1950s, I understood that I could not move forward in that direction, and therefore it was a closed door. I thought that by creating my works on the basis of triangulation and geometrization, as Giorgione and the best Renaissance painters did, I was not thinking deeply about the issue of structure, but extracting their basic forms of composition, which was almost plagiarism. We were taking from these great artists their power of invention, when what we had to do was to invent abstraction. That is why I moved away from my love for Giorgione and for the study of

55. Pierre Boulez. *Par volonté et par hasard*. Paris: Ed. Du Seuil, 1975, 70.

the typical triangulation of the Renaissance. I had to find a different way to structure the pictorial surface, otherwise I would remain tied to a centuries-old tradition and to the anthropocentrism I rejected. The human figure did not interest me; I was only interested in man as an idea, as the creator of ideas.[56]

AJ So it was in music that you found that new way to conceive the structure.

JS Even before, with the first *Repeticiones*. I really don't know what intuition led me to create those first *Repeticiones*. In *Repetición óptica Nº 2* [*Optical Repetition No. 2*] there was already an attempt to break away from the drawing tradition and from the limits of anthropocentrism. Moreover, the rigorous coding of pictorial elements that I attempted was not the only solution being attempted in those days for finding a way out of the stasis in abstract art. The Informalists of the day were also doing things. And I found that their reaction against abstract academicism through the informal approach was quite interesting, but then I understood that they were doing essentially the same thing. In reality, Informalism was almost like enlarging segments of a classical painting in order to re-encounter the pleasure of the vocation—the impastos of a Rembrandt, the brush stroke and color—without breaking away from the basic structures of figurative painting. I understood abstraction as a pure idea, because what is abstract in the consciousness of man, and particularly Western man, has nothing to do with representation. In principle, it has to be pure structure. And so I began to search for other activities with which I could achieve a relationship that would satisfy my notion of the abstract, and I found that relationship only in mathematics and music. But considering that I had neither the necessary education in science nor the time to study math for five years, I sensed that through music I could find a different way to handle pictorial elements, that would respond better to the concept I had of abstraction and that was a different way to decipher the universe.

AJ Nevertheless, the strictly serial experiences occupied you for a very brief time. They represented a circumstantial experiment that helped you organize and control the materials at your disposal, something like the organization of a work space, of your tools and materials, but the challenges of painting itself were still unresolved. Soon the issue of superimposing plots on transparent

56. "The painter is only a creator when the forms of his painting have nothing to do with nature." Kazimir Malevich, *De Cézanne au suprématisme. Lausanne, Switzerland: L'Age d'Homme,* 1974, 55.

planes and the resulting vibration would emerge. You then went from a pictorial practice that suggested external realities, like the apparent transparency of the square or the movement of a line in space, to one that activated pictorial phenomena and, in the case of movement, the displacement of the spectator.

JS That happened when I began to feel the need to introduce real space. *Muro blanco* [*White Wall*], of 1952–53, for example [Fig. 16], which is still a serial construction, may be linked to *Rotación*, of 1952. It is the same idea of a square that rotates in space, and that I tried to suggest with the inclination of planes downward and then upward, to the left and to the right. The difference this time was that it wasn't painted but created by the thickness of the square itself. I continued there with the goal of achieving a sort of symbiosis between the

Fig. 16. *Muro blanco* [*White Wall*], 1952–53.

wall and the paintings hanging on it, and it was with this in mind that I placed twenty-four white panels measuring fifty centimeters by fifty centimeters. They could have been another color, but white offered fewer suggestions outside of the idea, making it more neutral. Four of those small squares got lost at the Museo de Bellas Artes, probably during transport, when I had my exhibition.[57] So I tried to reconstruct them with Miguel Arroyo,[58] and I remember that I was never satisfied with the series that we rebuilt. Some day, perhaps, the original series will be reunited. I still hang on to the hope that one day it will be possible

57. The exhibition entitled *Soto. Estructuras cinéticas* opened on June 30, 1957, at the Museo de Bellas Artes de Caracas.

58. Miguel Arroyo (1920–2004). Visual artist, curator, and museum scientist who was the father of modern museum science in Venezuela. Director of the Museo de Bellas Artes de Caracas between 1959 and 1976.

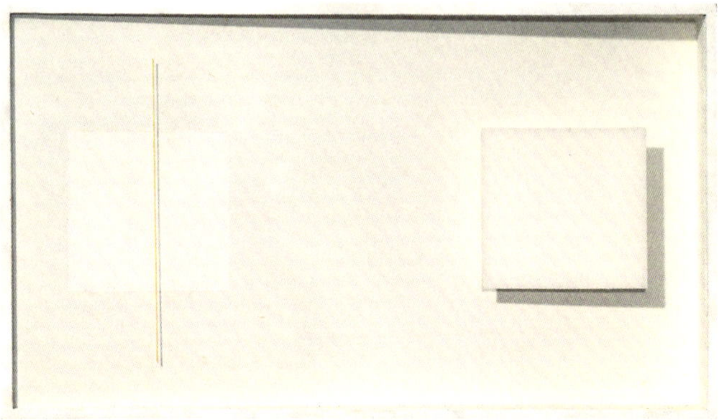

Fig. 17. *Dos cuadrados en el espacio* [*Two Squares in Space*], 1953.

to find the primitive result, since it isn't a problem of color. If you turn the twenty-four pieces over, you will find that the four restored ones are of a different kind of wood. However, it is not in that work where I really introduce space but in *Dos cuadrados en el espacio* [*Two Squares in Space*], of 1953 [Fig. 17]. That piece features two squares that are exactly equal: one is on the left side of the support and the other one is to its right on transparent Plexiglas, at a certain distance from the background. In front of the square on the left, I immediately placed a vertical line to materialize the space that may be observed between that square and the Plexiglas, whereas the one on the right creates a virtual cube by projecting its shadow on the background.

AJ It is interesting to note that these pieces, as in all of those that came after it for almost two years, the basic structure is the same one used by Malevich in *White on White*: that is, two similar or equivalent structures, one of which shifts with respect to the other.

JS It's true that I started with the goal of making Mondrian dynamic, but if you analyze my output of those years, you can see that it is imbued with Malevich's way of thinking. I wanted to work the square as something immaterial; that's why I thought about white or transparent colors, and even varnishes on Plexiglas. I tried to construct it through a repetition of small squares, or through a plot of dots. In *Desplazamiento de un cuadrado transparente* [*Displacement of a Transparent Square*], of 1953–54, you can clearly see that intent, and the foundation of what would lead me later on to superimpose one transparent plane over another [Fig. 18]. In fact, even before I started using Plexiglas, I saw each of those planes as true superimpositions. On top of a yellow square, two other

Fig. 18. *Desplazamiento de un cuadrado transparente* [*Displacement of a Transparent Square*], 1953–54.

squares move: one is composed of small squares and the other of dots, which makes them transparent. This is similar to what happens in *Desplazamiento de un elemento luminoso* [*Displacement of a Luminous Element*], of 1954 [Fig. 19]. I had seen Georges Koskas, when he was superimposing white dots over black dots on the plane. From there I got the idea of superimposing those plots of dots with the aid of Plexiglas. I remember one day I was at BHV (a French department store) and in the hardware and electrical appliances department I found a grid with round holes that was used, if I'm not mistaken, to hold radio parts or as a ventilation grille. So I decided to buy it because I was sure that I would be able to do something with it. I started out by copying all those dots, in white, on Plexiglas. Then I painted the grille black and placed it over a white background. The idea was to superimpose those two plots of dots, shifting them slightly.

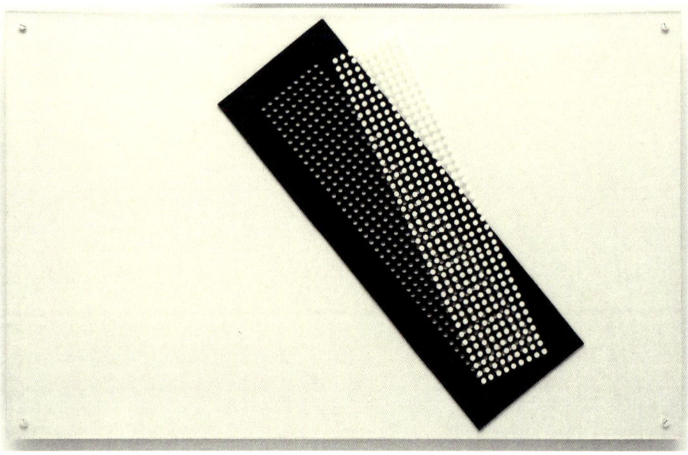

Fig. 19. *Desplazamiento de un elemento luminoso* [*Displacement of a Luminous Element*], 1954.

From that superimposition and displacement of two identical plots of dots, some shapes emerged that suggested the appearance of a third value. That piece, later on, would lead me to the work where I discovered a truly new situation: *Metamorfosis* [*Metamorphosis*], of 1954 [Fig. 20].[59] Superimposing a plot of dots over a plot of small squares, I discovered a phenomenon that left me floating on air for almost a week: when I superimposed the plots, luminous nuclei appeared, rotating and moving whenever I shifted position in front of them. When Vasarely saw this painting, he told me to call it "Andromeda" because of the sort of suns that seemed to be rotating. But I didn't want to do that, because it suggested a figurative base that had nothing to do with my work. I called it *Metamorfosis* because those luminous and immaterial dots had emerged from the superimposition of two similar elements. They were groups; I called them groups because several circular nuclei appeared, organized symmetrically.[60]

AJ It is interesting that you experienced such pleasure when, for the first time in your work, you created an effect of real movement and nuclei of light. I can't

59. In later conversations, Soto seemed to have doubts about the order in which *Desplazamiento de un elemento luminoso* and *Metamorfosis* were created. They were done in the same year and explore similar issues. Nevertheless, the structural coherence of *Metamorfosis* and its obvious influence upon later works lead us to believe that it came after *Desplazamiento de un elemento luminoso.*

60. "Only when the painter makes the spectator see more than is physically presented, will he be able to produce perceptive (psychological) effects." Josef Albers, "Op Art and/or Perceptive Effects," in *Yale Scientific Magazine,* November 1965.

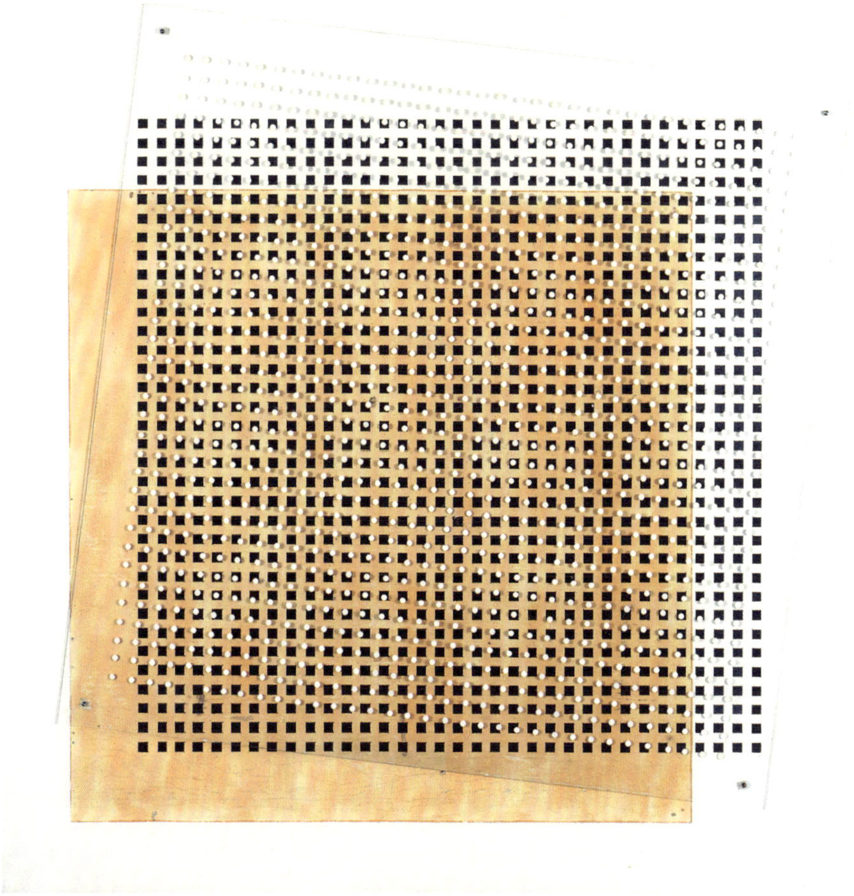

Fig. 20. *Metamorfosis* [*Metamorphosis*], 1954.

help but think that there is an important connection here with your childhood readings of Dante, where God was described precisely as circles of light, and with Malevich's *White on White*, which was the perfect way of capturing light on the canvas, to use your own words.

JS Maybe, and if you look closely, you will see that *Metamorfosis* is a combination of circles and squares . . . in a way connecting Dante and Malevich. The truth is that observing the superimposition of the dots, I realized that something new was happening, and so I tried to animate and give movement to what was happening there. Finally, I decided to separate them by about five centimeters, thus introducing real space and obtaining a movement that I still hadn't achieved with *Metamorfosis*, which led to *Puntos blancos sobre puntos negros* [*White Dots on Black Dots*], of 1954 [Fig. 21]. I then continued experimenting, and in some works I studied the cube, following the path of *Dos cuadrados en el espacio* [*Two Squares in Space*], of 1953.

By superimposing white and black squares, others painted with a varnish that allowed me to give them various densities of transparency until reaching the saturation of the white, I arrived at *Cubos sugeridos* [*Suggested Cubes*], of 1955, a piece in which I wanted to suggest the cube with a minimum of elements. Immediately I went on to *La cajita de Villanueva* [*Villanueva's Little Box*], also from 1955 [Fig. 22].

AJ Which is where, for the first time, you use the plot of lines that would characterize your later work.

JS Yes, this perhaps comes from the first *Repeticiones*, like that painting with the "rr's," where I wanted to achieve a vibratory state by repeating a single element. In *La cajita de Villanueva* there was something new besides vibration: that piece achieved an optical ambiguity that made it difficult to determine where the squares were. Sometimes the black square seemed to be in the background and at other times it seemed to be in the foreground.

AJ It is astonishing to see the perfect coherence of your process, one work leading to the next, one posing questions that would be solved or developed in the next one, with methodical precision. We can almost imagine you on par with the artist imagined by Paul Valéry, working meticulously, solving pictorial problems like a surgeon in his spotless white gown. For Valéry, as for you, I think, the artist's objective is not to express the emotions he feels in the creative work or in a particular experience, but to absolutely elicit them in the spectator, or

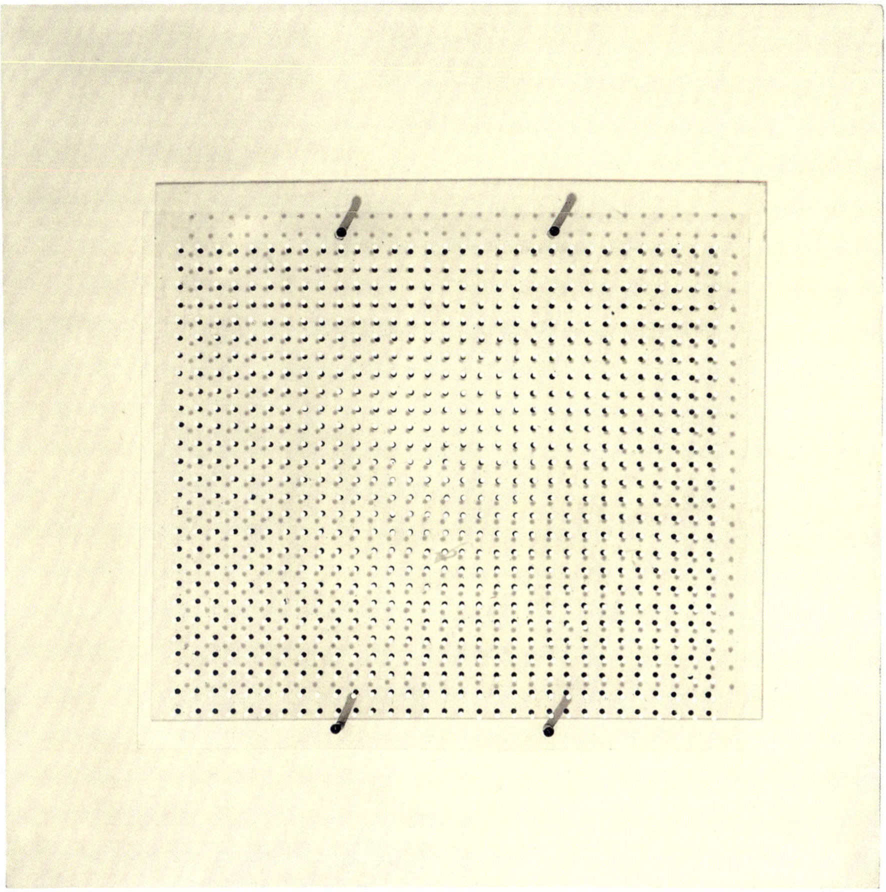

Fig. 21. *Puntos blancos sobre puntos negros* [*White Dots on Black Dots*], 1954.

even better, to awaken reflection in the spectator. Now, very few of your works from that time are known, and each one seems to follow the previous one with surprising accuracy. Did you make so few works then, or have many been lost?

JS No, that's right, I made very few pieces. You see, I didn't have a lot of time to work. Don't forget, I made a living from my guitar, playing at night, so I had very little free time. I would work during my very small margin of available time and I only executed those ideas that seemed fundamental to me. That was how it was, at least until 1957 when I really started to sell works and was able to make a living with my artwork.

AJ And what were you reading, what were your intellectual concerns?

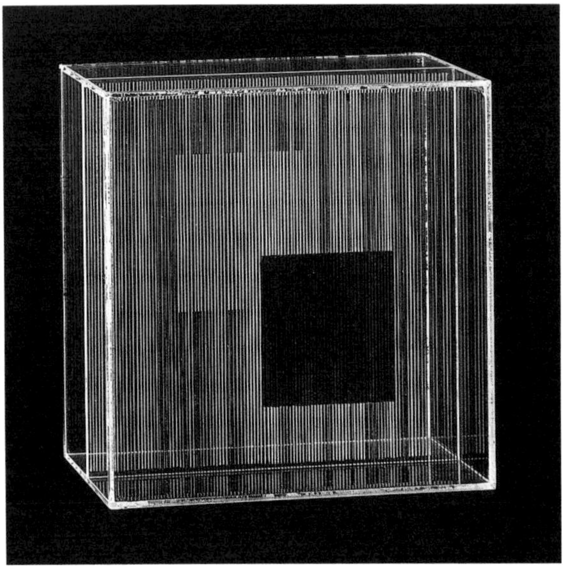

Fig. 22. *La cajita de Villanueva* [*Villanueva's Little Box*], 1955.

JS Music had allowed me to find structures that were independent of taste, but at that time my great concern was space-time and all the ideas originating in physics and mathematics. Now, since I didn't have the slightest idea about those things, because I hadn't studied anything after elementary school and then went straight to the School of Visual and Applied Arts of Caracas, whenever I met someone who knew about those things, I would ask as many questions as I could. That's what I did with my friend Jorge Vicente Ortiz, who was a mathematician. I spent entire nights with him talking about the new scientific ideas, through which I discovered a new concept of nature that was quite far removed from our usual notion of nature: about matter, energy, space, and time. Some time later I met David Medalla,[61] a very bohemian Filipino who seemed to be a genius in mathematics. I talked with him a lot about my scientific concerns, and one day he gave me a book in which, according to him, I would find everything I was looking for: *The New Scientific Spirit* by Gaston Bachelard.

AJ And do you feel that those scientific notions directly influenced you?

JS Absolutely. . . . From very early on, when I was studying in Caracas, I envisioned art not as an activity that was limited to producing aesthetic pleasure,

61. David Medalla (1942). A Filipino artist who uses a broad variety of media in his works. Painter, sculptor, performance artist. A fervent admirer of Piet Mondrian, Medalla was friends with Soto in the early 1950s and helped him understand some of the most important problems of modern physics.

but as something that contributed to human thought, just like science and philosophy. I have always thought that as artistic thought was considered equal to philosophy and science during the Renaissance and in Ancient Greece and Rome, so too should we reclaim that same level of respect for our field today. That's why, for me, an artist's activity was not and is not something impulsive destined to create what people call a personal language, the reflection of an exceptional personality. On the contrary: I am convinced that there are certain problems that are inherent to art, problems that correspond to specific historical moments, and only when we find answers to them will our work acquire a transcendent value for humanity.

TOWARD THE DEMATERIALIZATION OF BODIES

AJ The year 1955 was an important date in your personal history; it was the year of the first historic exhibition of Kinetic art, at the Galerie Denise René, where your international career really began.[62] Regarding your pictorial work, it was also the year of *La cajita de Villanueva*, which featured the plots that would characterize most of your later work, the spatial ambiguity produced by the superimposition of cubes over those plots, and *Espiral* [*Spiral*]. A first period of experimentation seems to have ended with that. A phenomenon similar to the passage from analytic to synthetic Cubism occurred in your work at this point: once the spatial and structural questions of the work were solved, color reappeared.

JS *Espiral* came about after seeing Duchamp's rotational work in the first exhibition, *Le Mouvement*, organized by Denise René [Fig. 23]. I wanted to do something similar, without the intervention of an engine. I did achieve it, by superimposing two spirals, one black and one white, with the spiral in the foreground spinning to the right. This induces an optical movement as we move in

62. In 1955, the French gallery owner Denise René had the idea of gathering in one exhibition a group of artists who, through different media and approaches, sought ways to incorporate real time and movement in the work of art. This exhibition marked the official birth of Kineticism, which would evolve considerably over the following decade. The orientation of these artists was, in reality, not at all uniform, and ranged from the irony of Duchamp, who saw a retinal, superficial manifestation of the arts in optics, to Soto, who believed that optical effects offered a way of suggesting deeper realities on the basis of the "real."

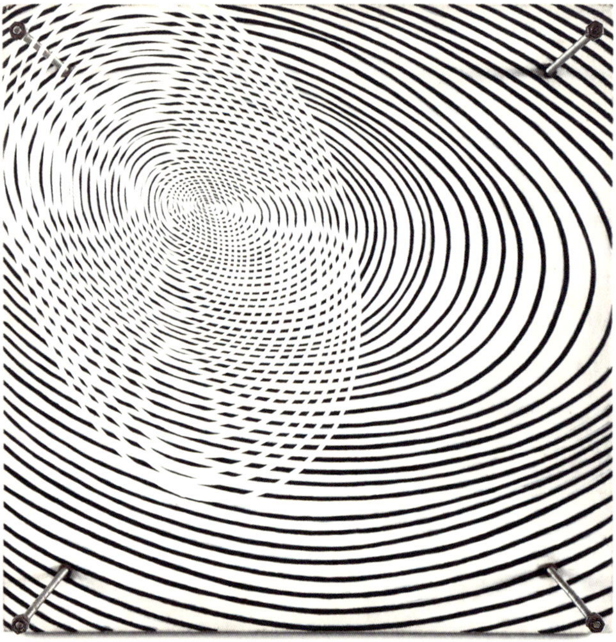

Fig. 23. *Espiral* [*Spiral*], 1955.

front of it, almost as if it were a stream of light coming out of the work. As for color, I said to myself that if it was the result of light, and I was working with luminous vibrations, why should I rule it out? So then I introduced color in its vibratory state.

AJ It was like going back to Impressionism, this time from pure structure, without the representation of landscape. Even the title of your work, *Luz plateada* [*Silvery Light*], of 1956, reuses the adjective you often employ when talking about Impressionism.

JS It's true, I wanted to put color in a state of motion, not as chromatic harmony, which is another academic vestige that I was running away from, just as I ran from composition and balance. What I was looking for was and is very far from achieving a beautiful harmony of colors. I only want to achieve those combinations in which color has greater vibratory strength, and where the spatial ambiguity that results from its superimpositions is evident [Fig. 24]. One of the

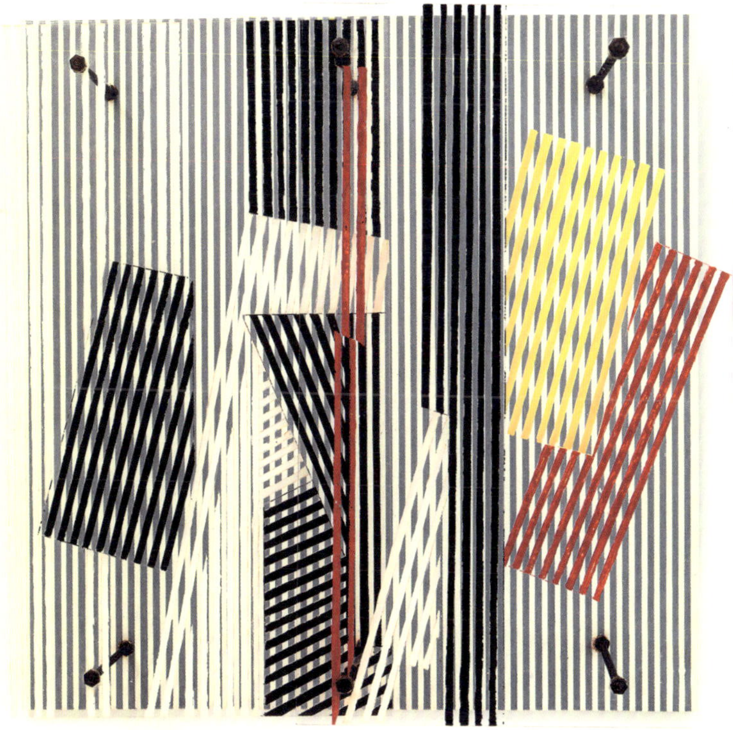

Fig. 24. *Doble transparencia* [*Double Transparency*], 1956.

great shortcomings of the public is that they always look for harmony, beauty in combinations, and they will never find that in my work.

AJ Nevertheless, one of your kinetic Plexiglas structures is called *Armonía transformable* [*Transformable Harmony*] [Fig. 25].

JS Yes, but I did it because it was the only way to attract people who didn't understand the essence of abstraction. If you didn't look for the right words, they would see in them anything but a work of art.

AJ Now, in that *Armonía transformable* something very important happens, something that marks a new phase in your work. Your painting is less and less the traditional plane where a "vision" is projected. With this I want to point out that rupture of the plane that served as a background, so that there was no longer figure and background, just a dynamic continuity that demanded an active participation on the part of the spectator.

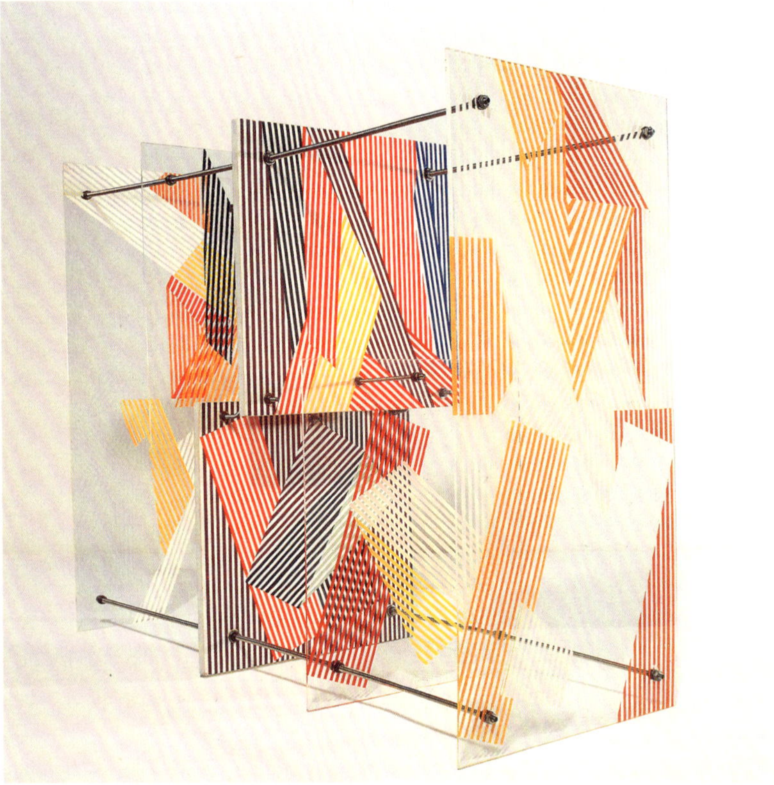

Fig. 25. *Armonía transformable* [*Transformable Harmony*] (side view), 1956.

JS Precisely, and that's why I did it on several planes. Though the rupture with the traditional figure-ground relationship had already occurred in *La cajita de Villanueva*. On the other hand, from the first *Repetición*, the one that's like a checkerboard, I was against that idea of the plane as a projection of a visual reality.

AJ In 1957, you abandoned Plexiglas to create your plots with metal rods welded together. That same year, for the first time, you superimposed a metal line over the background plot, opening the door to the *Vibraciones*.

JS That's exactly right, and that happened because I wanted to free myself of the Plexiglas. I have never liked to have ideas or a way of doing things imposed on me. When I feel that happening, I react, and that is when you find those abrupt changes in my process. Something similar was happening with Plexiglas. It was imposing itself on me so forcefully that it seemed essential to my work, and the

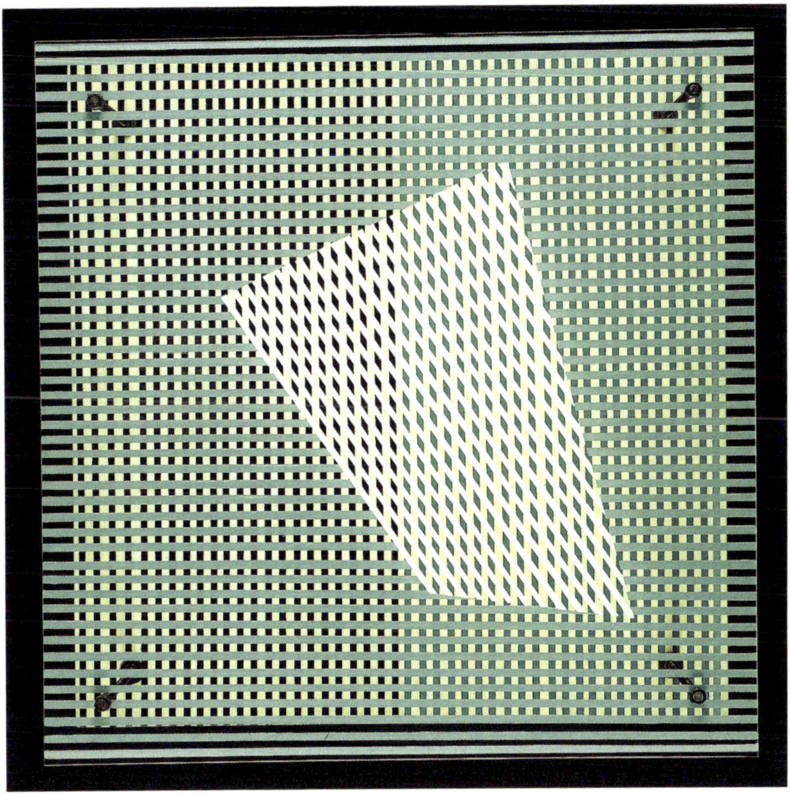

Fig. 26. *Trapecio* [*Trapezoid*], 1957.

public started seeing it as an aesthetic value, which bothered me, because I was only interested in it as a means to draw in space [Fig. 26]. That's why I invented that technique that allowed me to superimpose the plots through welded metal rods, without the additional element of the Plexiglas. The funny thing is that the result of the vibrations I obtained generated the same sensation as Plexiglas. I did that in Venezuela, when I presented my exhibition at the Museo de Bellas Artes. I gave the first of these pieces to Carlos Raúl Villanueva, because he loved it. He took it to the University and gave a lecture on it.

AJ An interesting thing begins to happen with those metal constructions: they are structures that, even through the technique used, can open up to the spectator, be penetrated, just like what ultimately occurred later on, around 1967.

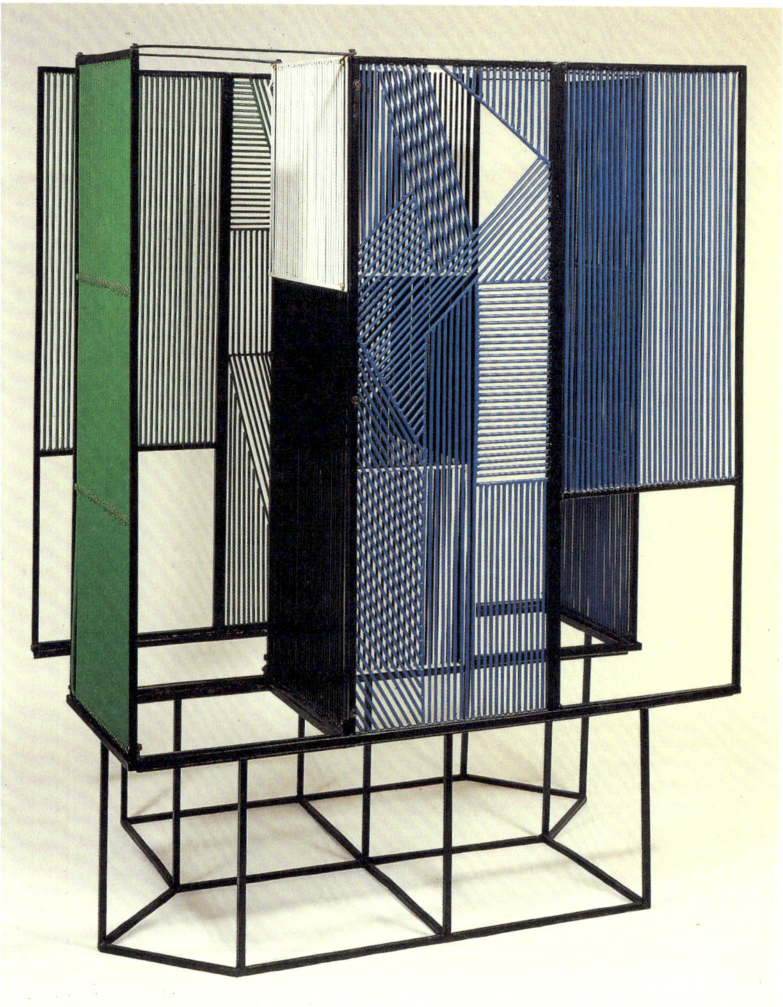

Fig. 27. *Pre-penetrable,* 1957.

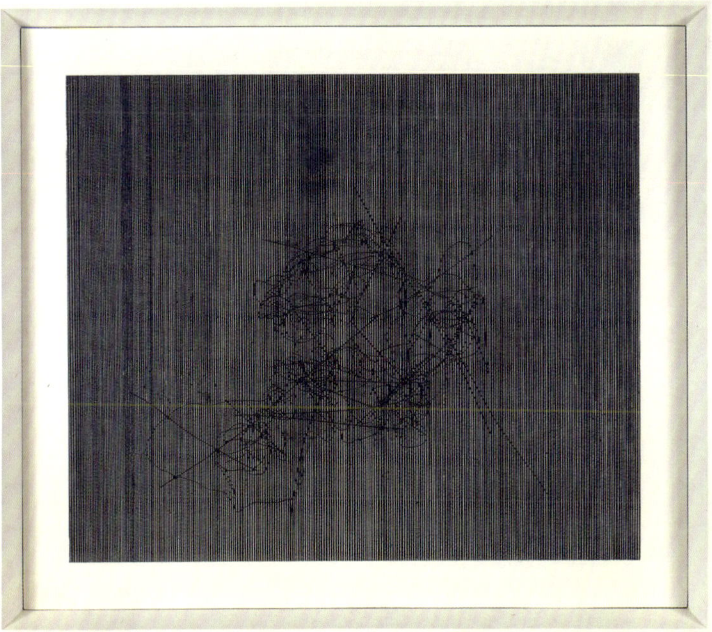

Fig. 28. *Vibración I* [*Vibration I*], 1958.

JS Of course, and that was what I was really looking for. One of them, *Pre-penetrable*, of 1957, which first belonged to Alfredo Boulton[63] and now resides in the Colección Patricia Phelps de Cisneros, was originally envisioned to be five times larger [Fig. 27]. They were models done on that scale because it was impossible for me to make them in the projected size. That's why I had so much fun watching Boulton's grandchildren playing inside it.

AJ Immediately after these kinetic structures, in which color tends to explode with all its vibratory force, you slowly abandoned color and focused on issues of a structural order, producing pieces that were often very sober, until in your Baroque period this was reduced practically down to white and black with a few discrete notes of color [Figs. 28–29]. How did this transition happen, and why?

JS The kinetic structures in Plexiglas were produced during a period that did not last very long, close to two years, but during this time I made many works.

63. Alfredo Boulton (1908–95). Venezuelan photographer, critic, and historian, and the author of *Historia de la pintura en Venezuela* (Caracas: Ediciones Armitano, 1964–72) as well as many monographs on Venezuelan artists, including one on Jesús Soto (Caracas, Ediciones Armitano, 1973).

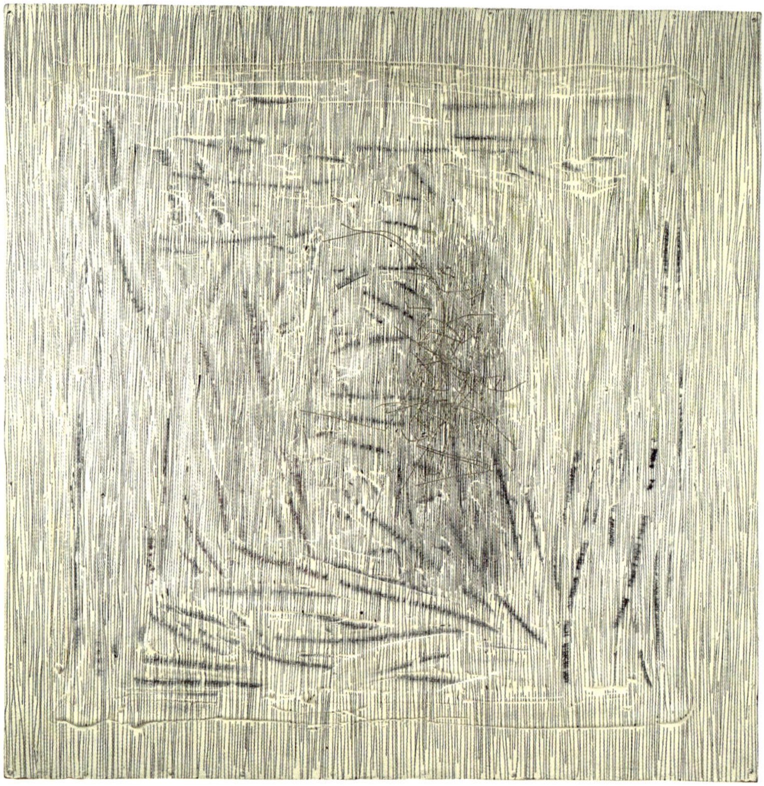

Fig. 29. *Vibración* [*Vibration*], 1960.

Then I felt the need to return to a sort of discipline based on the elements acquired. It wasn't a matter of abandoning color, but of putting it aside to solve other problems, like the one that appears in the work *Trapecio* [*Trapezoid*], of 1957. A rather strange thing happens there; when you face this painting you feel as if it were breathing. It expands and contracts like an accordion. It is an essential work, and perhaps one day I will study the issues it raises for me in greater depth [Fig. 26].

AJ We come now to an important group of works, those that represented Venezuela at our pavilion at the World's Fair in Brussels in 1958[64] and the great mural

64. Soto, through the intercessions of architect Carlos Raúl Villanueva, created an important collection of pieces for the Venezuelan Pavilion at the World's Fair held in Brussels in 1958. These works included *Mural de Bruselas* [*Brussels Mural*], now at the Museo de Bellas Artes de Caracas; *La Torre de Bruselas* [*The Tower of Brussels*], now at the IVIC; and *Muro de Bruselas* [*Brussels Wall*], also at the IVIC. This last piece was, in essence, his first *Escritura* [*Writing*].

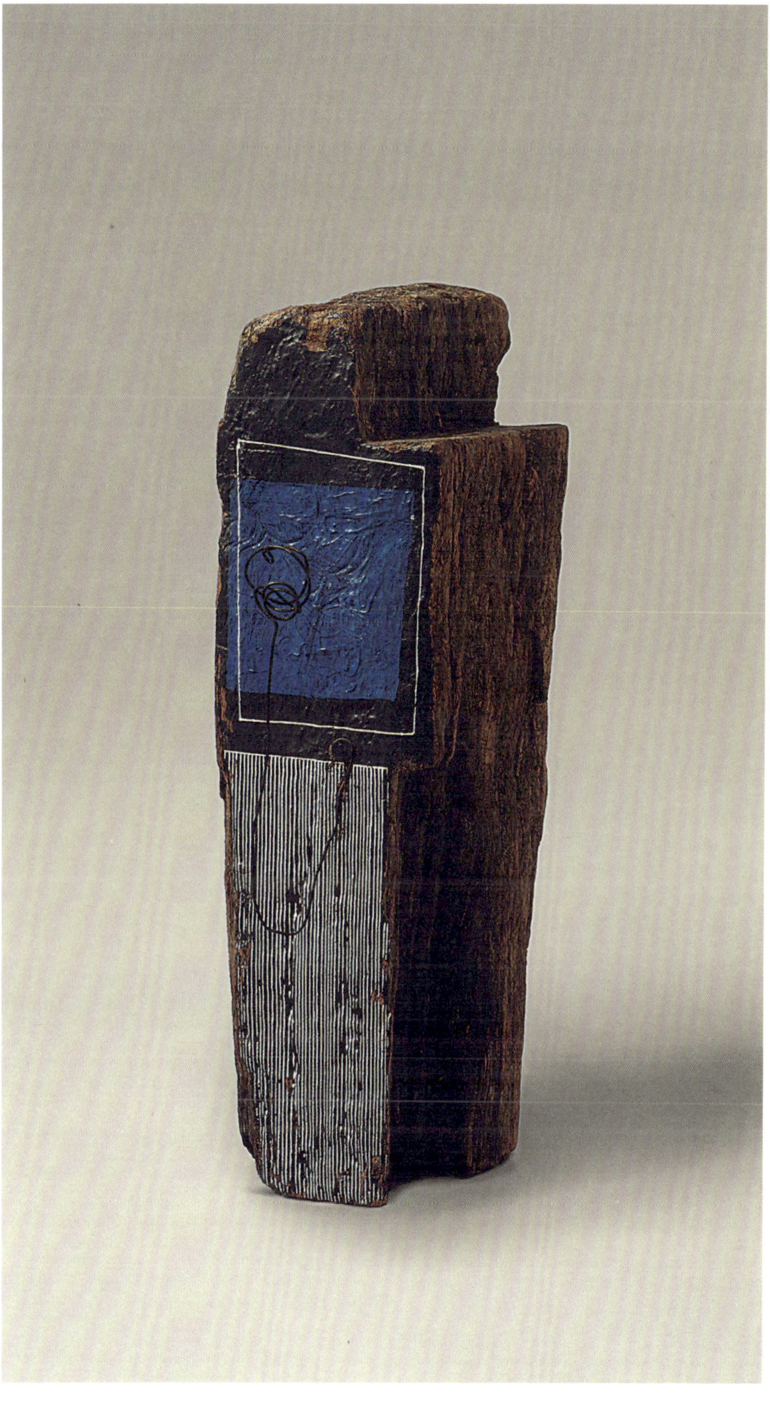

Fig. 30. *Tronco* [*Trunk*], 1960.

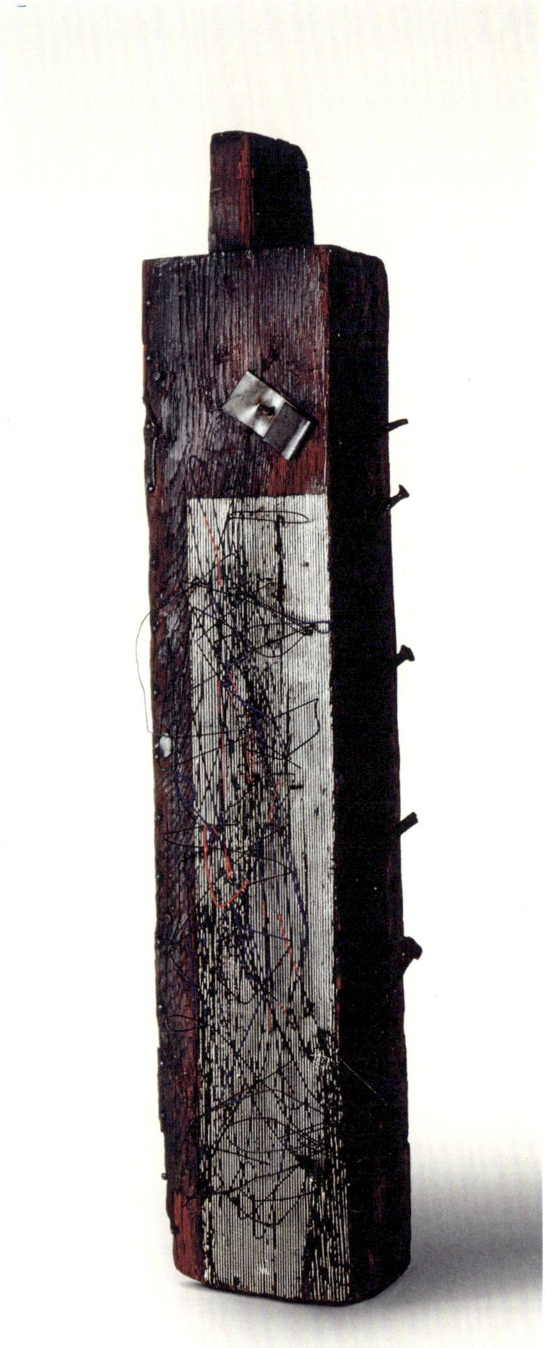

Fig. 31. *Leño* [*Log*], 1961.

JS As they were; they remained just as I found them, with their nails and all their features. The only thing I did was add a plot to them, to suggest the dematerialization of a specific element. I would then add some legs, some nails or bolts, but the wood remained as it was, with no intervention at all.

AJ It is interesting that construction materials or craftsmen's tools, like needles, are frequently found among the dematerialized elements.

JS I wanted to save the work done to those wood beams. The same thing happened with the needles. One day, while looking for materials, I came across a package of needles that I found very beautiful. Some were large, others were small and straight, and some were even curved. The same thing happened as with the wood: I wanted to save them by making a piece of artwork out of them. Something similar also happened with a series of metal structures, like the ones you can see, for example, in *Vibración III* [*Vibration III*], of 1960–61. When I bought my first apartment in Paris, on the rue du Temple, we had a small storeroom on the roof. The apartment had previously belonged to an artisan who made lampshades, and we found the storeroom full of beautiful metal structures. When I saw these lovely structures I didn't want to throw them all away, so I held onto a group of them, to use them in my work. They were cones, cubes, and circles so perfect that I could never have made them myself, so I integrated them just as they were. Sometimes I deformed them a little, or used only some of the circles. Those perfect circles that I used in the early 1960s come from that set.

AJ Many of these "Baroque" works, especially the vertical ones, seem to have an obvious relationship with synthetic Cubism [Fig. 32]. In these pieces, the shape seems to disappear, and you can often see fragments that, in certain cases, seem to approach the nudes and guitars often painted by the Cubists. I am thinking specifically of a piece *Vibración III,* in the Colección of Patricia Phelps de Cisneros, and *Sin título* [*Untitled*], of 1962, from the collection of the Museo de Arte Moderno Jesús Soto,[66] or where these circles you mention seem like the vestiges of a body or a guitar [Figs. 33–34].

66. Museum founded in Ciudad Bolívar, in southern Venezuela, by Jesús Soto. It was officially created in 1969 and inaugurated in 1973. The building in which it is housed is the work of architect Carlos Raúl Villanueva, and boasts some of the best museum structures in the country. The collection is comprised of two sets of artwork: the first group contains the personal work of Jesús Soto, and the second set contains the work of some of the greatest artists of the time, among them the French New Realism artists (Yves Klein, Daniel Spoerri, Christo, Armand, and others), and the Grupo Zero artists, in addition to a small historical nucleus, the highlights of which include drawings by Kazimir Malevich and Piet Mondrian and watercolors by Sonia Delaunay.

JS Maybe, but I didn't do it with that goal in mind. What was important for me was to bring all the trends that interested me—Tachism, New Realism, and others—to a space-time situation. That's why you see all those textures that are so obvious and the discarded materials, because I wanted to give those trends a greater importance, turning them into space-time situations . . . I wanted to make them more effective. That's why I confronted new realist textures and at the same time dematerialized them.

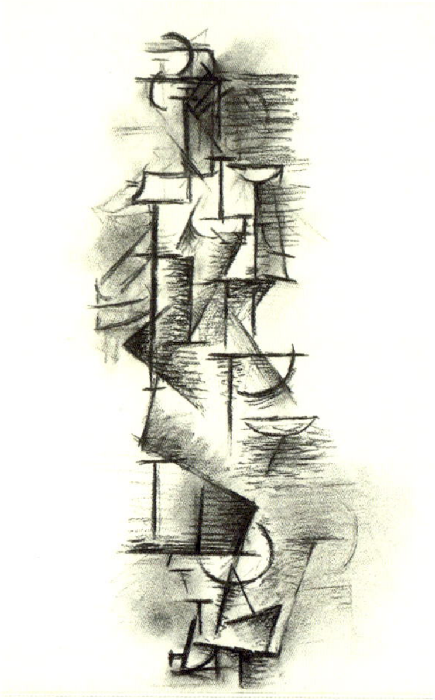

Fig. 32. Pablo Picasso, *Nude Woman,* 1910.

AJ In reality, it is a process that is similar to the one that led you to make Mondrian dynamic in 1950.

JS It is exactly the same process. . . . At least I tried; whether or not I succeeded remains to be seen, perhaps in the future it will become clear. That was what I was trying to do.

AJ Like in the 1961 mural at the Galería de Arte Nacional [Fig. 35].

JS Exactly, except that was a special case. When I returned to Caracas in the 1960s, *El Techo de la Ballena* [*The Roof of the Whale*][67] was active and a friend of mine, Daniel González,[68] told me: "Jesús, I have an idea, each of the artists creates a large work in the space of a day, and right away we'll exhibit them all together." I liked his proposition, because it was an action that would last eight hours.

67. *El Techo de la Ballena* was a movement of the Venezuelan avant-garde, active between 1961 and 1968. This collective united photographers, writers, painters, and designers who assumed a critical stance regarding political power and defended revolutionary processes as extreme as armed insurrection. Strongly influenced by Surrealism in literature and Informalism in painting, the group was aided by the activism of Adriano González León, Salvador Garmendia, Rodolfo Izaguirre, Daniel González, Edmundo Aray, and Carlos Contramaestre, among others.

68. Daniel González (1934). Venezuelan painter, sculptor, photographer, and graphic designer who was a prominent member of *El Techo de la Ballena,* for which he designed some of its best publications.

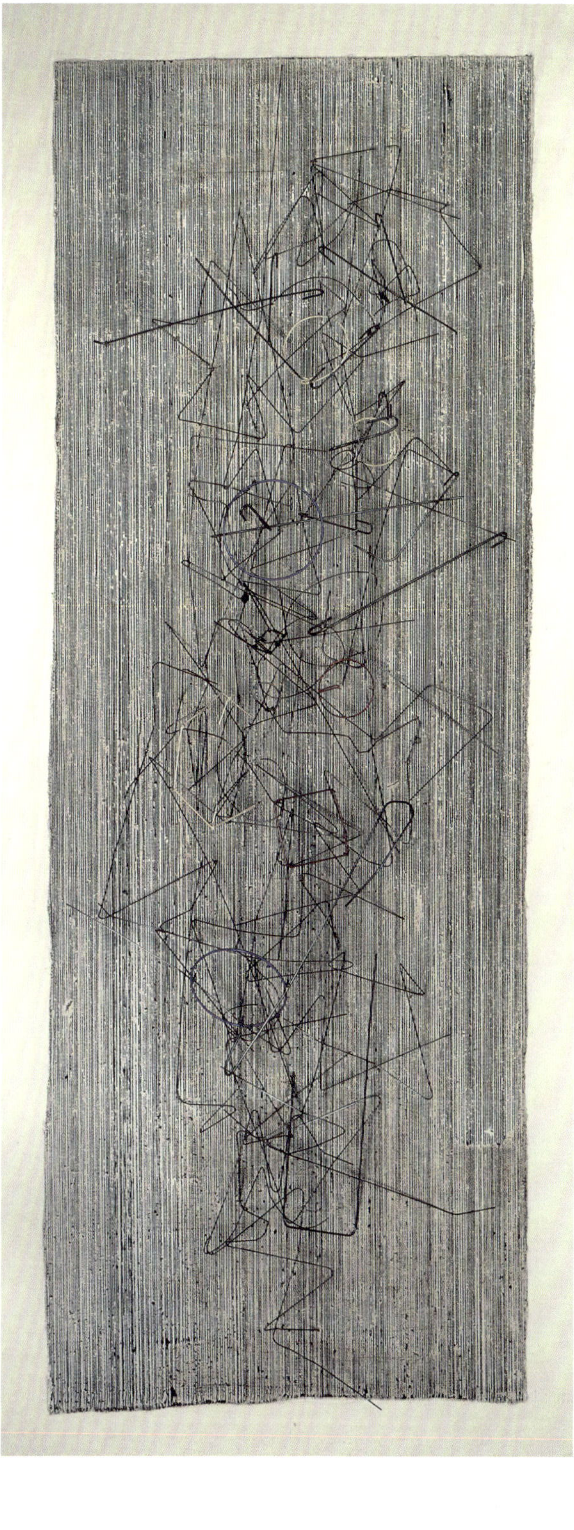

Fig. 33. *Vibración III*
[*Vibration III*], 1960–61.

Hans Neumann[69] loaned me a studio and I did it there. That's why you can clearly see that the left side of the mural is a typically New Realist situation and the right is a situation in movement, space-time. I found the materials for the left side in Hans Neumann's studio; it was equipment that he had stored there, and was quite expensive. . . . I remember Neumann said that it was worth around five thousand dollars. And I told him that the work would pay it back to him revalued. The rest of the materials, those on the right, I found in garbage dumps. The artist Ángel Hurtado[70] filmed the whole process.

AJ I think that your explanation of this Baroque period as the result of an unpaid debt to painting makes perfect sense; however, personal experience is always framed within a context from which it isn't easy to step away. Is there a parallel between your Baroque world, so to speak, and the French New Realism of the 1960s?

JS I met all those artists; they were my friends, and we exhibited together because we were trying to force a new situation. But deep down my attitude was different from theirs, and this became clear when we each began to forge our own individual paths after that particular historic moment. They were all very pure structuralists in the beginning. What happened was that during the 1960s people believed that man would become a prisoner of mechanics and technology, and that is in part the reason for that reaction, which was related to the French uprising of May 1968.

AJ Does that have to do with the negative feelings left over from World War II?

JS No. All the expressionism and gesturalism of those days might have emerged from World War II, but with regard to the French New Realists and myself, it was more about a different behavior; it didn't come from the guts.

AJ To what might you attribute this fear of becoming locked into the structures created by technology?

JS Well, literature and film began to generate a situation of fear regarding technology, and clearly artists are sensitive to those social tensions. But my case was the

69. Hans Neumann (1919–2001). Venezuelan industrialist and collector of Czech origin.

70. Ángel Hurtado (1927). Venezuelan visual artist whose work initially evolved within the context of abstract Informalism. He is the author of a considerable number of films on Venezuelan and Latin American art.

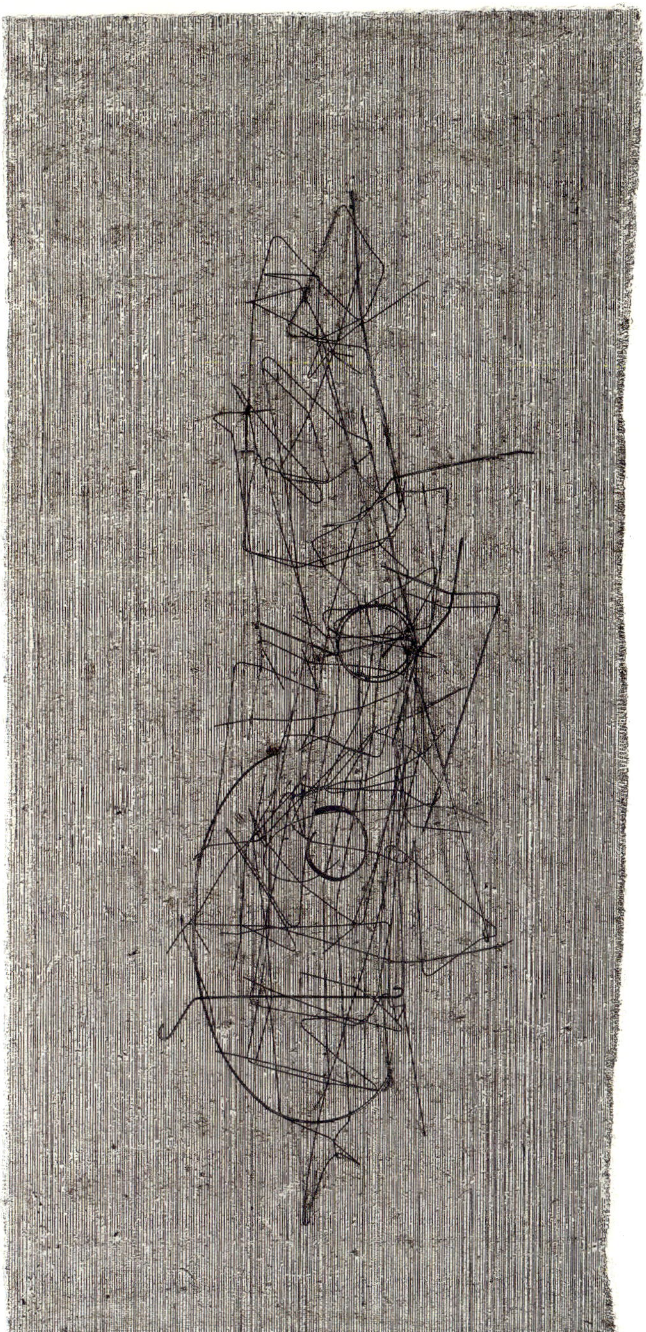

Fig. 34. *Sin título* [*Untitled*], 1962.

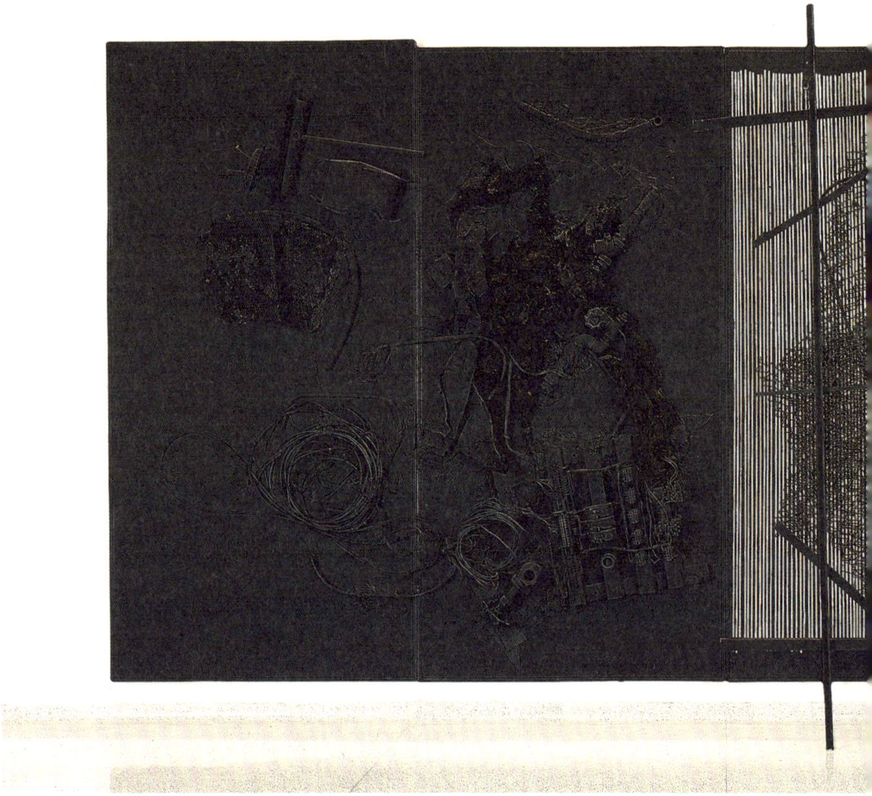

opposite of Tinguely and of the New Realists in general. We coincided temporarily, more because of form than substance, and that's why I couldn't ever fully adhere to their ideas. Tinguely, for example, was a brilliant and well-educated man who emerged from the most absolute perfectionism that is Switzerland. Switzerland was perfect in its economic and political system. That's why I think he reacted and began mocking machines, clocks, and mechanical perfectionism. If you look at them, his works are absurd mechanisms, halfway between contemporary technology and a sort of primitive mechanics.

AJ That attitude intensified toward the end of his life, when he started introducing pieces of skeletons in his machineries, whether real or manufactured.

JS Those concerns are a reaction to another problem. He started doing that after his first heart attack. That's when his fear of death began.

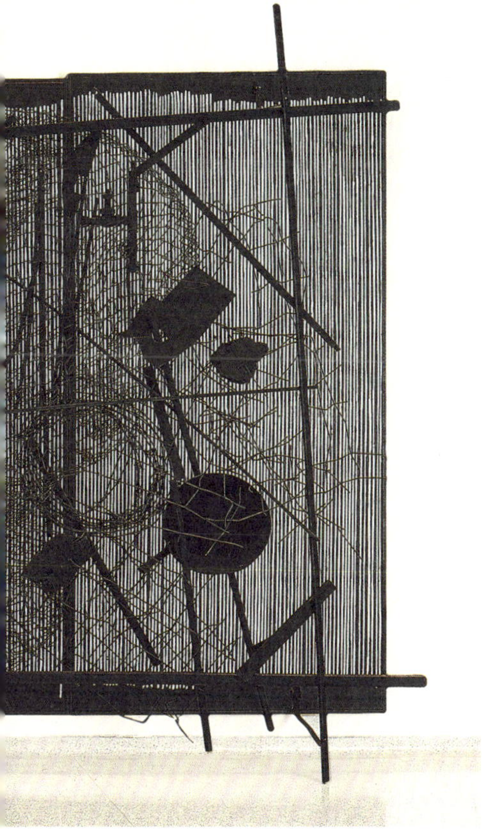

Fig. 35. *Mural,* 1961.

AJ No doubt, but Tinguely turns that personal fear into a symptom of our civilization. . . .

JS Maybe, but it has to do with a culture that is tired of doing things right, and Tinguely belongs to that culture. As a result, art is presented as a kind of antithesis to move the foundations of culture, like a call for regeneration. In Venezuela we don't have anything already made; we have nature on our side, but we are starting to tame it, and until we have a perfectly formed social structure, we have no right to destroy. We cannot act that way; we need to build first. That is why I have always defended the concept of structure, and at the very least that is what I hope to give my country. I don't know what value it may have, what intensity it may achieve, but at least I intend to leave it clearly and precisely. I want structure for Venezuela, and thus for Latin America. The most important thing, what concerns me the most, is to give my field a notion of what this country must be someday.

AJ On various occasions you have objected to the term "Baroque." Why do you believe this term does not define your work?

JS No, it doesn't define it. I began with contemporary artistic propositions or manifestations to which I wanted to give a space-time dimension, because I thought they could be more effective if we took them toward movement [Fig. 36].

AJ Yet you have been interested in Bach's music for years.

JS Yes, but Bach was not a Baroque musician, he was more of a structuralist. His problem was to obtain the greatest spectacle with the fewest elements—an immense job that had nothing to do with the Baroque.

AJ In your opinion, then, what would be the essence of the Baroque?

JS The Baroque, in all cases, sought movement.

AJ Once this inner need was fulfilled, in the so-called Baroque period, you once again began to control the pictorial elements you used. This occurred around 1962. Could you tell me how and why you did that?

JS Because I think that controlling the elements doesn't necessarily have to do with the behavior of the artist as a person. There came a time when I needed to restructure, and then I tried to avoid all distractions. The goal is not to create a structure in and of itself, but to figure out a way to capture universal values that you cannot capture otherwise. When you enter a world as vast as the one I was handling in those "Baroque" works, where you try to confront universal values, that universal consciousness that exists but is too colossal for human consciousness, you have to concentrate and limit the media you employ. Otherwise things start getting out of hand, you get lost. It's as if you needed to create controllable steps, antennae that can help you navigate that world a little better. The possibilities are not reduced; spatial ambiguity, vibration, the dematerialization of bodies, and everything that existed in that Baroque world are there, concentrated. For example, consider *Vibration: Cube bleu* [*Vibration: Blue Cube*], from 1962 [Fig. 37]. There you have space, movement, and the dematerialization

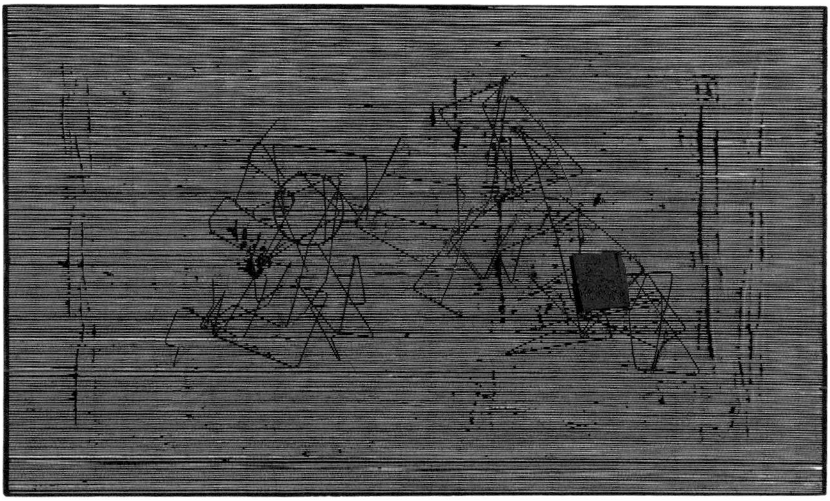

Fig. 36. *Hommage à Yves Klein* [*Homage to Yves Klein*], 1961.

of bodies. In earlier works, the cube could have been a branch or a needle; here it is concentrated in a cube, in a precise and controllable form.

AJ Another important aspect about this period is that you seem to re-engage in the process that stopped with the metal structures of 1956–57, to slowly arrive at the *Penetrable*, one of your most important contributions. Could you describe the process that took you from these first metal structures, which you would later term *Pre-penetrables*, to the *Penetrables* that we know today?

JS That was a very slow process that perhaps came from—and I'm saying this to myself now—the fascination I felt for what went on between the Plexiglas sheets of my first kinetic structures. I always wanted to get inside them. Later on, when I started working with the metal rods over the woven background, I started wondering what would happen if I put myself inside that vibration. If I started to superimpose the rods on several levels, like I did with Plexiglas twenty years earlier, maybe I could capture new values. This was what I tried to do at the Venice Biennale in 1966, although it wasn't truly a *Penetrable*. I took an angle and covered it with rods, trying to envelop the spectator. Then in 1966 and 1967 the idea of the *Penetrable* progressively emerged, by multiplying those rods until they covered the whole space and became an autonomous work [Fig. 38].

AJ If we were to try to write a short history of the *Penetrable,* I believe the next point on the timeline would be the exhibition Denise René organized for you in 1967, in which the rods invade a large part of the space, even beyond what happened in Venice, isn't that right?

JS In reality there were two exhibitions, one at the gallery on the Left Bank of the Seine, and the other at the gallery on the Right Bank. At the gallery on the Left Bank I exhibited my first *Penetrable*, although it was not more than a meter wide. It was small, but people could go in and they had a lot of fun; they played inside. It was a floor-to-ceiling metal *Penetrable* with wire rods that were unpainted, which gave them a very beautiful silvery color.[71] When you entered, since they were metal rods, they produced a sound like this (Soto lowers his head and makes a gesture with his hands, trying to describe an enveloping sound, like that of rain).

71. It is interesting to note the silvery quality of the metal rods. "Silvery" is the same term that Soto used to describe the light of the Impressionists.

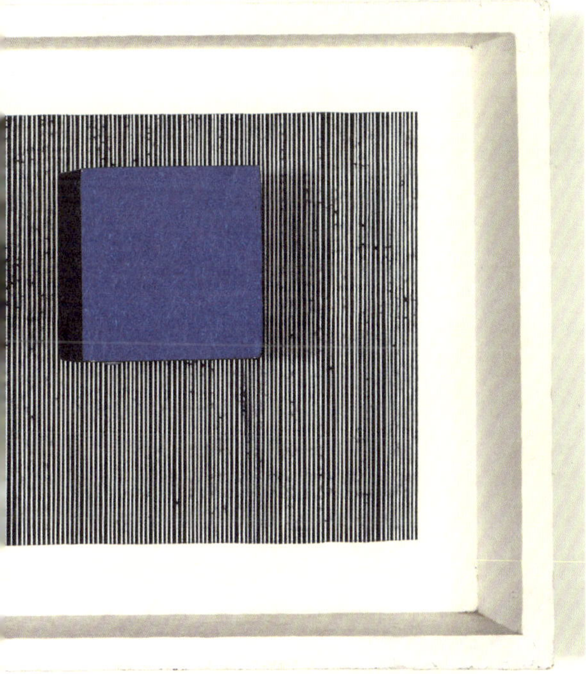

Fig. 37. *Vibration: Cube bleu* [*Vibration: Blue Cube*], 1962.

AJ To my understanding, it is significant that the core shape of your first *Penetrable* is a wide black cross, exactly like *Black Cross,* 1915, by Kazimir Malevich. It's as if this first *Penetrable* were telling us that, by entering that small area of light and sound, we were also penetrating the historic and visual boundary defined by Malevich, an area that also had an obvious mystical dimension [Fig. 39]. Doesn't this fact suggest the possibility of a very particular reading of the *Penetrable*, in the sense that it allows us to consider it a doubly redeeming device, both historical and metaphysical, so to speak?

JS I never thought of it that way, but it is a surprisingly seductive reading. In any event, I was trying to create truly enveloping works. That's what I called them: "enveloping." It was Jean Clay who started calling them *Penetrables*, perhaps because I told him that I had always wanted to penetrate that vibrating world of my Plexiglasses. For that reason I tried to make an enveloping wall at that first exhibition, a kind of half oval around the first *Penetrable*. I remember that the director of the Marlborough Gallery came to the exhibition and when he

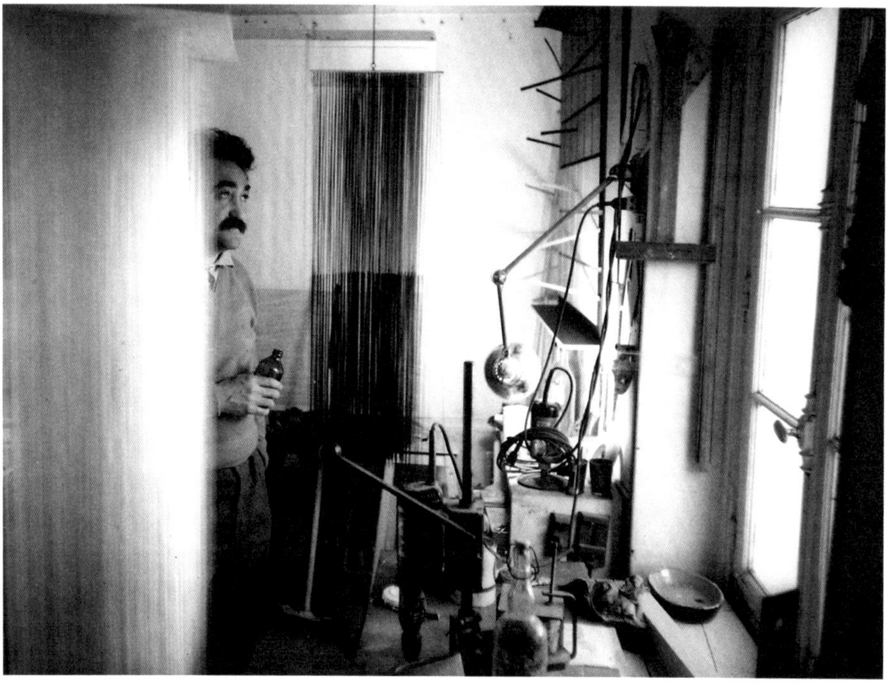

Fig. 38. Jesús Soto in his Paris studio on rue de Turenne, c. 1967.

saw the rods that ended close to the gallery window, he turned to me, surprised, and said: "It is like a dream."[72]

At the Right Bank exhibition I showed several pieces; some were of Plexiglas and there was also a suspended volume that was in fact the model I used for the large volume I exhibited at the Venezuelan Pavilion at the World's Fair in Montreal. Its support was a white square with a cross inscribed on it diagonally. The cross was narrower than Malevich's. . . . Villanueva liked it a lot. The sides of the cross formed a curve. I also did an enveloping work there that started on the ceiling and covered one of the walls of the gallery.

After that first *Penetrable* I made another one that was more autonomous, at the 1968 exhibition at the Fondation Maeght in Saint Paul de Vence. It was a large virtual cube with transparent striped walls. You entered it through a penetrable tower at one of the corners, and inside the cube you arrived at a circular

72. Because of the title that ultimately stayed with these types of pieces, they have traditionally been interpreted as penetrable works—in other words, structures that allow the spectator to penetrate the work from the outside. Soto's descriptions and the terms he used at the beginning present them as the active product of a "painting" that, on the contrary, seeks to absorb the spectator from the inside. This simple fact situates these works within a broad family of pieces that have traditionally sought to draw the spectator in as a participant in the work, just as Leon Battista Alberti described it in his treatise *On Painting*, dated 1435.

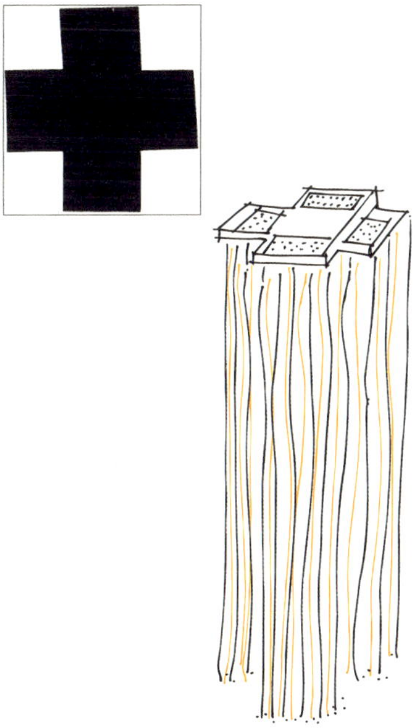

Fig. 39. Sketch of Kazimir Malevich's *Black Cross,* 1915, and Jesús Soto's first *Penetrable,* 1967.

space formed by the rods that covered the walls and corners of the cube. That circle was uncovered; it had no roof. Then I made other *Penetrables*, before the one I presented at my 1969 retrospective at the Musée d'Art Moderne de la Ville de Paris, but I don't remember details of their characteristics.

AJ What was your intention? What made you think of an entrance tower? Why did you leave the middle uncovered, like a roofless dome?

JS What I tried to do—I think—was join the tower of the cross, the one from my first *Penetrable*, with an enveloping space.

AJ Why not do it with the same height?

JS To mark the entrance . . .

AJ Do you realize that this structure is essentially the same as that of a Baroque church, with its clearly marked entrance and its inner dome metaphorically open to heaven?

JS No, I hadn't thought of it that way. And yet, it reminds me of an experience I had in Rome during my first exhibition at the Marlborough Gallery in the 1960s. I remember that a friend of mine, Sergio Tosi, took me to the Roman Pantheon, telling me "Come with me, I want you to see a world very similar to yours." When I entered, I was surprised to see the space of that perfect building dominated by the opening in the roof from which a stream of light descended . . . and through which you could see infinity [Fig. 40]. It is very similar to one of the *Penetrables* I made later on, in 1971 [Fig. 41][73], where a number of rods penetrate a plane that is open in the middle, like a stream of light descending from the ceiling, or like the stream that seemed to emerge from *Espiral*, of 1955, that came out of the painting, perpendicular to the two Plexiglas planes. . . . I conceive light like that, as a kind of intermediary between energy and matter. Energy is absolutely sublime, whereas light is already an initial loss of speed. . . . It's as if energy were becoming gradually less sublime until it becomes matter, its less sublime state. What I don't understand is why the sublime starts becoming less sublime as it becomes matter. . . . Even so, I believe that someday it will return to its original sublime state. . . .

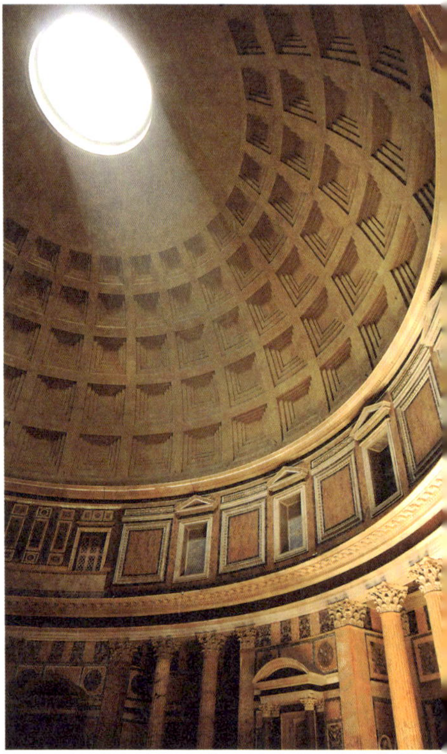

Fig. 40. Pantheon, Rome.

AJ Luis Enrique Pérez-Oramas pointed out to me that the *Penetrables* have been discussed in two different ways: either insisting upon the possibility of materializing or making evident what you call the plenitude of space, that "gelatin" you have often mentioned to me; or else emphasizing their ability to optically

73. Soto does not say he created that 1971 *Penetrable* thinking expressly of Agrippa's Pantheon, nor did I ask him about it at the time. In any event, the experience at the Roman Pantheon occurred before the *Penetrable*, which allows us to infer that, in fact, something of that experience did ultimately get expressed in the 1971 *Penetrable*.

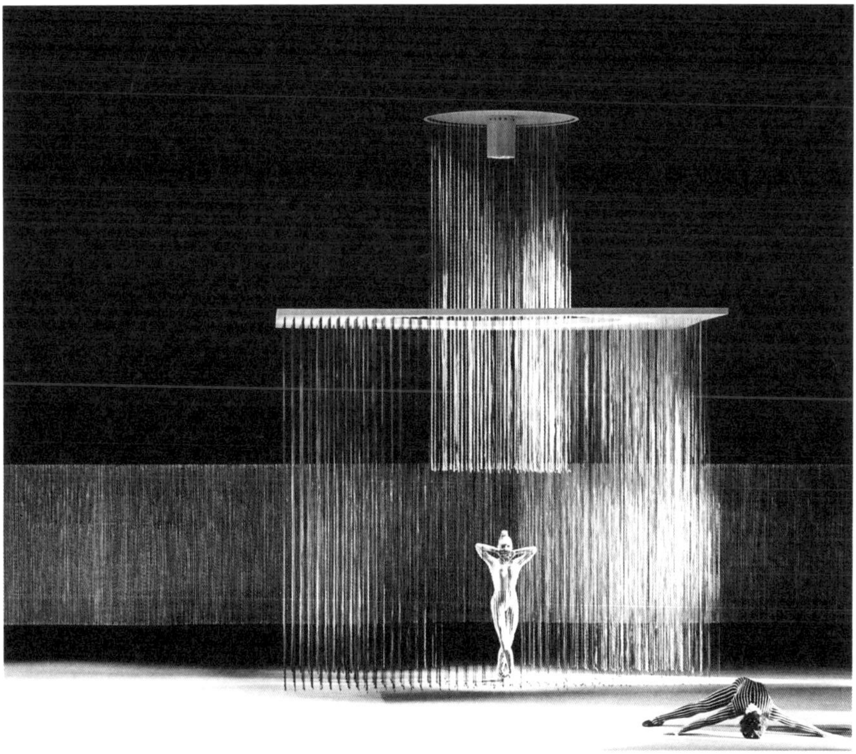

Fig. 41. Penetrable set design for *Violostries* (by Bernard Parmegiani), Ballet-théâtre contemporain de Paris, 1971.

dematerialize the bodies that penetrate them. For you, what is more important in the *Penetrable*, the possibility of making the density of space evident, or its dematerializing capacity?

JS The important thing is to show that space is fluid and full, because it has always been considered—as in the Renaissance—a place where things can be put, more than as a primal and universal value. I have often told you that I don't care about the elements; they are there only to make relationships evident. So what interests me primarily in the *Penetrable* is the density of space . . . and people feel it like that; when they enter a *Penetrable* they feel that it is another space, and they begin to play and move. I discussed it a lot with Yves Klein, because to his way of thinking the most important thing was the void. Of course, he said it from the perspective of Oriental wisdom, while I insisted upon the density of space, its plenitude.

AJ The *Penetrables* are conceived as structures that can encompass the entirety of a space. Now, if you had to make a *Penetrable* in an irregular space, would you cover all the existing space?

JS Of course: the *Penetrable* isn't even a work, it is an idea of space that can materialize in any situation and at any scale. . . . If it were possible, you could even cover the whole planet . . . that's not the important thing.

AJ Despite that, when you have the chance to do it in an open space, you invariably resort to the cube [Fig. 42].

JS Because that is the most obvious thing; if not, the public would perceive it as a sculpture or something drawn, and would ascribe to the form of the penetrable an aesthetic value it doesn't have in my work.

NO STAGE IS DEFINITIVELY CONCLUDED

AJ We might say that your mature period begins with the emergence of the *Penetrable* in the 1960s, a time in which you purge and develop your central concepts. This mature period also gave birth to your most recent work, the *Ambivalencias* [*Ambivalences*]. They emerge from a process of revision that is characteristic of your pictorial thinking.

JS After having worked in the 1960s and 1970s within a certain sense of moderation with respect to the use of color, I became interested again in this element, but from a different perspective than that of 1956–57. In those years I was interested in the possibilities of color combinations and vibrations, independent of or opposed to the traditional concepts of chromatic harmony. My purpose was not and has never been to find a beautiful harmony of colors, but to put them to work, to combine and blend them randomly, as if color were part of a magma in which man finds or creates the harmonies that interest him. Deep down, I wanted to let them coexist as they do in nature, with no preconceived concept of harmony. All the superimposed colors could create new colors. That is what I did, for example, in *Armonía transformable* [*Transformable Harmony*], of 1956. By the end of the 1970s I became preoccupied with color again. I have never been afraid to re-approach problems that could be improved or that I left unfinished, either because I focused on other types of concerns and could not

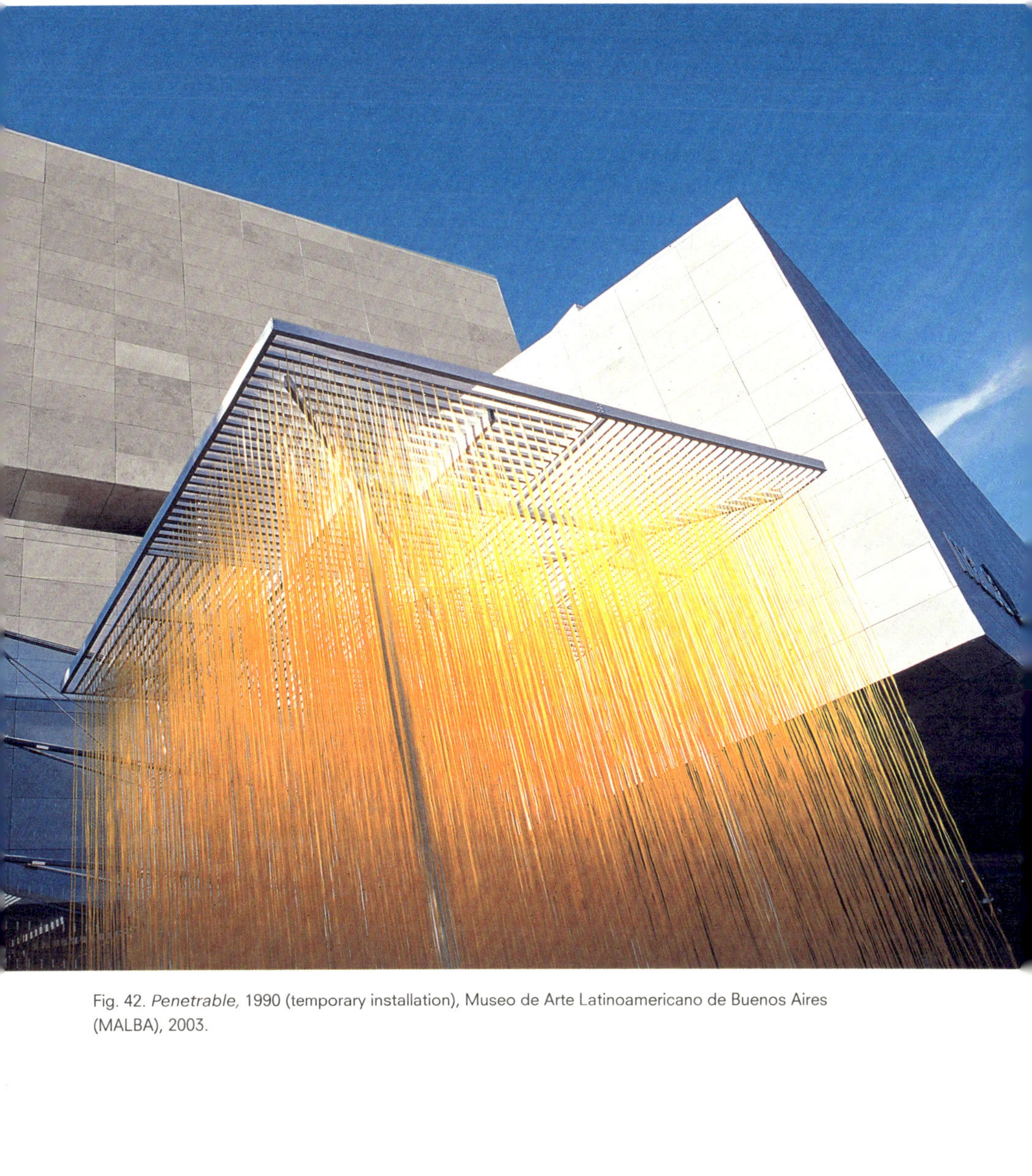

Fig. 42. *Penetrable,* 1990 (temporary installation), Museo de Arte Latinoamericano de Buenos Aires (MALBA), 2003.

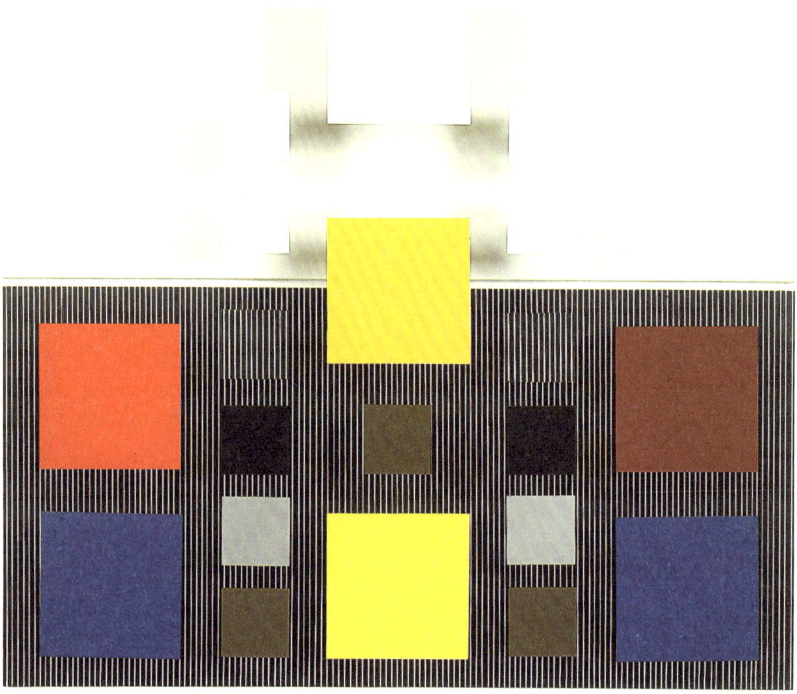

Fig. 43. *Planos ambivalentes* [*Ambivalent Planes*], 1981.

develop them, or because I didn't have the necessary technique or concepts to move them forward.

This is because I conceive art as a set of questions that must be solved by the artist, because they are problems posed by the age he lives in and not because he feels like doing it. The history of art takes you down that path, and you become a creator insofar as you find solutions to these questions. Artists in general are concerned about doing something personal and original, whereas I have always thought that, to the contrary, it is about something else: taking on the history of art and pushing it forward a little, taking a supplementary step within the issues it poses.

The *Ambivalencias* are the solution I found to a number of issues that were more or less implicit in [the work of] the great Western artists from the end of the nineteenth century onward, but that had not been developed. As a result of the *Fauves,* of individuals like Matisse, Léger, Delaunay, the Russian constructivists, and in general those who tried to use color independently of form and extra-pictorial content, the power and ambiguity of color become manifest, and we witness its capacity to generate the illusion of a space that is optically variable, as some dots seem to advance while others seem to recede. Later, Swiss artists and some Germans like Josef Albers proposed the independence of color, but without consciously solving what I have called the "spatial ambivalence of color." I then felt that color needed and demanded a space-time solution that could find a place within the spatial ambiguity that I was interested in revealing.

I then tried to introduce color no longer in its vibratory state, as I did in the 1950s, but with the color plane floating on the surface of the painting, so that the colors themselves might establish a chromo-dynamic relationship. The result is an obvious ambiguity of color in space. If you place a child in front of these works, he will see colors that advance while others seem to recede. Also, this situation is variable and reversible [Fig. 43]. Now, when the issue of chromatic ambivalence in space no longer satisfies me, I will focus on other concerns. It will never be a rupture, a denial of the problems posed previously. For me, there are no stages that are definitively concluded, and I feel completely free to take them up again when I feel the need.

AJ Nevertheless, there is a fundamental difference between revisiting issues that weren't sufficiently developed in order to move them forward or finding a new pictorial solution, and what I feel in some of your recent pieces, for example the *Leños* [*Logs*] that you are redoing now [Fig. 44].

Do you feel they represent an advancement? Wouldn't they indicate, on the contrary, the emergence of a different position regarding history? Wouldn't they introduce a certain lack of temporality regarding artistic issues?

JS Well, what happens is I make them for friends. . . . I have many friends who feel frustrated because they don't have one of these pieces, and when they find a piece of wood, I make them a *Leño*. . . . It's a matter of affection for my friends. . . .

AJ Do you consider them true creations or a sort of anachronistic fact?

JS No. They are developed like any other piece, and signed, but they bring together—and this is normal—the contributions of all the experiences I have had. I don't believe they are anachronistic, I don't think you can say that. . . . Art

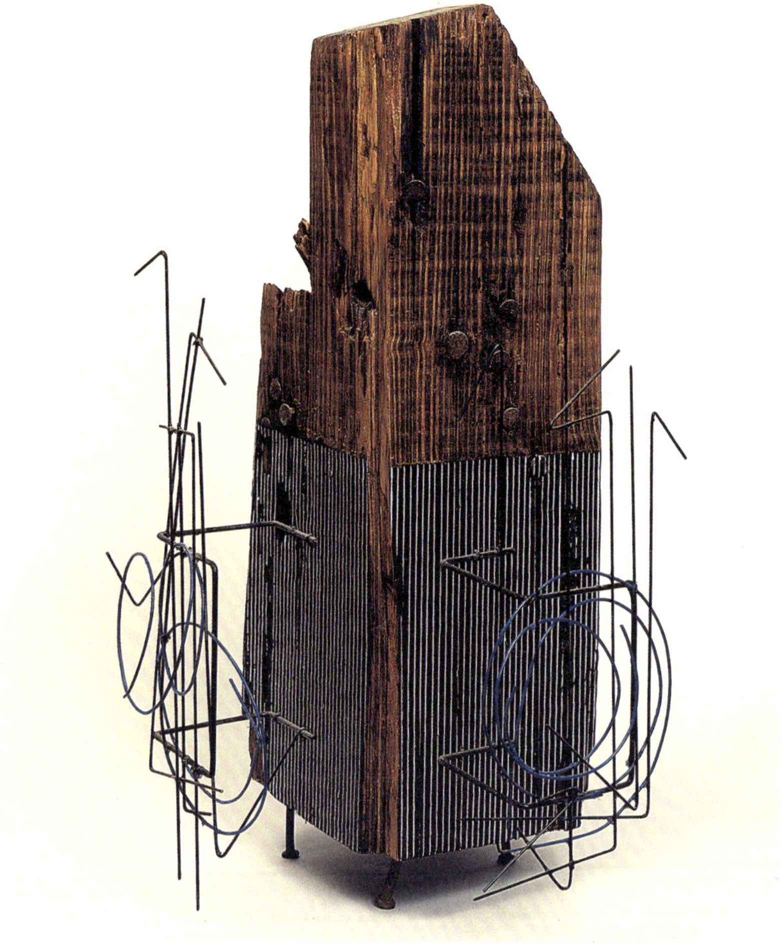

Fig. 44. *Leño* [*Log*], 2002.

is a timeless phenomenon; what happens is that it dates, it puts dates on pieces to allow history to situate it according to periods, but the Impressionist idea of atomizing light is still valid today.

AJ In a way, you are suggesting that the pictorial solution found by the artist can be dated and can be deemed material worthy of analysis by historians, while the problems it tackles are timeless.

JS Yes, those problems continue to be valid.

AJ Do you currently have some intuition of what you might do in the future?

JS I don't know, because I have never thought about what I'm going to do tomorrow. My head is full of many possibilities, which is logical when you are not reconstructing or aestheticizing on the basis of established values. I think we each have an infinite number of windows, eternal windows, from which we must decide where to leap. But I never do it wondering what I will invent tomorrow. I see art not as gratuitous invention, but as the intellectual development of man in history. I have not spent sleepless nights before knowing what I would do the next day; fortunately those dramas don't exist for me. If at a given moment I see the possibility of moving forward in a specific direction, I do it, but I never plan what I have to do, and in fact I don't feel any obligation to do anything tomorrow.

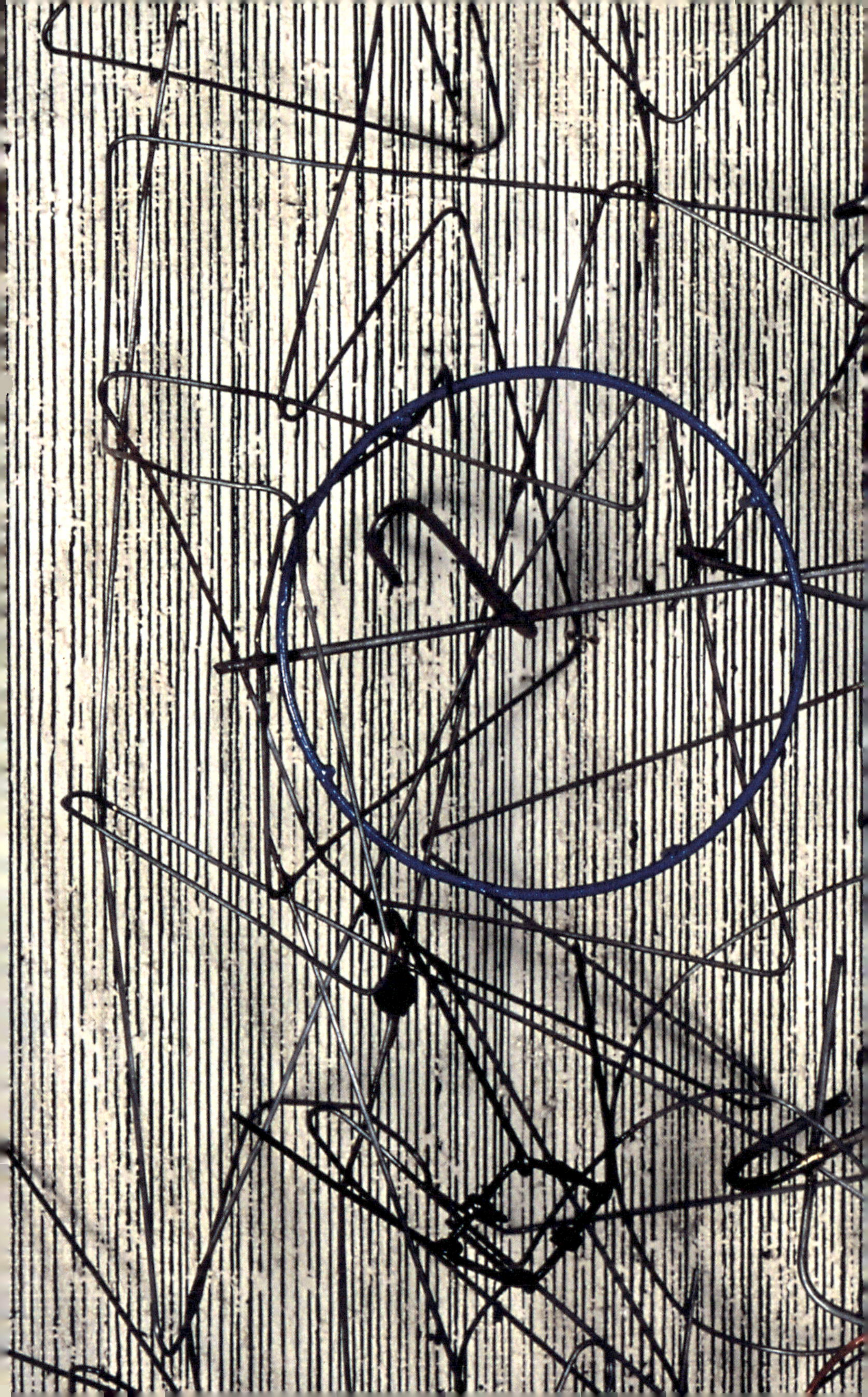

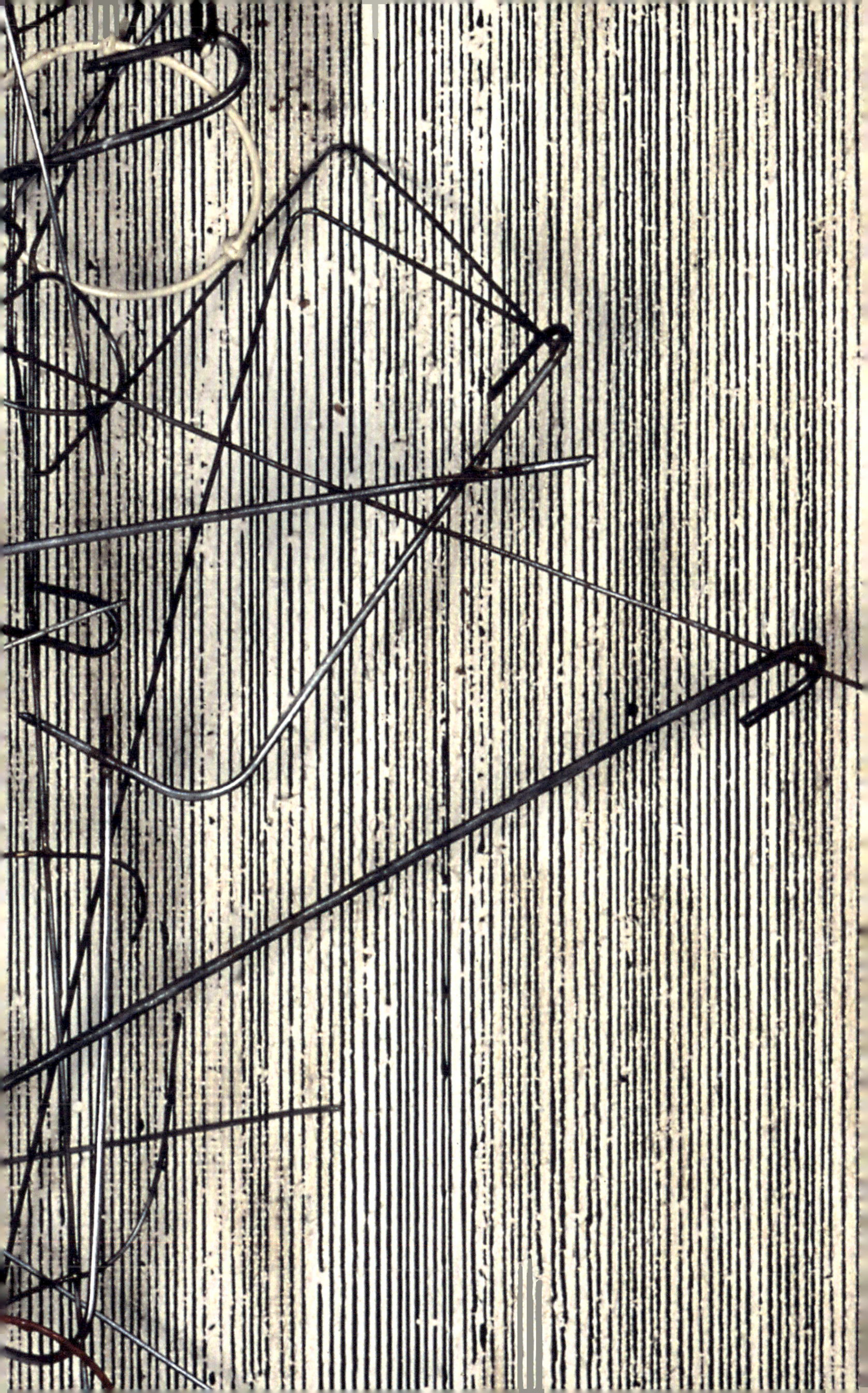

INTRODUCCIÓN

En 2001, la Colección Patricia Phelps de Cisneros (CPPC) publicó la primera versión de *Conversaciones con Jesús Soto,* de Ariel Jiménez, dentro de su serie *Cuadernos*. El libro fue considerablemente ampliado para la segunda edición en 2005, la cual constituye la base del presente volumen. Ambas ediciones fueron coordinadas bajo la dirección de Rafael Romero, el primer director de la CPPC y actual director emérito, y de Peter Tinoco, anterior presidente de la Fundación Cisneros, hoy en día su presidente emérito. Numerosos y significativos han sido los cambios ocurridos en la década que separa la primera publicación de ésta que aquí presentamos; quizás lo más notable sea la creciente apreciación, a nivel internacional, de las contribuciones de Soto y de otros artistas latinoamericanos pioneros a la historia del arte. La Colección Patricia Phelps de Cisneros ha sido, simultáneamente, testigo y promotor de estos cambios, organizando o apoyando exposiciones, otorgando préstamos de obras, realizando seminarios y publicaciones, con la misión de desarticular los estereotipos que por tanto tiempo han nublado la percepción del arte y la cultura latinoamericanos, y es por ello que nos sentimos muy orgullosos de poder relanzar este importante libro para que llegue a nuevos lectores.

Conversaciones con Jesús Soto es un proyecto con resonancia especial para la Fundación Cisneros/Colección Patricia Phelps de Cisneros, ya que Jesús Soto fue, de diversas maneras, un artista emblemático de la CPPC y por muchas décadas hubo una cercana amistad entre Soto y la Colección. Además este manuscrito fue la inspiración para la serie *Conversaciones*, que es en la actualidad la iniciativa más importante de investigación y publicación de la CPPC. Esta reedición constituye el cuarto volumen de la serie, después de haber dedicado libros a Carlos Cruz-Diez, a Tomás Maldonado y a Jac Leirner. De orígenes profundamente venezolanos, de Ciudad Bolívar, en el corazón del país, la incansable curiosidad de Soto lo llevó a París, y de allí a un ir y venir entre Venezuela y Francia, que lo convirtió, sin duda, en el creador venezolano más famoso y prominente en el escenario mundial. La incesante investigación de Soto sobre la forma, la luz y la vibración, se hizo sentir en cada continente donde se convirtió en el ícono de un arte que podría ser objetivo y sugestivo, científico y poético, todo al mismo tiempo. Fue un ejemplo vital para muchos artistas jóvenes que luchaban por escapar de los prejuicios folclóricos asociados con Latinoamérica, que la definían apenas como una tierra de conflicto y exotismo. Soto significó

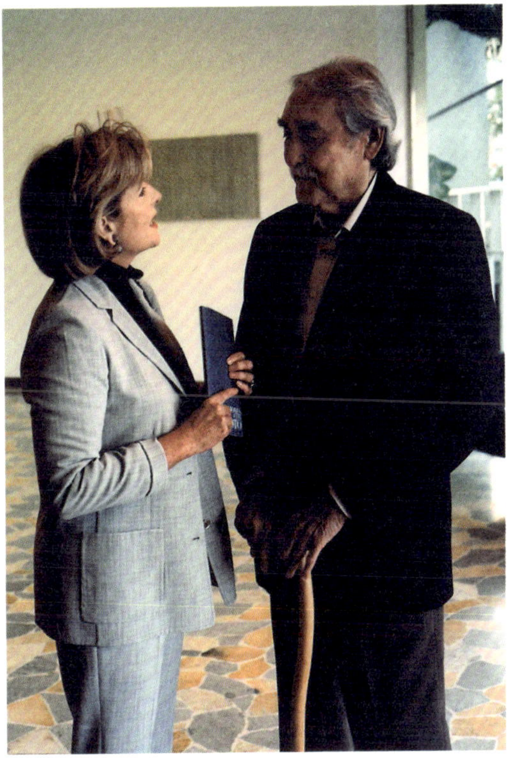

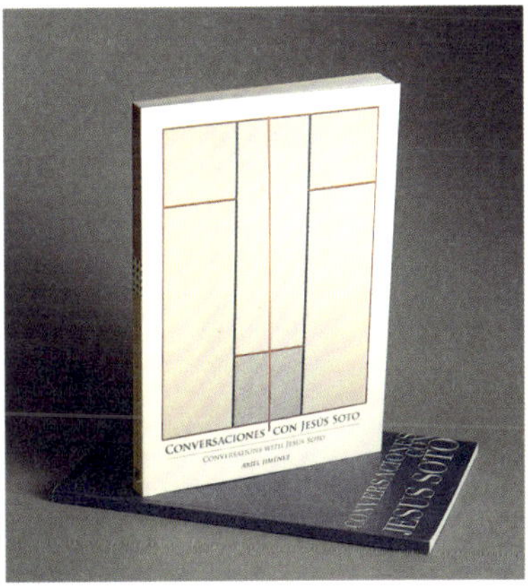

Arriba: Primera (2001) y segunda (2005) ediciones de *Conversaciones con Jesús Soto.*

A la izquierda: Patricia Phelps de Cisneros y Jesús Soto en el lanzamiento de *Conversaciones con Jesús Soto* el 6 de febrero de 2002 en Caracas.

un modelo progresista y optimista de una América Latina que podía dialogar sin restricciones con el resto del mundo, y su obra y trabajo fueron prueba de que ello era posible. Esta creencia compartida fue también la razón de la empatía natural entre la familia y la Fundación Cisneros y Soto durante toda su vida, así como de una alianza de profundo respeto y admiración mutua.

Es preciso agradecer a Ariel Jiménez, curador jefe de la CPPC, por su visión en la ejecución de la serie *Conversaciones* y por su cuidada edición y ensamblaje del manuscrito definitivo. Jiménez y Soto se conocieron en 1977, y en los años ochenta Jiménez ocupó el cargo de asistente en el estudio del artista en París, logrando tener una perspectiva única acerca de los aspectos filosóficos y prácticos de la obra de Soto. Fue en 1995 cuando ambos comenzaron formalmente estas conversaciones, las cuales continuaron con gran intensidad por años. Jiménez es considerado una autoridad internacional en cuanto a Soto se refiere; además fue nombrado director del Museo de Arte Moderno Jesús Soto, ubicado en Ciudad Bolívar, durante los últimos años de vida del artista, un cargo que ejerció de manera simultánea con sus funciones en la CPPC. La producción de esta edición revisada y corregida fue supervisada por Ileen Kohn

Sosa y Donna Wingate, quienes adicionalmente examinaron el manuscrito y las traducciones con María Esther Pino y Kristina Cordero. Damos las gracias al equipo de Marquand Books por su esmerada atención a los detalles y a la calidad del resultado. Por último, agradecemos muy especialmente a la Sucesión Soto, por su colaboración en este proyecto.

El testimonio contenido en la presente obra es la más completa y detallada descripción de la obra de Soto, explicada en las propias palabras de su creador, y ha proporcionado valiosa información a estudiantes e investigadores. Ante el creciente interés en la obra de Soto y en el arte geométrico y cinético en general, esperamos que este volumen continúe instruyendo e inspirando a un público, cada vez más numeroso, interesado en las obras e ideas de Soto.

Gabriel Pérez-Barreiro

Director, Colección Patricia Phelps de Cisneros

NOTA AL LECTOR

Para esta tercera edición de *Conversaciones con Jesús Soto* hemos introducido una serie de cambios que, sin afectar en esencia el texto publicado en vida del artista, lo enriquecen y hacen más fluida su lectura.

La primera modificación se limitó a reemplazar las palabras repetidas, en particular aquellas que, por su cotidianidad, empleamos a veces inadvertidamente, y que pueden ser reemplazadas por otra sin afectar el sentido del texto. Se le prestó por supuesto una atención especial a esta intervención, sobre todo para no afectar aquellos términos que revisten una importancia crucial en el pensamiento de Jesús Soto, como los calificativos que emplea para referirse a los conceptos de espacio, tiempo, materia y energía.

La segunda intervención tuvo que ver con la reubicación de una pregunta y su respuesta, colocándolas en una secuencia cronológica más coherente con los procesos del artista, con lo que la posición de algunas imágenes se hizo también más fácilmente legible para el lector.

El resto de las modificaciones introducidas en esta edición se restringen al material de apoyo, como las imágenes y las notas que acompañan al texto. En este sentido, no solo ampliamos el número de imágenes reproducidas, sino que repensamos la relación entre una obra y otra, y entre éstas y el texto, siempre con el objetivo de facilitar su lectura y de enriquecer la comprensión que el lector pueda hacerse de Jesús Soto y de su procesos creativos. Se agregaron algunas notas a pie de página, se eliminaron otras y, en ocasiones, las más largas fueron incluidas como intervenciones del entrevistador.

Con todo ello, esperamos presentarle al público interesado por el arte latinoamericano una versión más completa de estas conversaciones con Jesús Soto.

Ariel Jiménez

JESÚS SOTO

EN CONVERSACIÓN CON

ARIEL JIMÉNEZ

El misterio es lo más hermoso que nos es dado sentir. Es la sensación fundamental, la cuna del arte y de la ciencia verdaderos. Quien no la conoce, quien no puede asombrarse ni maravillarse, está muerto. Sus ojos se han extinguido.

A mí me parece que tal es la función principal del arte y de la ciencia: despertar y mantener vivo ese sentimiento en todos aquellos que estén dispuestos a recibirlo.

Albert Einstein
Mi visión del mundo

IR A CARACAS

ARIEL JIMÉNEZ Cuando se piensa en lo que podía ser Ciudad Bolívar[1] hacia los años veinte, esa pequeña capital regional aún dominada por la presencia del paisaje, sin museos, sin ninguna actividad que pudiera alimentar la vida intelectual de un joven pintor, no podemos dejar de pensar en aquella frase con la que Freud describe la actividad artística como un hecho sicológicamente misterioso. ¿De dónde, por qué vías surge en efecto en un joven la vocación artística en un medio donde nada parecía hacerlo posible? ¿Qué noción del arte podía hacerse un joven en la Ciudad Bolívar de los años veinte?

JESUS SOTO Cuando comencé a pensar en el arte y a sentirme concernido por el problema creativo, encontré en realidad muy poco, casi nada, en Ciudad Bolívar. Conocí un teatro que fue destruido durante la época de Juan Vicente Gómez.[2] Llegué a verlo de niño, cuando tenía unos cuatro años de edad, aunque no recuerdo cuándo lo destruyeron. En él se producían espectáculos interesantes para un centro de ese tamaño. Actuaban zarzuelas, daban recitales; había un cierto movimiento de carácter nacional e inclusive internacional. Ciudad Bolívar era entonces una especie de puente entre Europa y el interior del país, debido esencialmente a la explotación de una serie de productos que ya no ocupan un puesto importante en nuestro mercado, pero que entonces sí era considerable: las plumas de garza, la sarrapia y el caucho. Todo eso pasaba por la ciudad, que era el puerto internacional a donde venían a buscar esa mercancía. Siempre he pensado que Ciudad Bolívar era una especie de pequeño Manaos[3] donde sucedían cosas poco comunes; allí llegaban artistas que venían directamente del extranjero sin pasar por Caracas. Para ellos era más cómodo bajarse en Trinidad y tomar los barcos del Orinoco [Fig. 1], que venirse a Caracas hasta donde no existía comunicación por carretera, mientras que por mar estaba a más de quince días de trayecto en los barcos costaneros. Yo llegué a montarme

1. Capital del Estado Bolívar, situada al borde del río Orinoco, al sureste de Venezuela.

2. Dictador venezolano oriundo del Estado Táchira en Los Andes (1857–1935). Gobernó al país entre 1908 y 1935. Creó la primera red de carreteras nacionales e inició la explotación industrial del petróleo.

3. Ciudad ubicada al noreste brasileño, en plena selva amazónica. Tuvo una importancia económica considerable durante el siglo XIX, gracias esencialmente a la explotación del caucho. Se le conoce principalmente por su célebre Teatro Amazonas, donde se presentaron estrellas como Caruso y Sarah Bernhardt.

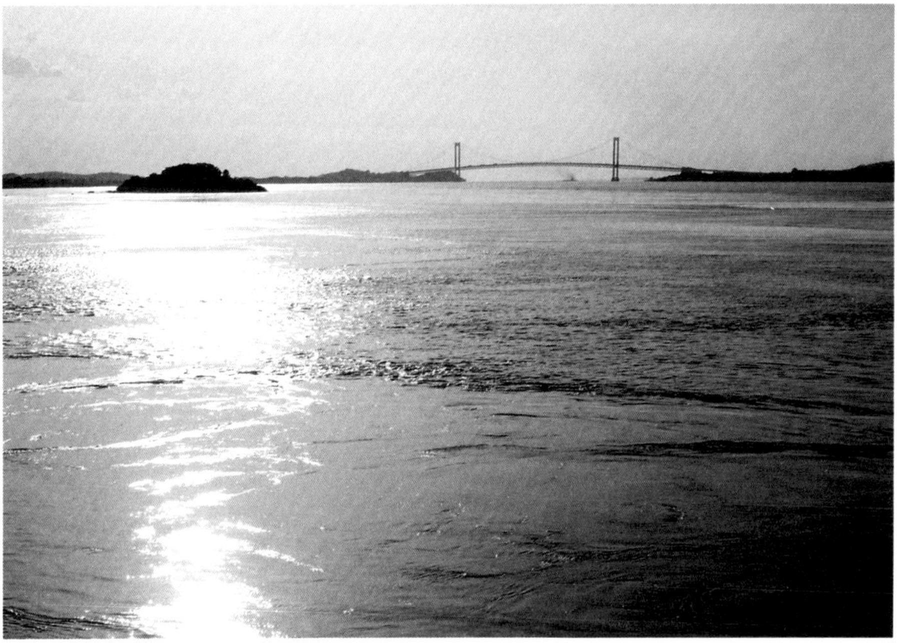

Fig. 1. Puente sobre el río Orinoco, Ciudad Bolívar.

en uno de esos barcos; así pude conocer cada uno de los pueblitos de la costa, entre Ciudad Bolívar y el puerto de Maracaibo.[4]

AJ Algo similar sucedía con capitales regionales como Puerto Cabello[5] y Maracaibo, que mantenían un contacto con el exterior relativamente independiente de la capital nacional.

JS Eran centros regionales bastante independientes de Caracas. Incluso, los jóvenes de Ciudad Bolívar que no podían ir a estudiar a Europa, no se dirigían a Caracas, sino que estudiaban en las escuelas privadas de Trinidad. Allí se formó mucha gente hasta que se construyeron las carreteras entre Caracas y Ciudad Bolívar. . .

4. Capital del Estado Zulia, situada al extremo noroeste de Venezuela, al borde del lago que lleva su nombre.

5. Es el puerto más importante de la costa venezolana por el volumen de carga que moviliza y por servir de puerta de entrada a la zona industrial centro-norte del país. El puerto y la ciudad del mismo nombre están ubicados en el llamado golfo Triste.

Soto recordaba todavía la construcción de las carreteras que por primera vez, durante el régimen gomecista, permitieron un contacto fluido con la capital.

Eso ocurrió después de la Primera Guerra Mundial. Yo era muy niño. Una tía mía vivía con un militar de la guarnición que vigilaba la construcción de la carretera, y me llevó a pasar unos quince días con ella. De ese modo pude visitar a los presos en la noche. A mí me aceptaban, primero porque era niño, y segundo porque estaba viviendo en la casa de uno de los jefes. Allí dormía un esbirro que cuidaba a los presos. Yo quise conocerlo y los presos me lo enseñaron. Te estoy hablando de un sitio que se llama La Canoa, que queda entre El Tigre y Ciudad Bolívar. Más tarde supe que otro grupo de presos trabajaba cerca de Valle de la Pascua, en Palenque.[6]

AJ Es indudable que sus memorias infantiles están más íntimamente unidas a las experiencias sencillas que podía tener un niño en el ambiente rural de Ciudad Bolívar que a las de una vida culturalmente rica. Esa interacción privilegiada con la naturaleza que Alejandro Otero[7] calificó de "contacto con la elemental realidad del mundo",[8] lo marcarían por ello con una peculiar intensidad, al mismo nivel que las escasas lecturas que entonces ampliaban su horizonte intelectual.

JS Una de las experiencias que recuerdo con mayor entusiasmo no es de Ciudad Bolívar, sino precisamente de una casa que mi tía poseía en el campo, donde yo pasaba a veces mis vacaciones y donde viví algún tiempo. En la casa de mis primos yo debía trabajar como cualquiera de ellos. A cada quien se le asignaba una tarea y el trabajo que me encomendaron a mí era el de mensajero. Montado en un burro, tenía que ir de una casa a la otra, y recuerdo cómo me maravillaba ver la vibración del aire por la reverberación del sol sobre la tierra. Era algo que

6. Una de las más crueles conductas de la dictadura gomecista consistía en obligar a los presos políticos, junto a otros condenados, a efectuar trabajos públicos, en particular la red de carreteras nacionales que se emprendió durante su mandato.

7. Alejandro Otero (1921–90). Artista plástico venezolano originario del Estado Bolívar. Iniciador de la pintura abstracta en Venezuela. Miembro fundador del grupo y la revista *Los Disidentes*, editada en París (1950) por jóvenes artistas e intelectuales venezolanos. Entre sus principales obras se encuentran: la serie de las *cafeteras* (1947–51), los *coloritmos* (1955–60) y sus *esculturas cívicas* (1968–90).

8. Citado en la cronología de Alexander López para el catálogo de la exposición *Alejandro Otero*. Museo de Arte Contemporáneo de Caracas, 1985, 12.

no me cansaba de ver, esa masa vibrante que flotaba en el espacio y que brillaba sobre los caminos.

Tampoco olvido las alucinaciones visuales que tuve durante una enfermedad. Eso sucedió en mi casa. Tuve unas fiebres altísimas, tal vez la fiebre amarilla, no sé, lo cierto es que eso me hacía percibir cosas muy extrañas que me fascinaban y me producían un gran placer, hasta el punto de que no deseaba curarme, porque prefería verlas. La visión consistía en que, observando a una persona, de repente la veía reducirse rápidamente hasta convertirse en un pequeño punto luminoso. El punto crecía luego y restituía su imagen. Eso lo recuerdo claramente, como si fuera hoy.

Otra de las experiencias que nunca he podido olvidar, es la increíble destreza de los indios que pescaban en el Orinoco con arco y flecha. Ellos no le disparaban directamente al pez, en línea recta, sino que lanzaban sus flechas al aire para alcanzarlo tras describir una curva en el espacio. Era increíble que dieran en el blanco de esa manera. Muchas experiencias de este tipo me marcaron por siempre, y, por supuesto, la lectura de los escasos libros que pude encontrar en Ciudad Bolívar me dejaron algunas de las memorias más felices de mi infancia.

Recuerdo particularmente unos cuentos japoneses provenientes de Chile. Uno de ellos contaba la historia de un hombre a quien le habían dicho que en una playa encontraría la piedra filosofal que transformaría en oro todo lo que tocara con ella. El hombre se puso de inmediato a recoger todas las piedras (había miles) que encontraba en la playa, y a tocar con ellas su anillo de hierro. Lo hizo con infinidad de piedrecillas, sin encontrarla. Poco a poco fue reduciendo el ritmo de la búsqueda hasta que llegó a hacerlo ya pocas veces, y casi automáticamente, seguro convencido de que no podría encontrarla. Sin embargo, una mañana, al levantarse, observó que su anillo era de oro, y comprendió que seguramente había sido transformado por alguna de las piedras que recogió, y enseguida botó, inadvertidamente. Es un cuento que me impactó muchísimo porque el hombre había encontrado la piedra filosofal, pero la costumbre le impidió darse cuenta de ello. No pudo reconocerla. La metamorfosis que esperaba se había dado, sorpresivamente, y no supo verla. . .

Soto no quería perder la ocasión de su propia metamorfosis. . .

Otro cuento se refería a la experiencia de un pescador quien, al zambullirse un día en el mar, se encontró, al salir, con un espectáculo increíble. Su pueblo había desaparecido por completo, nadie habitaba ya el lugar. La desolación del sitio y el envejecimiento de las piedras amontonadas, parecían indicarle que fuera del agua (donde él creía haber permanecido pocos segundos), habían transcurrido cientos, tal vez miles de años. La imagen de este hombre confrontado a dos coordenadas temporales radicalmente diferentes, me dejó loco, y se quedó anclada en mi memoria.

Él también, justamente, se sentía vivir entre dos coordenadas temporales radicalmente distintas; entre esa historia prestigiosa y lejana de Europa y el tiempo sin historia de su país natal.

AJ Al escuchar estos relatos de su infancia: la reverberación del sol en las carreteras solitarias, las alucinaciones donde las personas se hacían luz, la transmutación de la materia y del tiempo, es imposible no pensar en lo que sería su producción madura, por completo dedicada a la búsqueda de esa "esencia inmaterial" del universo. La teoría de la relatividad, la ciencia moderna, vendrían después a legitimar ante el adulto las experiencias del niño en la soledad intemporal, sin historia, de su infancia campesina. Éstas no fueron por tanto las únicas lecturas que parecen haber tenido una influencia durable en usted. Arnauld Pierre menciona igualmente, en el catálogo del Jeu de Paume,[9] la lectura de *La divina comedia* de Dante.

JS Es verdad, la leí cuando tenía unos doce o trece años. Me montaba en un árbol, solo, al fondo de mi casa, de modo que nadie pudiera molestarme ni burlarse de mí. Me lo prestó una tía que tenía algunos libros. Recuerdo, como si fuera hoy, la injusticia que me parecía eso de que Virgilio se quedara en una especie de limbo, sin poder ingresar al Paraíso, por no haber recibido el bautismo. Retuve sobre todo la angustia que sentía, y que iba creciendo, a medida que se anunciaba el encuentro de Dante con Dios. Sentía una angustia muy rara, muy fuerte, por el temor que me producía la imagen que pudiera tomar Dios. . . ¿Cómo sería, cómo lo vería Dante? Esa posibilidad de que Dios pudiera tener una figura, de que pudiera parecerse al Dios barbudo de Miguel Ángel, ese Dios amenazante que dice: "Tú debes hacer eso, porque a mí me da la gana", me angustiaba de una manera que todavía hoy, sesenta años más tarde, recuerdo con precisión. Tanto, al menos, como el gran alivio que experimenté cuando descubrí que Dios era solo luz –es decir, energía– que no tenía ni forma ni cuerpo material. Sentí un gran alivio. . . Claro, mi cultura era extremadamente

9. Citado en el catálogo de la exposición individual de Jesús Soto organizada por la Galerie Nationale du Jeu de Paume. París, 1997, n35.

pobre. Afortunadamente Dante lo escribió para que gente humilde pudiera entenderlo. . . y yo lo comprendí como podía hacerlo un campesino.

Cada vez que Soto menciona la luz, se apresura a precisar que ella es, también, energía. Y es que en el adulto se daría luego una especie de superposición entre dos interpretaciones posibles: la religiosa, esa que le proporcionan sus lecturas infantiles de Dante, donde la luz materializa de algún modo una imagen idónea de Dios, su más pura manifestación sensible, y la científica, donde solo es una expresión de la energía, fuente y principio de todo lo que existe. En ambos casos, la luz se convertiría en un principio explicativo e incluso legitimante. A pesar de no ser un hombre religioso, ambas lecturas le acuerdan a la luz un valor trascendente. Atraparla y en cierta forma producirla desde la pintura, lograr su aparición real en la obra sería, para el adulto, una meta plástica y una doble fuente de legitimación, a la vez metafísica (el término religioso *le molesta) e histórica.*

AJ Su preocupación inmediata era, no obstante, la pintura, la posibilidad y la necesidad de darle forma visible a las cosas, aunque sus posibilidades parecían dramáticamente limitadas desde el punto de vista técnico. ¿Cuáles fueron sus primeros contactos con el mundo de la imagen, qué noción de la pintura podía ser la suya entonces?

JS En las paredes de mi casa pude ver algunas reproducciones de Millet, como *El Ángelus* o una de esas parejas sobre el sol poniente. Había incluso una de las vírgenes de Murillo. En Ciudad Bolívar no existía mucha gente interesada en esto, pero pude ver en los libros algunas reproducciones del Renacimiento, además de los pintores históricos de Venezuela, que me interesaban bastante: Arturo Michelena,[10] Martín Tovar y Tovar,[11] Antonio Herrera Toro[12] y el más moderno entre ellos, que era Tito Salas.[13] Recuerdo que estaba muy interesado en ellos.

10. Arturo Michelena (1863–98). Pintor académico venezolano, cuya producción cuenta entre los más importantes conjuntos iconográficos dedicados a la independencia nacional. Entre sus obras destaca *Miranda en la Carraca*, de 1896.

11. Martín Tovar y Tovar (1827–1902). Pintor académico autor, junto a Arturo Michelena, de algunas de las más emblemáticas imágenes de la independencia venezolana. Su obra más significativa es sin duda la *Batalla de Carabobo* (1888), realizada por encargo del gobierno nacional para el Salón Elíptico del Palacio Federal.

12. Antonio Herrera Toro (1857–1914). Otro de los grandes pintores académicos venezolanos que contribuye a forjar la iconografía de la independencia. Trabaja para Tovar y Tovar en la *Batalla de Carabobo*. Fue director de la Academia de Bellas Artes de Caracas. En contra de su gestión como director se rebelan los jóvenes artistas que fundan el Círculo de Bellas Artes en 1912.

13. Tito Salas (1887–1974). Pintor venezolano, autor del mayor y más conocido conjunto iconográfico sobre la vida de Simón Bolívar. Entre sus obras destacan los conjuntos de la Casa Natal de Simón Bolívar y del Panteón Nacional.

De pequeño los copiaba y los estudiaba, en blanco y negro, eso sí, en vista de que no dominaba la técnica del color. La primera vez que pude ver una paleta y un caballete fue a los diecinueve años, cuando llego a la Escuela de Artes Plásticas y Artes Aplicadas de Caracas.[14] Hasta entonces solo los había visto en las revistas y en el cine.

AJ No es difícil imaginar la importancia que pudo tener el cine, mundo de la imagen en movimiento, en un joven que aspiraba a ser pintor y cuyo conocimiento del arte se limitaba a las escasas reproducciones vistas en la casa materna, en los libros y revistas que caían en sus manos, provenientes de Chile y de España. De sus experiencias con el universo del cine recuerda sin embargo, y en particular, el contacto circunstancial que pudo tener con el color.

JS En esa época funcionaban tres cines: el América, el Mundial y el Royal, todos del mismo dueño. Cuando tenía unos dieciséis años, aprendí a dibujar bien las letras; por eso, cuando se retiró el señor que hacía los letreros, me dieron el puesto. Yo era un muchacho, y aquello fue una verdadera graduación, que me dieran el único trabajo remunerado de la ciudad para un pintor. Trabajaba mucho en el día y en la noche pintaba los carteles. Algunas veces debía pintarlos en la mañana, porque el señor no sabía cuál era la película que iba a pasar y no me lo decía sino a las 5 a.m. Entonces había que empezarlos a esa hora de modo que estuvieran listos a las 7 a.m. Adquirí una técnica y una velocidad tan grandes que no comprendo cómo podía hacer tantos carteles en un periodo tan corto. Eran carteles grandes, de 1,5 metros. Yo iba pintando mientras otra persona los retiraba y los colocaba a un lado.

Asimismo, un señor amigo mío sabía utilizar el difumino. Yo llegué a ver algunos dibujos suyos hechos con esa técnica y le pedí que me enseñara. Eso resultó maravilloso, porque con él podía lograr el claroscuro con todas las sutilezas posibles. También iba a menudo al cine, casi todas las noches, aprovechando que me daban las entradas gratis. Allí encontraba una serie de amigos que me estaban esperando para ver lo que había hecho, y eso me estimulaba muchísimo. Yo seguía dibujando y utilizaba los carteles del cine para hacer más de lo que me pedían. El dueño me reprendía, decía que gastaba mucho pigmento y que perdía mi tiempo inútilmente, cuando él solo necesitaba que le pintara los letreros; pero en el fondo creo que lo apreciaba. En todo caso, fue

14. Fundada en 1835 como Escuela de Dibujo, pasa luego a llamarse Academia de Bellas Artes durante el período de Guzmán Blanco, para finalmente transformarse en la Escuela de Artes Plásticas y Artes Aplicadas de Caracas en 1936.

una experiencia que aproveché para manejar el color. Eran pigmentos en polvo, bellísimos, que se mezclaban con engrudos de almidón. Con ellos aprendí a mezclar los colores. Lo curioso es que esos colores que usaba cada día al pintar los carteles, porque eran los más baratos, son en el fondo los que he empleado y empleo aún en mi obra. Utilizaba mucho el azul cobalto, tal vez un poco más azulado que el que uso ahora. Allá lo llamaban azul marino. Manejaba el negro, el blanco, el verde (ese verde oliva que ves en mis *vibraciones*), el amarillo y especialmente el rojo ladrillo, que era el más barato de todos. Esos eran los colores disponibles para trabajar día a día, y es posible que se hayan quedado grabados en mi retina, el caso es que son además los que mejor funcionan en mi pintura.

AJ Se podría esperar, en vista de la escasez de imágenes que podían alimentar su apetito de joven pintor, que las películas vistas durante aquellos años tuvieran un impacto considerable en su obra posterior, y sin embargo, usted afirma que ninguna película tuvo una influencia decisiva.

JS Retuve todas esas películas como una gran masa donde sobresalen a veces algunas imágenes por su poder imaginativo más que discursivo. No recuerdo alguna que me haya interesado por el tema. Me gustaban mucho las películas cómicas. Amé realmente al Charlot de Chaplin, sin saber que era un genio, porque nunca me lo presentaron así, sino como un hombre que divertía. Pero a mí me fascinaba su mímica. Cuando era muchacho iba al cine casi a diario, no solamente cuando trabajé, sino después también, y vi muchas películas en blanco y negro, mudas por supuesto, que son las que mejor conservo en la memoria. Hay algunas incluso que me gustaría ver nuevamente, en especial aquella donde aparecía una negrita con dos moñitos en la cabeza. Durante el invierno, en los Estados Unidos, ella estaba esquiando y, de repente, se encuentra perdida en el bosque. La asustaban todos los ruidos que oía: los pájaros, los búhos y todos los rumores del bosque. Entonces se le ve esquiando y buscando por dónde salir, cuando cae en un cementerio. En ese preciso instante su miedo era tan grande que cuando cantó un búho, abrió la boca y sacó la lengua, donde llevaba pintado un corazón. . . No sé qué película era, ni cómo se llamaba, pero mi impresión fue tan grande que la he recordado toda mi vida. Cosas, imágenes como esa, me marcaron profundamente. Lo cierto es que no pensé que el cine fuera un arte; era otra cosa, un espectáculo divertido, una simple distracción. Yo vine a saber que el cine alcanzaba una dimensión artística cuando llego a París, con la cinemateca. Ya en Venezuela se empezaba a hablar del cine desde una perspectiva artística, pero en el fondo lo seguía considerando como un espectáculo divertido y nada más.

AJ Es quizás por eso que sus evocaciones del cine están más ligadas a las experiencias plásticas que pudo hacer durante su trabajo de cartelista y a las posibilidades que eso le proporcionó para su carrera. El mundo del cine le abrió una puerta hacia la pintura por sus experiencias concretas con el pigmento y por los contactos que le procuró.

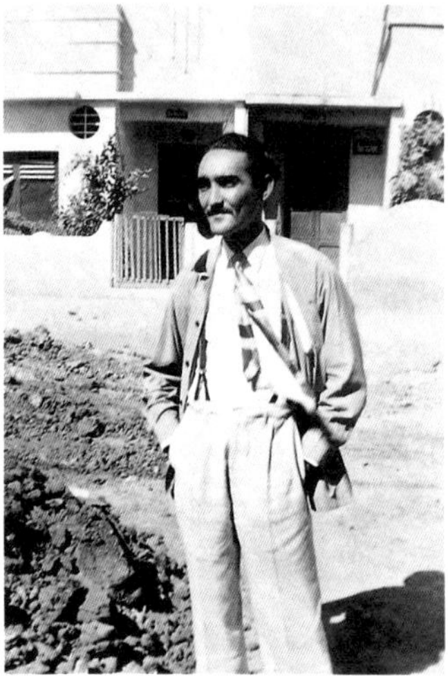

Fig. 2. Jesús Soto durante sus estudios en Caracas, c. 1943.

JS Es cierto, porque es gracias a eso que logro conseguir mi beca de estudio y que puedo irme a la Escuela de Artes Plásticas y Artes Aplicadas de Caracas [Fig. 2]. Mi empeño y mi entusiasmo trajeron como consecuencia que algunos amigos empezaran a hablar de mis posibilidades, hasta que alguien insistió en que pidiera una beca. Puesto que no conocía a nadie que pudiera ayudarme a conseguirla, unos amigos lograron que el Obispo de la ciudad me recibiera. Y fui, con todas mis dudas, a verlo. Recuerdo que le enseñé algunas copias de desnudos y, luego de ver mis trabajos, pensó, eso creo, que tenía algún talento. El caso es que me dio una recomendación muy bonita con la que me fui a ver al Secretario de Estado, que sí era un hombre interesado por la cultura. Fui entonces a verlo y me dijo: "Me parece bien que quieras irte a estudiar. Pero nosotros no tenemos becas para arte, ven mañana o pasado mañana, a ver qué puedo hacer". Cuando volví, me dijo: "Mira, Soto, lo único que conseguí es una beca para maestros, aunque es muy pequeña, son solo noventa bolívares". No importa, le dije, usted me da eso y yo feliz, ya veré cómo me las arreglo. "Antes tendrás que ir a ver al Presidente del Estado (era el título que se le daba entonces al gobernador). Él tiene que endosarlo". El Presidente del Estado era un humanista, un historiador. Siempre recordé su nombre de memoria, aunque no tuviera idea de su importancia. Mucho más tarde supe quién era, en Venezuela, Mario Briceño Iragorry.[15]

Al igual que otros jóvenes de su generación, Soto se dirige a Caracas con esa inmensa sed de aprender que suele nacer en quienes han vivido la extrema aridez

15. Mario Briceño Iragorry (1897–1958). Historiador, ensayista, abogado y diplomático venezolano. Miembro de las academias de la Historia y de la Lengua. Entre sus múltiples actividades destaca su cargo como gobernador del Estado Bolívar entre 1943 y 1944.

cultural de las zonas rurales. Una sed que opaca cualquier otro apetito, que se impone como única e ineludible urgencia y orienta su vida en una sola dirección, toda su energía entregada a satisfacer la necesidad de ver y de comprender aquello que cautivaba, sin saber por qué, su mirada.

Llegué con mi beca de 90 bolívares, decidido a dedicarme al arte. Ya que el dinero no era suficiente, intenté ganarme la vida haciendo lápidas de cementerio, porque aprendí a hacerlas en los talleres de la Escuela. Con eso ganaba dinero para comprar ropa y esas cosas que uno necesita. Luego encontré unos primos que trabajaban como joyeros en Caracas. Ellos me recibieron en su casa, porque se dieron cuenta de que estaba pasando trabajo. Con ellos me quedé hasta que terminé mis estudios en la Escuela. Lo importante es que pude hacerlos, y que los hice completos. De día estudiaba en la Escuela, y por las noches tomaba los cursos destinados a la formación de profesores.

Venía con las escasas referencias que pudo tener en Ciudad Bolívar, decidido a aprender, abriendo grandes los ojos.

Mi admiración por los pintores históricos de Venezuela era grande, y creo que vine a Caracas con la intención de seguir su camino; no en tanto que pintor histórico, pero sí naturalista. Todo eso se me olvidó cuando vi una naturaleza muerta de Georges Braque, que me impresionó muchísimo, aunque no podía comprender por qué. La vi al entrar a la Escuela, creo que el mismo día de mi llegada. Claro, ya yo había visto la reproducción de algunos cuadros modernos en las revistas que pude conseguir en Ciudad Bolívar. Recuerdo además un libro que gané en un concurso de cuentos, durante mis estudios de primaria. Un español enviado por el Ministerio de Educación llevó una serie de libros que fueron repartidos como premios durante el concurso. Yo gané el concurso como contador de cuentos y obtuve de premio un libro donde se reproducían algunas poesías e imágenes modernas; eran cuadros con una técnica próxima a la de Sorolla.[16]

AJ Y sin duda impregnadas del espíritu impresionista.

JS Sí, aunque de un impresionismo donde la luz era marrón, no como el Impresionismo francés, donde la luz es plata. A la vez, tuve la oportunidad de coleccionar

16. Joaquín Sorolla (1863–1923). Pintor realista e impresionista español. Su obra capta la luz del mediterráneo y las costumbres populares del pueblo español con un particular colorido y una luz a menudo amarillo-rojiza.

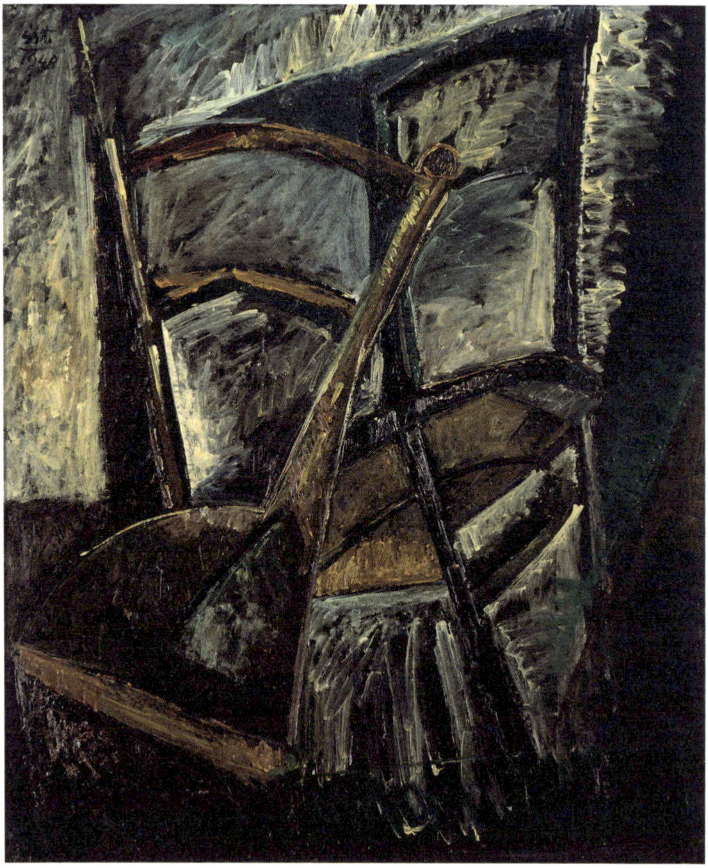

Fig. 3. *Sin título,* 1948.

unas revistas que venían de Chile. De allí venía mi preocupación por esa manera de pintar, pero no estaba seguro de lo que quería hacer. De modo que cuando me voy a Caracas, llego con la idea de hacer una pintura inspirada en los clásicos venezolanos, y también con el sabor que había despertado en mí ese libro sobre poesía moderna. Por supuesto, cuando ingreso a la Escuela de Artes Plásticas y Artes Aplicadas de Caracas, y veo en el caballete esa naturaleza muerta de Braque, recibí un impacto enorme. Inmediatamente empecé a preguntarle a mis compañeros, y sobre todo a los más avanzados, sobre el significado y la importancia de esa obra y de su autor. Primero consulté a Alejandro Otero, que era mi paisano, y quien me dio una buena explicación. Después le pregunté a los profesores. . . Al principio me sentí muy satisfecho con las explicaciones que me dieron, pero enseguida quise conocer más detalladamente sobre el Cubismo y toda esa historia de la cuarta dimensión. Entonces me dijeron que antes tenía que estudiar mucho, que sin preparación no podría entender. Lo esencial es que quería comprenderlo, porque a partir de ese impacto mi problema fue hacer una obra que fuera más allá de lo conocido [Fig. 3].

AJ El Cubismo y la cuarta dimensión se habían convertido para los alumnos de la Escuela en una de las preocupaciones mayores de su formación intelectual. Su oscuridad manifiesta, amparada sin duda por el prestigio de la ciencia, parecía resumir el misterio de la pintura y del mundo moderno que Soto quería comprender. ¿Es esta experiencia la que lo lleva a interesarse por la ciencia?

JS Bueno, tal vez porque no me daban buenas explicaciones y yo quería saber con exactitud por qué un pintor era más importante que otro, cuando los dos se parecían. Eso me preocupaba, y cuando llego a Caracas quise comprender por qué Cézanne, por ejemplo, tenía una importancia superior a la de otros pintores que me parecían de una eficacia mayor. Luego entendí que, en buena medida, era la historia que iba aclarando el desarrollo de la pintura por periodos e iba situando a los artistas. Eso era ya, en mi opinión, un aspecto científico. Enseguida comenzaron a hablarme de la cuarta dimensión, lo que sin duda agudizó mi interés por la ciencia.

AJ En cualquier caso, esta preocupación por el tiempo y por la organización de la superficie pictórica tal y como la descubre en el Cubismo, es ya evidente en las piezas que realiza durante los últimos años de la escuela y posteriormente en Maracaibo. [Figs. 3–4]

JS Por supuesto, porque capté inmediatamente en Cézanne el problema del tiempo, tal y como lo comprendí en el Impresionismo cuando me dijeron que ellos pintaban la luz en diversos momentos del día para probar que cambiaba constantemente. Así fui acumulando una serie de pequeños elementos sobre el tiempo, el movimiento y el espacio que más tarde se despertaron y me ayudaron a comprender. También me interesaron muchas cosas que podía ver en revistas, especialmente en las chilenas. Allí pude ver reproducciones de artistas que pintaban a la manera de Picasso durante su periodo griego, que me fascinaron. Todo me preparaba para comprender el arte moderno. El concepto, también, de la perspectiva renacentista tuvo mucha influencia en mí. La idea de crear un espacio virtual dentro de una especie de gran cubo me parecía una invención maravillosa, y cuando descubro que en el Cubismo ese cubo renacentista, esa perspectiva monocular, se transforma en un espacio multifocal, poliocular, por decirlo de algún modo, eso fue una revolución maravillosa. Por eso es que cuando conozco al Klee de las ciudades y del equilibrista, donde cada casita, cada cubito respondía a un punto de fuga diferente, me maravilló la posibilidad de aprehender esa otra noción del espacio.

Las artes plásticas llegaron a ser en su caso el campo donde podía buscar una respuesta a las incógnitas que se le presentan en principio a todo niño cuando intenta comprender qué es el tiempo, qué la materia y el espacio, lo finito y lo infinito. Las obras de los artistas, inscritas en la historia, eran ejemplos de lo que había sido hecho, e indicios del camino que debía seguir. La escuela le ofrecía la posibilidad de indagar en ese mundo de la historia, aprendiendo a ver, aprendiendo a hacer.

Comencé mis estudios en 1942,[17] y seguí el mismo método que los alumnos mayores, como Alejandro Otero. En mi opinión, lo importante era la actitud no restrictiva de los profesores. Ellos orientaban sin imponerse, y si uno tenía inquietudes le daban la libertad de investigar. Cuando comenzaba una tela, un paisaje por ejemplo, empezaba haciéndolo más o menos como lo veía, y después iba buscando una forma sintética de hacerlo. Mi profesor de paisaje, que era Rafael Ramón González,[18] me decía: "Voy a dejar que hagas lo que quieras, tú me enseñas eso al final". Luego discutíamos y él me decía lo que pensaba sobre el trabajo. A veces, viendo mis paisajes, me preguntaba: "¿No ves los violetas escondidos en la sombra, no ves la variedad de tonos que se esconden en ella?. . .". Y yo ponía los violetas y los tonos que el profesor me decía, porque era el profesor, pero en verdad nunca pude ver esos tonos. Yo no comprendía al Impresionismo en Venezuela. No podía ver esas gamas de color en el paisaje. Lo vine a entender cuando llego a Francia y veo la luz europea, esa luz plateada de Monet que sí puedo comprobar en el paisaje. El segundo año ya no hacía falta esperar a los profesores; escogía un motivo cualquiera y se lo llevaba una vez terminado. De modo que iba a verlos cada quince días aproximadamente, salvo si hacía en mi opinión un cuadro interesante; entonces se lo llevaba inmediatamente y ellos me daban su opinión. Jamás me imponían una manera de hacer las cosas.

Al tercer o cuarto año, no hablábamos con ellos de profesor a alumno, sino como compañeros, de pintor a pintor. . . Eso era maravilloso para los

17. Soto dice haber recibido su beca gracias al apoyo de Mario Briceño Iragorry en 1942, pero la biografía de Iragorry indica que fue gobernador del Estado Bolívar entre 1943 y 1944, con lo que es probable que Soto haya obtenido su beca en 1943 y no antes.

18. Rafael Ramón González (1894–1975). Importante paisajista venezolano. Fue profesor de paisaje en la Escuela de Artes Plásticas y Artes Aplicadas de Caracas. Su obra contribuyó en gran medida a hacer del cerro El Ávila un tema central en la paisajística nacional.

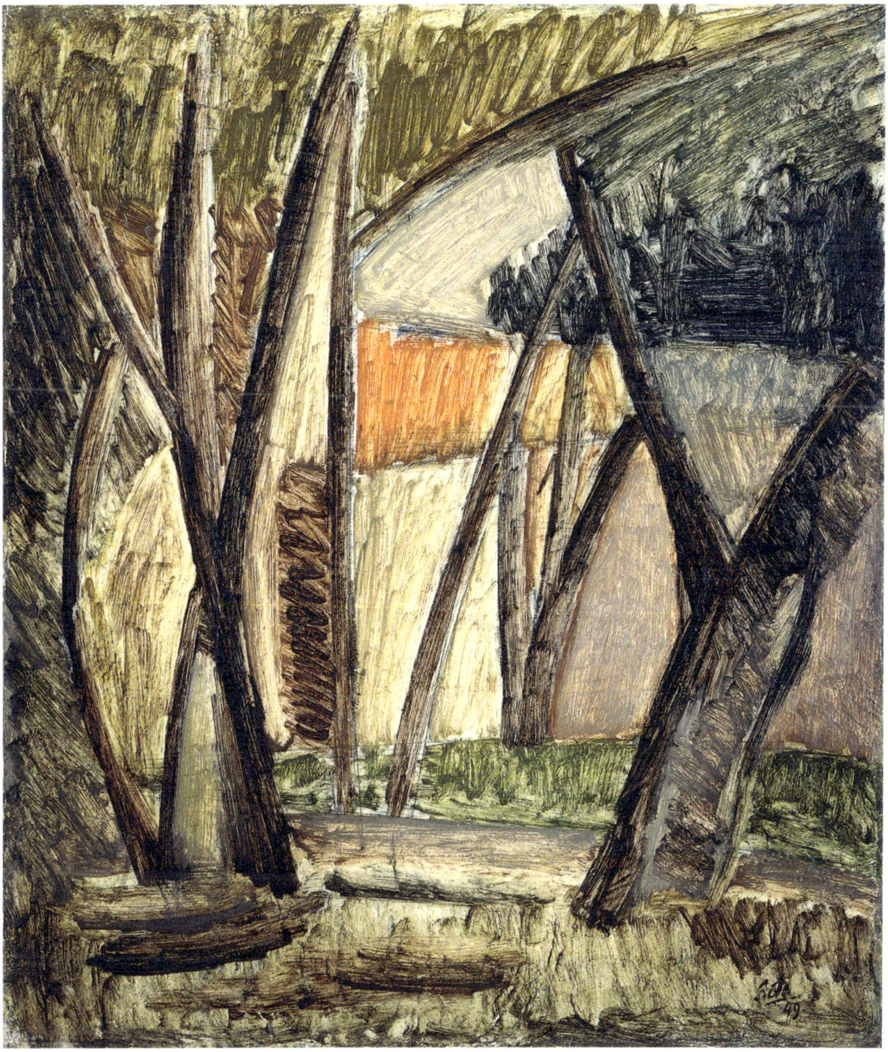

Fig. 4. *Sin título (paisaje),* 1949.

alumnos con inquietudes, así no tenían que pasar cuatro o cinco años repitiendo y copiando, aprendiendo técnicas o problemas que no les servirían después. Sin embargo, los alumnos que querían tener una formación estrictamente académica encontraban la posibilidad de hacerlo. Más que una escuela en el sentido académico del término, era un gran taller colectivo, una peña de artistas. Y eso era enriquecido con una buena formación intelectual, aprovechando la experiencia de los profesores que podían viajar, y de aquellos que habían leído mucho, como el director de la escuela, Antonio Edmundo Monsanto.[19]

AJ El arte viene del arte, toda obra tiene un árbol genealógico en el que se inscribe como en una familia de formas, con sus antepasados cercanos y lejanos, sus ramas truncadas y su descendencia, cuando la tiene. ¿Tuvo alguno de ellos un peso preponderante en su formación?

JS Creo que todos me aportaron lo mejor de ellos. Te he venido hablando del paisaje, pero allí estaba Marcos Castillo[20] quien, en el dominio del color, me enseñó muchísimo. También aprendí mucho de un artista lamentablemente mal recordado: Juan Vicente Fabbiani.[21] Si Castillo me instruía en la manera de enriquecer cada centímetro cuadrado de la tela, gracias al color, Fabbiani me enseñaba el sentido de la síntesis, el pintar sin insistir en los detalles. La formación era por eso muy variada y había dónde escoger.

AJ Alejandro Otero solía decir que el regreso de Héctor Poleo,[22] proveniente de México, causó un verdadero impacto en su generación. Él les aportaba una manera diferente de enfrentarse al paisaje, con aquellos frotados finísimos que tomó del Muralismo mexicano, en particular de Diego Rivera. ¿Tuvo eso alguna influencia en su caso?

19. Antonio Edmundo Monsanto (1890–1948). Modesto pintor, de obra escasa. Fue miembro fundador del Círculo de Bellas Artes y director de la Escuela de Artes Plásticas y Artes Aplicadas de Caracas (1936–48). Durante este periodo tuvo una influencia decisiva en la formación de los principales artistas abstractos venezolanos.

20. Marcos Castillo (1897–1966). Fue uno de los principales exponentes de la llamada Escuela de Caracas, considerado uno de sus mejores coloristas. Fue profesor de Jesús Soto y de la mayoría de los artistas abstractos de los años cincuenta.

21. Juan Vicente Fabbiani (1910–89). Pintor venezolano conocido esencialmente por sus desnudos. Fue profesor de la Escuela de Artes Plásticas y Artes Aplicadas de Caracas. Su tendencia a la síntesis formal tuvo considerable influencia entre los artistas abstractos de los años cincuenta.

22. Héctor Poleo (1918–89). Artista plástico, cuya obra, influenciada en un primer momento por el Muralismo mexicano, tuvo gran impacto entre los jóvenes artistas de la década del cuarenta. Durante la Segunda Guerra Mundial, abrumado por el desastre, su pintura se acerca al Surrealismo.

JS A mí en realidad lo que me interesó y me sigue interesando de Héctor Poleo es su periodo surrealista, aunque en ese momento él llega con sus ideas muralistas y con unas obras que yo admiraba, porque estaban bien ejecutadas, solo que ese no era el camino que quería seguir. Tal vez se deba al impacto que causó en mí aquella naturaleza muerta de Braque, y a esa libertad que buscaba a través de las pocas imágenes descubiertas en Ciudad Bolívar. . . , algo menos temático. Nunca hice una pintura temática.

AJ Y aun así, al igual que muchos artistas latinoamericanos, usted debió tomar parte en las discusiones donde se intentaba pensar la función social del artista. Toda aquella discusión sobre lo local y lo universal implícita en los propósitos de Héctor Poleo, y que formarían luego el eje central de *Los Disidentes*,[23] debieron tener alguna influencia en su pensamiento.

JS Indudablemente. Las grandes reuniones que se organizaban en el grupo de Alejandro Otero, Pascual Navarro[24] y otros, y a las cuales asistíamos los alumnos de las generaciones más jóvenes, como Carlos Cruz-Diez,[25] Guevara Moreno[26] y yo, tuvieron algún impacto sobre mí. En ningún momento, eso sí, llegaron a hacerme creer en la necesidad de subordinar la libertad del artista a la problemática política. La gran preocupación entre nosotros estaba ligada a la necesidad de descifrar el Cubismo y la complicación que significaba toda aquella historia de la cuarta dimensión. No podíamos comprenderla, aunque presentíamos que era algo de una importancia trascendente. Yo vine a entenderla mucho después, cuando me lancé en la investigación del movimiento en los años cincuenta: esa era la cuarta dimensión que buscábamos. El tiempo y la obra de cada uno, creo, han demostrado no solamente que la mayor parte de los estudiantes de condición decidieron irse por la vía del Postimpresionismo, sino que en Venezuela esta vía ha dado mejores resultados que la del americanismo influenciado por el Muralismo mexicano.

23. *Los Disidentes*. Nombre de una agrupación y una revista de arte editada en París (1950) por artistas e intelectuales venezolanos entre los cuales figuran Alejandro Otero, Mateo Manaure, Narciso Debourg, Perán Erminy y J.R. Guillent Pérez, entre otros.

24. Pascual Navarro (1923–85). Artista plástico. Miembro fundador de *Los Disidentes* y de la revista homónima, donde escribió polémicos artículos sobre la pintura venezolana.

25. Carlos Cruz-Diez (1923). Artista cinético venezolano, compañero de estudios de Jesús Soto. Su obra madura se centra en el estudio del color y en el intento por presentarlo como realidad física independientemente de toda intención representativa o simbólica. De allí que sus obras más conocidas se titulen *Fisicromías*.

26. Luis Guevara Moreno (1926–2010). Pintor venezolano. Fue miembro fundador de *Los Disidentes*. Durante los años cincuenta hizo una considerable obra abstracta que luego abandonaría para centrarse en la figura humana. Formó parte del movimiento Madí.

AJ Eso tiene que ver con lo que fue y sigue siendo la orientación esencial del país: modernizarse, salir del subdesarrollo. Son quizás pocos los países donde, como en Venezuela, "lo moderno" tenga un prestigio tan grande. A ello se agrega que nosotros no tenemos un pasado precolombino tan fuerte y presente como en México y Perú. Venezuela vive orientada hacia el futuro.

JS Sí, pero en ese momento los políticos te presentaban como único futuro el mundo del socialismo y, en arte, al Realismo socialista. La fuerza política obligaba a irse por ese camino. Aun así, a mí nunca me interesó, y es cierto que tampoco fui un apasionado del comunismo ruso. No fui un creyente y Stalin siempre me dio terror. Y traté de meterme, créeme, porque la atracción y la presión intelectual eran demasiado grandes. Había tanta gente inteligente involucrada en eso que yo creía estar equivocado, solo que jamás logré convencerme y defendí constantemente la independencia del artista ante las directrices ideológicas. En París iba a sus reuniones con mi guitarra, porque quería apoyarlos, aunque repitiéndoles que con la pintura no podía hacerlo, porque no entendía su camino. Ellos, en cambio, me castigaban con palabras desagradables y yo les decía: Si soy un hombre del pueblo, lo que haga debe salir del pueblo y debe serle útil; pero no hubo nada que hacer, cada vez me respondían acusándome de ser un traidor a mi clase [Fig. 5].[27]

Cosas como ésta me enfriaron paulatinamente. Yo me decía que tal vez tenían razón, pero no los entendía y no podía seguirlos. Nunca acepté la intromisión de la política en el arte, ni en la literatura ni en la canción. La imagen del artista comprometido me produjo siempre un malestar. Era buscar una protección de la sociedad, lo que no sucedió con el arte abstracto, que no ha sido protegido por nadie. Ha sido atacado o, en el mejor de los casos, soportado, pero no ha existido ni existe un régimen político o una agrupación que lo vea como lo que debe ser el arte del presente o del futuro. Sin embargo, el arte comprometido sí ha gozado de esa protección y la sigue teniendo. Eso no significa que critique ese tipo de situaciones, cada quien tiene derecho a tener su actitud ante la vida. Yo sigo pensando que el arte es más importante que cualquier posición proselitista o cualquier agrupación de tipo ideológica. La ideología termina siendo una carga de prejuicios, mientras las artes son un aporte positivo para la humanidad. Y si no parecen importantes, no molestan a nadie.

27. No solo grandes pensadores como Hegel y Marx impusieron la idea de una historia única, orientada hacia una futura liberación de la humanidad, sino que durante la primera mitad del siglo XX los acontecimientos históricos (la Revolución bolchevique, luego la china y por último la cubana) permitían pensar que la humanidad se dirigía ineludiblemente hacia ese futuro, un futuro claramente identificado con las sociedades comunistas.

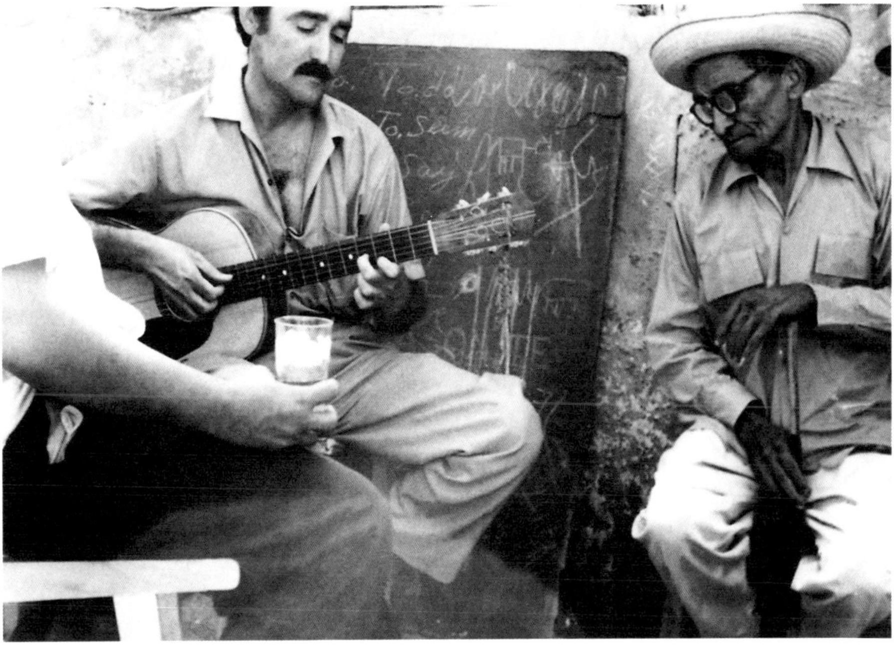

Fig. 5. Jesús Soto tocando guitarra con su tío Pedro Soto. Ciudad Bolívar, 1961.

AJ Un caso patético de esta entrega a las ideologías y su inevitable desencanto posterior, es sin duda el de los artistas rusos a principios del siglo XX. Ellos creyeron ver en la revolución artística que impulsaban un movimiento paralelo al de la revolución social, y pensaron ingenuamente que así sería percibido por las clases dirigentes. El arte, la ciencia y el pueblo organizado, llevarían a cabo la gran revolución que exigía la historia. No obstante, fueron rechazados y marginados, reducidos al silencio y condenados, cuando no se suicidaron. Hoy, mientras el sistema político que los condenó ha terminado en una impresionante catástrofe, sus obras siguen siendo una de las más bellas conquistas del siglo.

JS Estás hablando del caso más doloroso, puesto que el único arte que estaba a la altura de los ideales que movían al comunismo de los años 1917 al 1927, era el que ellos hacían: Malevich, Tatlin, Mayakovsky y los demás. Si querías romper con todos los parámetros históricos y sociales del mundo burgués, debías romper también con sus ideales artísticos. Y sin embargo, el arte oficial del comunismo fue el más tradicional y convencional de la historia. Lo que pasa, en cualquier régimen, es que el arte y la ciencia están siempre más avanzados que la política. Los políticos, incluyendo los de jerarquías elevadas, no llegan nunca a la capacidad visionaria del artista. Imagina lo que debió significar, en el caso de hombres convencidos como Malevich, tener que volver a pintar aquellas figuras convencionales. . . Una verdadera tragedia. Eso demuestra que no debemos ponernos al servicio de una causa partidista, cualquiera que ella sea. Y si la sociedad no considera a la actividad artística como una necesidad inmediata, por lo menos que no condenen al artista a la cotidianidad. Que lo dejen tranquilo, que él, en general, está viendo más lejos que ellos.

INVENTAR LA ABSTRACCIÓN

No deja de ser cierto que los artistas modernos, inclusive cuando no pretendían hacer otra cosa sino encontrarle soluciones a los problemas que les planteaba la plástica de su época, tuvieron una conciencia clara de su responsabilidad social. Al hacer su obra creían contribuir con la construcción de un orden nuevo para el mundo. Un ejemplo claro de esta posición la encontramos en Kasimir Malevich cuya obra, totalmente abstracta, era sin embargo pensada como una más de las batallas que se daban entonces contra el pasado, ya anacrónico, de la humanidad. Por eso afirmaba que: "La Revolución de Octubre, destruyendo las bases del antiguo Estado, ha reconocido, en parte, a los renovadores del arte. . . Hoy tenemos al ejército del principio nuevo de la vida económica y tenemos ya las vanguardias del arte. La vida económica del nuevo mundo ha sacado adelante la comuna. La creación del nuevo arte ha sacado adelante el Suprematismo del cuadrado".[28] Era una lucha contra las formas pasadas que debía darse a la vez en el espacio virtual de la tela y en la vida colectiva, y cuando Soto tuvo ante sí la responsabilidad de educar a los jóvenes en Maracaibo, respondió también a ese llamado. En 1947 termina sus estudios y se va a Maracaibo, donde asume la dirección de la Escuela de Bellas Artes. Entonces intenta implantar un nuevo sistema de estudios abierto a las prácticas de su tiempo.

JS Lo intenté, claro, pero fracasé. Mientras yo hablaba de Picasso, que era mi mayor preocupación en ese momento, dado que no conocía nada más avanzado después del Cubismo, el resto de los profesores y alumnos se interesaban

28. Kasimir Malevich. *De Cézanne au Suprématisme*. Lausanne, Suiza: Ed. L'Age d'Homme, 1974, 139–41.

por los pintores *pompier*.[29] Yo insistía en que debíamos estudiar a Picasso y a su generación. Incluso conseguí que el Ministerio de Educación me enviara unas reproducciones, pero no logré que nadie se interesara, y por eso me fui de allí. Las únicas personas en las que logré sembrar esa inquietud fueron dos poetas; uno se llamaba César Rincón y el otro Esnor Rivera. Ellos estudiaban medicina, y una parte de sus estudios les exigía clases de dibujo. De manera que se acercaron a la escuela buscando al profesor que daba esa materia y se encontraron con las piezas más o menos cubistas que estaba haciendo. A ellos les parecía increíble que aquello se estuviera haciendo en Venezuela, y me contaron que habían leído mucho sobre poesía moderna e incluso sobre el Cubismo, y no pensaron que en el país pudiera haber algún interés por ese tipo de pintura. Luego vino un periodista chileno, se estableció en Maracaibo, y los convenció de que el Cubismo era la manifestación de una sociedad decadente y que lo verdaderamente importante era el Realismo socialista.

Un hecho fundamental hacía imposible la comunicación entre él y sus compañeros, profesores y alumnos de la Escuela de Bellas Artes de Maracaibo. Mientras ellos se interesaban por el arte realizado, por sus expresiones históricas, Soto buscaba en ellas indicios de lo que podrían ser sus formas posibles. El arte no era para él un medio de expresión, sino un modo de pensar, una manera de responder a las interrogantes de la historia. Y si estas interrogantes eran diferentes, diferente debía ser la forma que tomara el arte de su tiempo.

Esta apertura conceptual "hacia lo posible" es sin duda lo que le permite asimilar la experiencia fortuita que surge durante una conversación en Maracaibo, experiencia oral que se convertiría en una verdadera guía para su trabajo plástico: su primer contacto con el concepto del Cuadrado blanco sobre blanco *de Kasimir Malevich* [Fig. 6].

JS Fue un encuentro totalmente casual. Yo era amigo de Lya Bermúdez[30] y de su esposo, y siempre nos reuníamos a conversar. En una de esas ocasiones apareció una muchacha, prima suya, que acababa de llegar de un viaje por Europa y Nueva York, y le pregunté sobre lo que había visto durante el viaje. Entonces me contó que había conocido a Picasso, que no le entusiasmaba mucho, aunque

29. Denominación peyorativa empleada para calificar al arte oficial y académico francés durante la segunda mitad del siglo XIX. Se supone que el término hace referencia a la cercanía entre los cascos o yelmos empleados en muchas de estas pinturas de corte histórico y mitológico y los cascos de los bomberos franceses. *Pompier* significa bombero en francés.

30. Lya Bermúdez (1923). Escultora y pintora venezolana. Fue amiga y alumna de Jesús Soto mientras éste dirigía la Escuela de Bellas Artes de Maracaibo (1947–50). En 1993 inauguró el Centro de Arte de Maracaibo Lya Bermúdez.

Fig. 6. Kasimir Malevich, *Suprematist Composition. White on White* [*Composición suprematista. Blanco sobre blanco*], 1918.

creía ver algo en él. "Pero –me dijo– cuando me presentan un cuadro blanco con otro cuadro blanco encima, creo que se están volviendo locos. Eso no es nada, ahí no hay nada que ver"... Ella no podía entender, pero eso fue para mí una verdadera revelación, esa obra se convirtió desde entonces en una fuente de inspiración: era la forma más perfecta y pura de atrapar la luz en una tela. Cuando llegué a París no conocía siquiera el nombre del autor, por eso digo que su aporte fue de orden conceptual. Cuando la vi por primera vez, casi diez años después, no me aportó nada adicional a lo que imaginé en Maracaibo. Logré comprender su importancia y asimilar su contenido sin necesidad de verla.

No podría haber mejor ejemplo que éste para afirmar que gran parte del interés que pueden tener las estructuras de Soto no proviene precisamente de las ilusiones ópticas que ponen en juego, sino de lo que se sugiere o intenta hacerse visible en ellas. La dimensión pues de lo sublime, de todo aquello que, según la frase de Jean-François Lyotard, podemos concebir, pero no podemos ni ver ni hacer ver.[31] *Y es que en esa somera descripción del* Cuadrado blanco sobre blanco *de Malevich, Soto descubre intuitivamente un punto de contacto con sus preocupaciones más íntimas,*

31. Jean-François Lyotard, *Le postmoderne expliqué aux enfants*. París: Ed. Gallilée, 1986, 27.

en particular con ese ejemplo clásico de lo sublime descrito en La divina comedia: *el encuentro de Dante con Dios, un dios descrito precisamente por círculos de luz sobre luz. De ahí que el haber oído hablar de esta pieza haya sido suficiente. El deseo de ir a París, el centro donde habían surgido el Impresionismo y el Cubismo, y donde debía, sin duda, surgir un arte nuevo, se le hizo entonces patente, se convirtió en una urgencia.*

Yo estaba buscando una beca, porque con lo que ganaba allá no me era posible reunir dinero y pagar el pasaje. Ese mismo año conseguí mi beca y me fui a París. Llegué directamente al apartamento de Guevara Moreno e inmediatamente me puse en contacto con mis amigos de la escuela: Alejandro Otero, Pascual Navarro, Mateo Manaure,[32] Carlos González Bogen[33] y Narciso Debourg.[34] Con su ayuda comencé a organizar mi vida y encontré una pequeña habitación que compartía con el poeta Lira Sosa.[35] Como él hablaba un poquito mejor el francés que yo, logramos entendernos con la señora, quien nos alquilaba la habitación y nos daba la comida. Inmediatamente tuve que empezar a trabajar con mi guitarra, porque la beca de Maracaibo solo me cubría los gastos del cuarto y además no me duró sino un año. Sin embargo, me organicé rápidamente, y por eso no me traumatizó perder la beca al cabo de un año. Cuando aumentaron el alquiler de la pequeña habitación que ocupábamos, nos mudamos a una buhardilla. Cerca de allí conseguimos un pequeño restaurante popular donde, cosa increíble, se comía por cien francos de la época. Eso estaba lleno de españoles y de gente muy pobre. Más tarde Alejandro Otero me consiguió un cuartico pequeño, donde me alojé por algún tiempo. El único problema consistía en la instalación sanitaria del apartamento superior; el desagüe se encontraba justo en el centro de la habitación y cuando se tapaba el *water*, aquello se desparramaba en medio de la pieza. Luego, gracias a mi sueldo de guitarrista y a la ayuda de mi profesor de guitarra, Alexandre Lagoya,[36] pude instalarme en otro

32. Mateo Manaure (1926). Artista plástico venezolano. Nace en Uracoa, Estado Monagas. Fue miembro fundador del grupo *Los Disidentes* (1950). En 1952 participa en el proyecto de integración de las artes liderado por el arquitecto Carlos Raúl Villanueva en la Universidad Central de Venezuela. En 1960 abandona la pintura abstracta y regresa a temas de corte nacionalista.

33. Carlos González Bogen (1920–92). Escultor y pintor venezolano. Fue miembro fundador de *Los Disidentes*. Durante los años cincuenta realiza una considerable obra abstracta que luego abandona (1966) para dedicarse a temas de contenido político.

34. Narciso Debourg (1925). Artista plástico venezolano. Miembro fundador de *Los Disidentes*. Desde entonces ha realizado una considerable, aunque escasa, obra abstracto-geométrica.

35. José Lira Sosa (1930–95). Poeta surrealista venezolano originario del Estado Monagas.

36. Alexandre Lagoya (1929–99). Guitarrista francés. En 1950 creó, junto a su esposa la guitarrista Ida Presti, el dúo Presti-Lagoya.

apartamento que se encontraba en un tercer piso de la Rue du Temple. Allí organicé mi vida, me casé con Hélène en 1952, y nacieron mis hijos.[37]

AJ Su vida entera se organizaba en torno a las exigencias de la pintura. ¿Aparte del contacto con sus amigos venezolanos, en qué dirección se orientan sus intereses en el medio cultural francés?

JS Lo primero que hice fue preguntarle a mis amigos sobre la actividad plástica de la ciudad; las galerías que frecuentaban, los museos que conocían, etc. Enseguida conocí a las cuatro o cinco galerías donde se encontraba lo más interesante, entre ellas, la Galería Denise René.[38] Con el mismo objetivo fui al Musée d'art moderne de la Ville de Paris [Museo de Arte Moderno de la Ciudad de París], pero ahí no pasaba nada, aquello era pobrísimo. Te estoy hablando del año 1950, cuando llegué a París. A principios del año siguiente me fui a Holanda con Fernando Rísquez,[39] donde por fin veo a Mondrian, a quien no conocía sino por reproducciones, inclusive cuando me sirvió de punto de partida para mis primeras experiencias abstractas.

AJ Normalmente, el paso a la abstracción representó, en la mayoría de los artistas que lo vivieron, un lento proceso plástico. Fue el caso de Kandinsky, de Mondrian y de Theo van Doesburg a principios de siglo, y también el de Alejandro Otero, a finales de los años cuarenta, a partir de sus *cafeteras*.[40] No obstante, ese proceso se da en usted intelectualmente; es decir, sin que estuviera secundado por la práctica y en el transcurso de algunos meses.

JS Lo que pasa es que yo sabía que la abstracción existía (recuerda que Otero expone sus *cafeteras* en Caracas antes de mi viaje a París), pero no sabía cómo se había llegado a ella. La estaba buscando y lo que pensaba era justo, solo que era un pensamiento de los años 1910–15, que consistía en sacar la abstracción

37. El 5 de abril de 1952 Soto se casa con Hélène de Robert, con quien tendrá cuatro hijos: Isabelle, Christophe, Anne y Florence.

38. Importante galería fundada en París por Denise René (1945). Fue uno de los principales espacios para la defensa del arte abstracto y cinético durante los años cincuenta, sesenta y setenta en Francia. Allí se organizó, en 1955, la primera exposición cinética *Le mouvement*, donde participan Jesús Soto, Yaacov Agam, Víctor Vasarely, Alexander Calder, Jean Tinguely, Marcel Duchamp y Paul Bury, entre otros. En esta galería se llevó a cabo la primera exposición dedicada en Francia a Piet Mondrian (1957).

39. Fernando Rísquez (1926). Reconocido psiquiatra venezolano y autor, entre otros libros, de *Homeopatía y psiquiatría*. Presidente de la Liga Medicorum.

40. *Las cafeteras*: Serie pictórica producida por Alejandro Otero en París (1947–51) y expuestas en el Museo de Bellas Artes de Caracas, en 1949, provocando polémicas. Se trata de un conjunto de obras donde, paulatinamente, el artista pasa de la pintura representativa a la abstracción. Es la primera manifestación de la abstracción en el país.

del Cubismo, no inventar una abstracción. Quería eliminar los elementos para encontrar el verdadero sentido de la pintura. Claro, yo venía leyendo mucho, porque mi inquietud era averiguar lo que había sucedido después del Cubismo. Aimée Battistini[41] me ayudó muchísimo en esto. Entre las cosas que me mostraba había reflexiones sobre la abstracción, Mondrian y luego Malevich, a quien conocí a través de la revista *Art d'Aujourd'hui*. Yo me preguntaba por qué y cómo habían llegado estos artistas hasta ese punto. Así descubrí los árboles y las catedrales de Mondrian, y entonces entendí su evolución hacia la abstracción. Fue cuando me dije que tenía que ir de allí en adelante. De la misma manera que ellos habían llegado a la abstracción a través del Cubismo, yo debía partir de esa abstracción para seguir adelante. Tenía claro además que mi trabajo de ese momento no era importante, porque esa investigación ya había sido resuelta. Mi problema era cómo ir más allá. . .

Otero conocía también la abstracción, y sin embargo llega a ella paulatinamente, siguiendo, viviendo en carne propia el proceso que otros experimentaron antes que él, señalando en su práctica la imposibilidad de todo gesto voluntarista. Soto, por el contrario, pretende detectar el estado más avanzado de la abstracción (a sus ojos el movimiento de mayor significación en el siglo XX) para lanzarse a la aventura de crear una obra que pudiera continuar esa tradición, haciéndola avanzar. Una concepción lineal de la historia guiaba su pensamiento.

A partir de allí me impongo una disciplina de estudio muy consciente. Yo, que vengo de una enseñanza dibujística, me impongo un abandono total del dibujo representativo. Era algo así como comerse las gallinas con las plumas para quitarse las ganas de comerla. Entonces me dedico a estudiar el dilema de la abstracción a partir del artista que, a mi entender, había llegado más lejos en esa vía: Piet Mondrian [Fig. 7].[42] Lo primero que intenté fue hacer de sus composiciones una situación dinámica, sacarlas de la bidimensionalidad. Yo entendí que Mondrian había tenido dificultades con la bidimensionalidad en el cruce de las verticales y horizontales, donde se producía una vibración. Por eso me dije que si él tuvo ese tipo de inconvenientes, el camino no debía ser el de insistir en la bidimensionalidad sino llevarlas a una dimensión diferente.

41. Aimée Battistini (1916–89). Artista plástica venezolana, oriunda de Ciudad Bolívar y de una familia de origen corso. Instalada en París desde 1928, inició a la abstracción a los jóvenes venezolanos fundadores de *Los Disidentes*. Su apoyo fue igualmente considerable para introducir a Soto en el mundo de la abstracción.

42. Jesús Soto y sus compañeros asisten a los cursos y conferencias del Atelier d'Art Abstrait, creado en París por Jean Dewasne y Edgar Pillet en 1950. El programa de fin de año anunciaba diversas conferencias sobre Mondrian y el Neoplasticismo. El impacto de estas conferencias debió ser grande, pues entre finales de 1950 y principios de 1951, tanto Otero como Soto emprenden el viaje a Holanda para encontrarse con la obra de Mondrian.

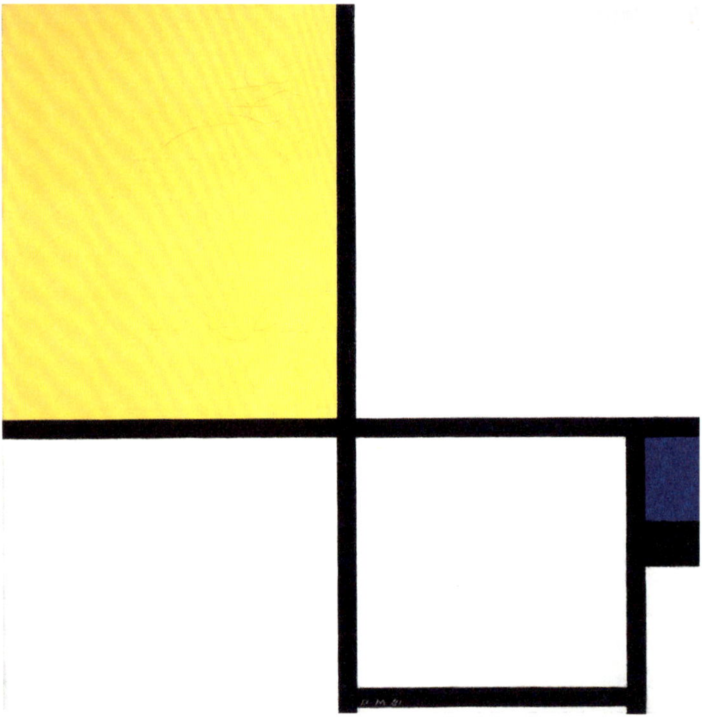

Fig. 7. Piet Mondrian, *Composition No. II, with Yellow and Blue* [*Composición N° II, con amarillo y azul*], 1931. ©2011 Mondrian/Holtzman Trust c/o HCR International Washington, DC

Eso fue un proceso bastante rápido, comencé dinamizándolas con diagonales y líneas curvas, siempre en el plano [Fig. 8]. Más tarde me doy cuenta, al conocer los *boogie-woogie*, de que ya él había intentado dinamizarlas, salir de la bidimensionalidad. Cuando descubro esto, se acaba en mi caso "el problema Mondrian" y empieza otro proceso, esta vez a partir de la música y de otros artistas como László Moholy-Nagy.[43] Él escribió un libro importante sobre el movimiento, solo que estaba en inglés, y tuve que leerlo con una amiga que me iba traduciendo. Cada noche leíamos una parte del libro. Así pude entender lo que buscaba Moholy-Nagy con la idea del movimiento. Después de la serie donde intenté dinamizar a Mondrian, hice un conjunto a partir de conceptos no dibujísticos, como la repetición y la progresión. Me dije que no podía seguir dibujando de manera impulsiva, o con esa libertad intuitiva de la dibujística tradicional. Entonces pensé que debía encontrar una manera de trabajar que

43. László Moholy-Nagy (1895–1946). Artista de origen húngaro, autor de una obra compleja y variada. Pintor, escultor, fotógrafo, cineasta, escenógrafo y diseñador gráfico. Profesor y teórico de la Bauhaus. En 1947, después de su muerte, se publica su libro *Vision in motion*, cuya lectura, en 1953, tiene un considerable impacto en la obra de Soto.

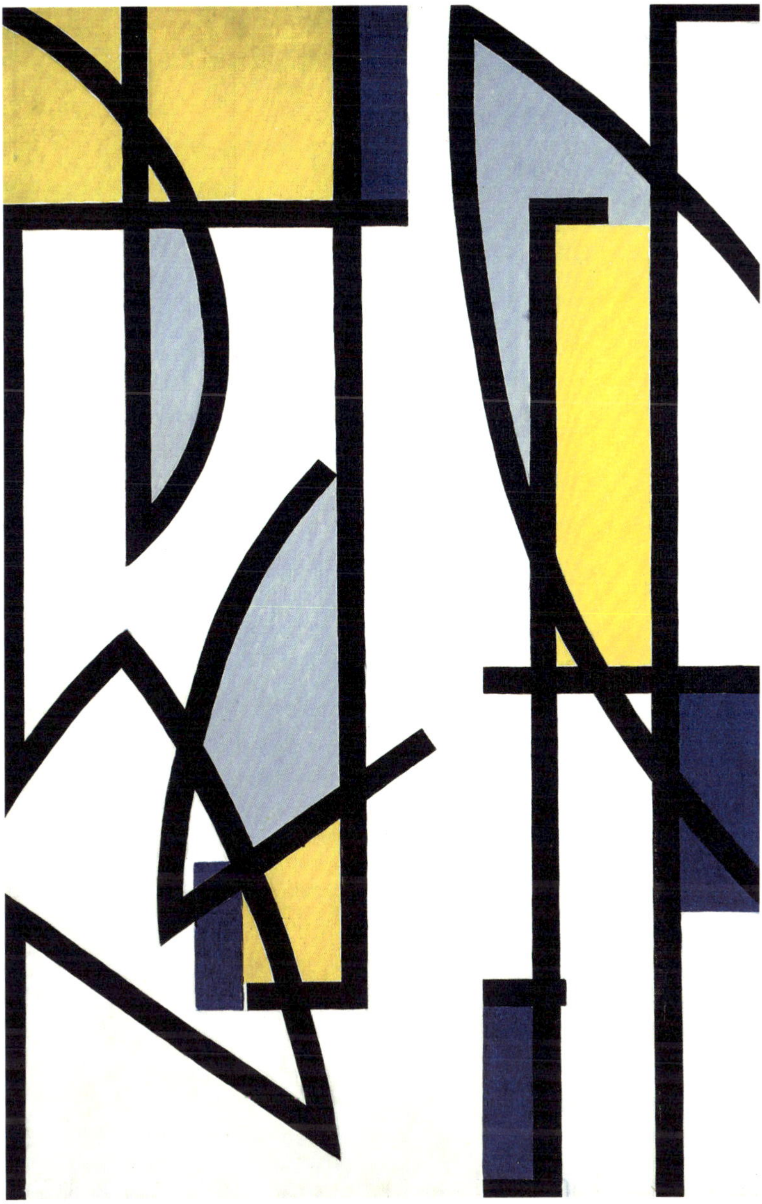

Fig. 8. *Composición dinámica,* 1950–51.

se opusiera a la llamada sensibilidad, que era necesario cambiar de escritura, y eso lo encontré en los elementos repetitivos. Una de las primeras piezas que hice es una repetición amarilla, *Repetición óptica Nº 2*, de 1951 [Fig. 9]. Hice varias *repeticiones*, pero se han perdido casi todas. Ésta es una de las pocas que quedan. Es una estructura construida por la repetición de diagonales que yo confrontaba con verticales. Enseguida hice otra que me interesó mucho más, porque era desequilibrada. En ese periodo venía a menudo a mi casa el Dr. Rísquez, y él me decía que esa obra sugería un ruido ascendente, algo así como la erre francesa. . . *rrrreee*. Por eso la llamábamos "la obra de las erres"; ella producía una sensación a la vez visual y auditiva.[44]

Las reflexiones de los artistas modernos sobre los límites de la pintura como medio de representación, se desarrollan paralelamente a un interés creciente tanto por sus posibilidades inventivas, como por su capacidad para sugerir realidades que existen más allá de los sentidos. Sugerir lo audible a través de la pintura, un arte de la visión, es una de esas tentativas por superar sus límites.

Yo estaba buscando un estado vibratorio a través de la repetición. Me interesaba el problema vibratorio y el estudio de la luz, lo que me fascinaba en Velázquez, y que los impresionistas, por quienes he sentido toda la vida un gran respeto, estudiaron muy conscientemente. Por eso, cuando voy a Holanda, me sorprenden (aparte de Mondrian, por supuesto): Vincent van Gogh y Johannes Vermeer. Van Gogh me demuestra que la oscuridad de los tonos no tiene nada que ver con el hecho de ser holandés, y Vermeer me sorprende por su capacidad pasmosa para expresar la luz, como si hubiera vivido en el trópico, en un lugar completamente distinto.

Recuerdo en particular un paisaje suyo que representa la ciudad de Delft, una tela que siempre he recordado al lado de *Las Meninas* y de las grandes obras que me marcaron. Aquello era casi un vitral, luminoso, de una luminosidad que nadie ha logrado conseguir. Seurat lo intentó luego por otros medios, sin conseguirlo. Eso me hizo comprender que quien se interesa por la luz la pinta en cualquier lugar, aunque no viva en el trópico. . . y el caso de Armando Reverón[45] es clarísimo. Él la pintaba de memoria. No la pintó porque vivía en

44. Soto se refiere aquí, probablemente, a *Repetición y progresión*, de 1951.

45. Armando Reverón (1889–1954). Fue uno de los principales artistas de la llamada Escuela de Caracas, sin duda el paisajista más potente y original de la pintura venezolana durante la primera mitad del siglo XX. Sus obras de los periodos "blanco" y "sepia" (según categorización de Alfredo Boulton) cuentan entre las más destacadas realizaciones de la pintura moderna latinoamericana. Aquí se manifiesta una de las contradicciones de Soto, contradicción que dice mucho de los conflictos que marcan a innumerables artistas latinoamericanos a la hora de pensar su realidad histórica. Cuando se trata de pensar la luz en Reverón, Soto opinaba que no existía relación alguna entre su obra y la luz de su entorno tropical. Le molestaba pensar que Reverón haya

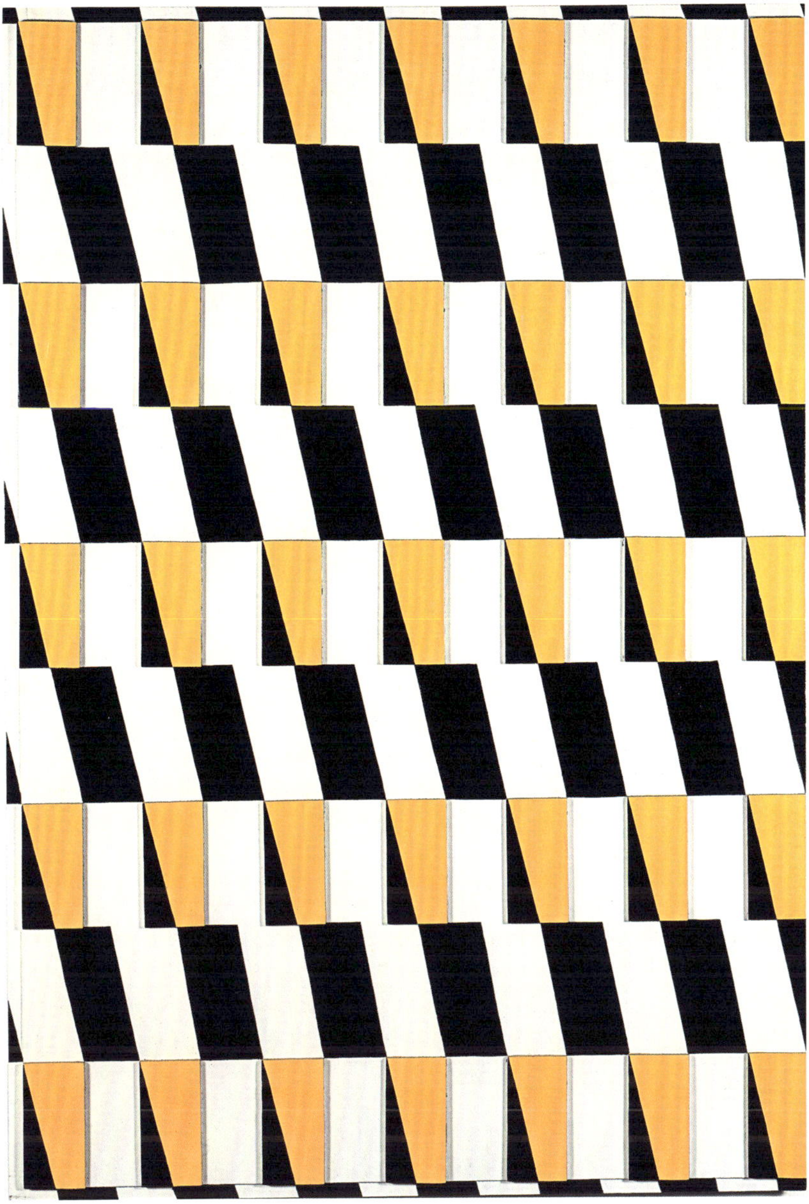

Fig. 9. *Repetición óptica N° 2,* 1951.

podido pintar la luz de Venezuela. Para él, Reverón solo pintó una idea de la luz, un concepto universal, y lo hizo "como hubiera podido hacerlo Vermeer en Holanda". Sin embargo, cuando intenta pensar el Impresionismo, afirma que él no podía comprenderlo en Venezuela, porque no lograba observar en el paisaje las gamas que veía en las obras de Monet. Lo entiende, afirma, cuando viaja a Francia y puede constatar que esa calidad plateada de la luz en Monet era la del paisaje francés. ¿Ahora, si Monet pintó la luz de Francia e hizo con ello una obra universal, por qué no hubiera podido hacer lo mismo un pintor como Reverón ante la luz del trópico?

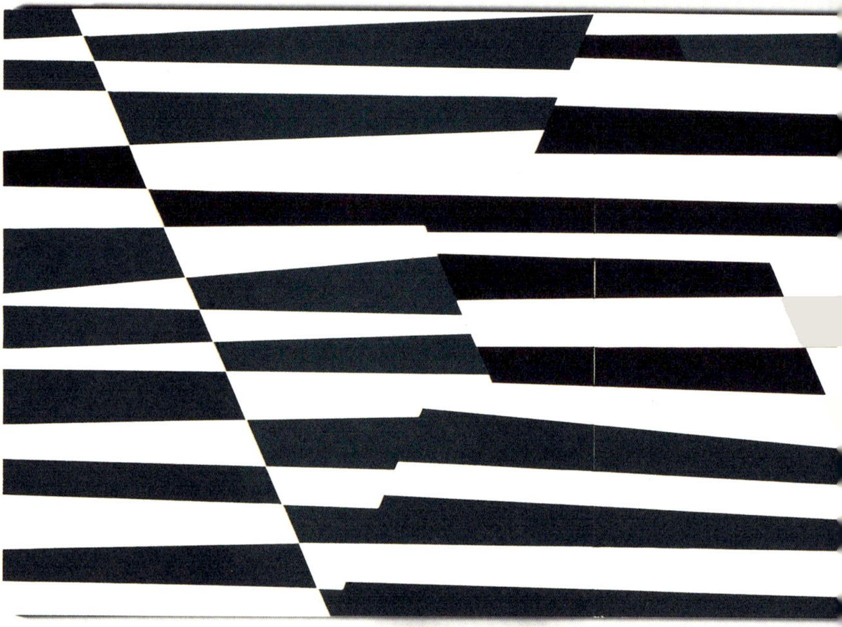

Fig. 10. *Muro óptico,* 1951.

Venezuela, sino porque se interesaba por ella, y lo hizo como lo hubiera hecho Vermeer en Holanda.

En ese momento, te decía, a la vez que me interesaba por los estados vibratorios, intentaba romper con los códigos esenciales del arte figurativo; por eso quería acabar con las nociones de composición y equilibrio, dos de los grandes códigos clásicos de la pintura representativa. Entre las cosas que intenté, se encuentran esas primeras *repeticiones* de las que te hablé, donde ya no existe el concepto de composición, pues se trata de un orden que puede repetirse hasta el infinito y donde cada segmento es igual al todo. La obra era solamente el fragmento de una realidad infinita.

AJ Precisamente, esa noción de la obra como un fragmento del universo viene de los impresionistas, donde el cuadro parece compuesto a través del visor de una cámara fotográfica. Ya no es la confección de una totalidad autosuficiente, ese orden donde la composición, la forma de un cuerpo o de un árbol en el paisaje se plegaban al discurso o al tema tratado. Los impresionistas, por el contrario, no solo pintaban un fragmento del espacio, sino que pretendían captar un instante fugitivo en condiciones atmosféricas específicas, con una luminosidad y

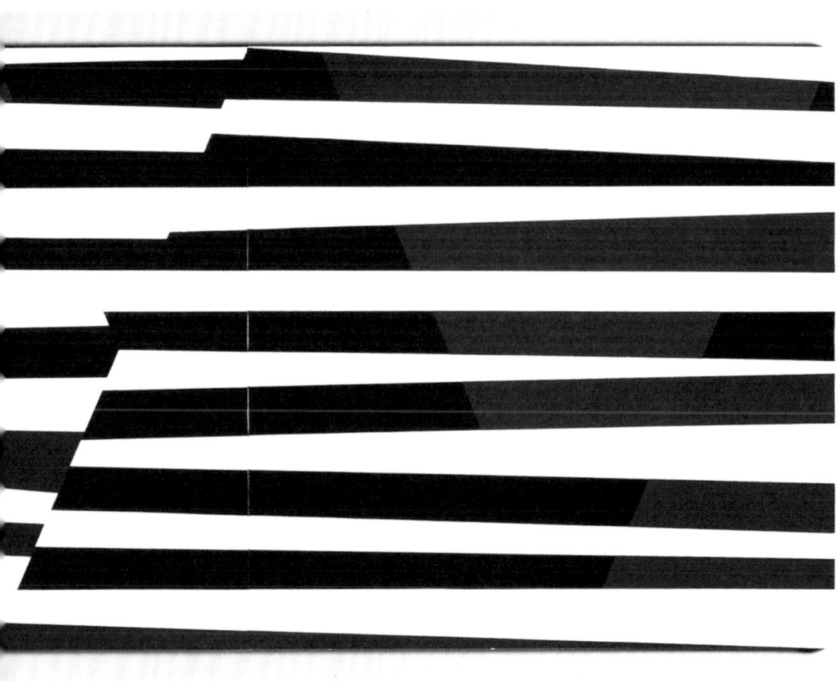

un colorido precisos. De allí, en parte, esos personajes cortados por los bordes, indicando claramente su continuidad fuera de los límites de la tela.

JS Por supuesto, y de ahí viene mi amor por los impresionistas, por ocuparse prioritariamente de la luz y su vibración, y de ella como la esencia de todo, y no del objeto, la forma y el tema, como lo pretendían los académicos. Paralelamente a estas *repeticiones*, o tal vez un poco antes, hice una serie de piezas en las que buscaba una estructura similar a las que observé en Cézanne mientras era alumno de la Escuela de Artes Plásticas y Artes Aplicadas de Caracas. No sé con qué intención él hacía esas cosas, lo cierto es que pude observar que, en algunos paisajes, comenzaba por la izquierda con mucha densidad, e iba licuándolo todo hacia la derecha. Ese modo de proceder se me había quedado grabado y me valí de él en un panel llamado *Muro óptico*, de 1951 [Fig. 10].

AJ Era buscar la vibración de los impresionistas a través de la estructura compositiva de Cézanne.

JS No precisamente a partir de su estructura compositiva. En mis pinturas de entonces no existía una composición en el sentido clásico de la palabra, se

Fig. 11. *Sin título (Progresión),* 1952.

trataba de una especie de progresión de la densidad pictórica de izquierda a derecha.

AJ Lo importante, en cualquier caso, es que esa progresión de la densidad sugería ya un elemento nuevo, es decir, el tiempo, lo que formaliza en las diversas *progresiones* y *repeticiones* que hace durante los años de 1951 y 1952 [Fig. 11]. Inmediatamente después de estas *repeticiones*, usted concibe *Rotación*, de 1952, [Fig. 12] que me parece capital, no solamente porque es el inicio de sus piezas seriales, surgidas directamente de la música, sino también porque en ella se manifiesta por primera vez un rasgo que será característico de su producción posterior; la presencia de un elemento fijo y uno móvil.

JS La idea era la de hacer un cuadrado en movimiento. . . pero, ¿cómo podía hacerlo, cómo podía sugerir la sensación de movimiento? Al principio pensé en hacer un cuadrado transparente –como lo hice en otras ocasiones– con la intención de convertirlo en algo más abstracto, porque lo que me interesaba era la idea del cuadrado. Luego decidí hacerlo en blanco sobre un fondo casi blanco. De esa manera, aparte de utilizar la lección de Malevich, le daba más importancia a la superposición de dos valores luminosos que a las formas en sí. Por otra parte, el cuadrado representaba –y representa todavía para mí– la forma más genuinamente humana, en el sentido de que ella es una pura creación del hombre. El cuadrado, y las figuras geométricas en general, son pura invención del espíritu humano, son una creación netamente intelectual y lo que me interesa particularmente en ellas es que no poseen una dimensión específica. No se encuentran limitadas por las relaciones de escala que existen entre el hombre y los diversos objetos y seres de la naturaleza. Una casa, un árbol, poseen dimensiones más o menos definidas, tienen una medida, mientras que una figura geométrica puede ser infinitamente pequeña o infinitamente grande, no tiene limitaciones de orden métrico y, en consecuencia, escapan completamente al antropocentrismo tradicional del arte occidental.

Hay, en este interés de Soto por las figuras geométricas y los volúmenes perfectos como el cubo, la pirámide y la esfera (esas formas universales a partir de las cuales podrían engendrarse todas las demás), una cierta dimensión platónica que comparte con la mayoría de los artistas abstracto-geométricos.[46]

Por estas razones decido utilizar el cuadrado. Luego, buscando hacer visible el movimiento, decido repetir una serie de cuadrados sobre la superficie con una separación igual a la medida de un cuadrado. Materializando uno de sus bordes por medio de una línea negra y haciendo que ésta pareciera desplazarse alrededor del cuadrado, logré sugerir la idea de que cada uno de ellos giraba sobre sí en el sentido de las agujas del reloj. Al llegar a la mitad me di cuenta de que ya no necesitaba del cuadrado blanco, y que bastaba con hacer girar la línea negra. Buscando siempre una mayor abstracción, pensé en reducir la línea a sus dos extremos, indicándolos por un par de puntos que giraban en el mismo sentido. Por último, ya al final, quise representar esos puntos y hacer una especie de resumen de todos sus movimientos, una suma, y los representé como si se tratara de su proyección ortogonal sobre el plano, lo que generó esas líneas continuas de puntos.

46. Mondrian también, por supuesto, como en principio todo artista abstracto-geométrico, le acuerda a estas formas perfectas un carácter universal. "El artista de mañana. . . podrá partir cada vez más de lo universal, mientras que el artista de hoy tenía que partir de lo natural (lo individual)." Piet Mondrian. *La nueva imagen en la pintura*. Murcia: Colegio Oficial de Aparejadores y Arquitectos Técnicos, 1993, 95. Originalmente publicado en la revista *De Stijl* N° 11, septiembre 1918, 127–34.

Fig. 12. *Rotación,* 1952.

AJ Hablando de esta pieza, Luis Enrique Pérez-Oramas[47] me hizo observar que si seguimos la secuencia de las líneas que sugieren el movimiento del cuadrado, encontramos que el paso de una línea de cuadrados a la siguiente, en el sentido vertical, se hace por medio de un salto equivalente a dos columnas. Es decir, que en su borde derecho faltan dos columnas de cuadrados que no fueron representados, lo que crea un espacio virtual o invisible que explica el salto existente entre una línea de cuadrados y la siguiente.

JS Eso respondía a la noción de la obra abierta, tal y como Umberto Eco lo señala en sus libros, solo que lo hice mucho antes que él. *Rotación* responde a esa idea de que la obra puede ser cortada en cualquier lugar, o que podía continuar indefinidamente sin que yo tuviera necesidad de pintarlo.

47. Luis Enrique Pérez-Oramas (1960). Curador, ensayista y poeta venezolano. Autor de numerosos textos sobre arte moderno europeo y latinoamericano. Es actualmente curador de arte latinoamericano en el Museum of Modern Art, Nueva York.

AJ Sin embargo este no es exactamente el problema de Umberto Eco, pues lo que pasa en *Rotación* es que no fueron representadas dos columnas de cuadros, o sea que tienen más relación con las líneas de puntos no pintadas en las experiencias seriales (*Estudio para una serie*, por ejemplo), que con las *repeticiones*, que sí son verdaderas obras abiertas.[48]

JS Tal vez, pero lo que a mí me interesaba en ese instante era la intuición de que no hacía falta representar todo lo que proponía, y esas situaciones podían continuar indefinidamente en cualquier dirección. Ahora, *Rotación* tenía otra función, que era conseguir que los resultados de la serie pudieran extenderse hasta el muro. Era una especie de reacción mía, con el propósito de darle igual importancia al muro de sostén (la pared) que a las estructuras fabricadas en mi taller.

AJ Este es el momento en el que hace la maqueta con la que debía participar en las experiencias de integración a la arquitectura liderizadas por Carlos Raúl Villanueva en la Universidad Central de Venezuela.[49] Es una obra bien peculiar, pues parece unir las experiencias realizadas en tiempos diferentes. Tiene por ejemplo el problema de la progresión, que ya había trabajado por separado, a lo que se une el tema del color y el de la rotación de los pequeños cubos [Fig. 13].

JS Sí, es un mural que no llegué a realizar y donde intentaba sugerir también la idea de un cubo en movimiento, como en el caso de *Rotación*. A eso le agregué esas líneas de color que se expanden hacia la derecha y hacia la izquierda, en una progresión sin límites determinables. Lo interesante es que el color ya respondía a una preocupación serial, ya estaba codificado.

AJ ¿Y por qué no pudo construirla?

JS Bueno, por razones políticas, de oposición a la dictadura militar. Mis amigos

48. Una obra abierta, según Umberto Eco, sería aquella que incorporaría en su estructura plástica una cierta inclinación a lo incompleto, a lo inestable y sobre todo un llamado a la intervención del espectador a diversos niveles y grados. Esa intervención del espectador podría ser psicológica o física, lo importante es que la obra no se presente como una forma completa y cerrada sobre sí misma, sino como un proceso abierto continuamente y que permita aislar nuevos perfiles y nuevas posibilidades de una forma. Así, la obra abierta tiende a colocar al espectador como centro activo de una red de relaciones inagotables, no necesariamente orientadas desde la obra. Ver más en Umberco Eco, *Opera aperta*, Milano: Edit. Bompiano, 1962.

49. Carlos Raúl Villanueva (1900–75). Arquitecto venezolano formado en Francia, sin duda la principal figura de la arquitectura moderna venezolana. Su obra más densa e influyente es la Universidad Central de Venezuela construida entre 1944 y 1964 (declarada por la UNESCO Patrimonio Cultural de la Humanidad en el año 2000). Allí emprende un ambicioso proyecto de integración de las artes que alcanza su momento de esplendor a inicio de los años cincuenta. Participaron, entre otros artistas: Alexander Calder, Henri Laurens, Fernand Léger, Alejandro Otero, Anton Pevsner, Víctor Valera, Víctor Vasarely y Oswaldo Vigas.

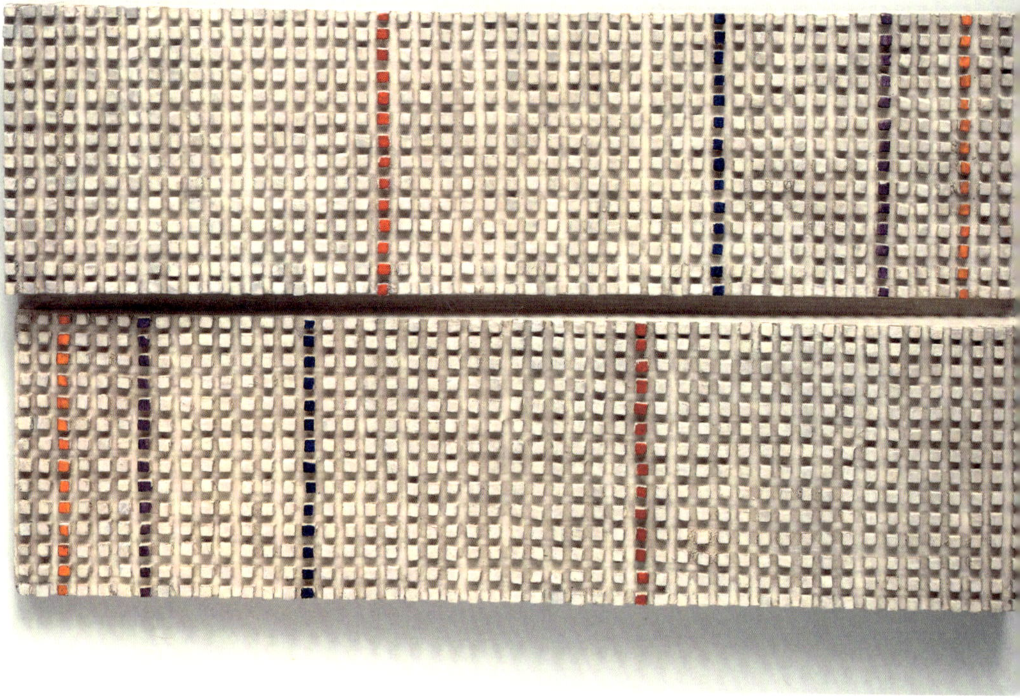

Fig. 13. *Sin título (Maqueta para mural Universidad Central de Venezuela),* 1952–53.

artistas me decían que no debíamos colaborar con un régimen militar, y decidí no hacerla. . . Al fin, ya ves, ellos hicieron la suya y la única que no se hizo fue la mía.[50]

AJ Ahora, por el hecho mismo de que estamos ante una maqueta, y también porque la expresión del movimiento *en* o *desde* la pintura comporta no pocas y muy interesantes ambigüedades, me gustaría precisar cómo concebía usted el movimiento aparente de estos cubos y la expansión de las líneas de color. ¿Se daba, en su imaginario, de modo simultáneo, o se producía por etapas? Es decir, ¿deberíamos imaginar esta pieza como un espacio donde los cubos, en su conjunto, estarían simultáneamente en movimiento, o se trataría de un movimiento que pasaría de un cubo a otro, de manera que solo uno estaría

50. Entre 1952 y 1958, el general Marcos Pérez Jiménez gobierna a Venezuela de manera dictatorial, hasta que un golpe de Estado cívico militar lo derroca el 23 de enero de 1958.

moviéndose a la vez? Supongamos que queremos animarlos en un video, ¿cómo deberíamos hacerlo?

JS No, yo creo que el objetivo era hacerlo como en *Rotación,* que un cuadrado giraba primero, luego el otro, y así sucesivamente. . . , todos esos movimientos debían sugerir la idea de un cubo girando en el espacio.

AJ Éstas son, si no me equivoco, sus últimas producciones antes de pasar a las experiencias propiamente seriales. Ya se siente en ellas un gran rigor; cada línea, cada punto, responde a una intención precisa. Lo que me interesa particularmente en sus próximas piezas, es que en ellas se manifiestan dos aspectos a mi entender fundamentales en el arte moderno. Uno de ellos es la relación entre la música y la plástica. Desde Gauguin, y más tarde Kandinsky y Klee, la música le ofrece al pintor ejemplos de lo que puede ser una construcción plástica no descriptiva. A la vez, la pintura le proporciona diversas posibilidades constructivas a la música, como lo vemos por ejemplo en el caso de Pierre Boulez, quien habla, en 1950–51, de la influencia que tuvieron en él ciertas piezas de Paul Klee. El segundo aspecto que me interesa es el que se refiere a la necesidad de trascender los límites antropocéntricos de las artes visuales, atacando la perspectiva, la composición y el gusto.

JS No es precisamente Pierre Boulez quien despierta en mí el interés por conocer las nuevas estructuras musicales. Él me interesó sobre todo por el concepto de la revolución musical, por la voluntad de revolucionar el fenómeno artístico-sonoro. Para entonces creó *Le marteau sans maître*, en cuya estructura no tenía cabida el sistema armónico tradicional. Tuvimos una buena relación e, incluso, me invitó a trabajar con el *Stockhausen Festival* en Alemania. Lamentablemente, ya me había comprometido con el pabellón de Venezuela en Bruselas, y no pude hacer ambas cosas. Eso nos separó y desde entonces no nos hemos vuelto a ver. Mi conocimiento de las nuevas estructuras musicales, el sistema dodecafónico y las experiencias seriales, las descubro a través de un libro de René Leibowitz.[51] Él, quien había sido discípulo de Anton Webern, escribió un libro sobre el sistema dodecafónico que leí y estudié religiosamente,

51. René Leibowitz (1913–72). Director de orquesta, compositor y ensayista francés de origen polaco. A finales de la Segunda Guerra Mundial, cuando la música dodecafónica de Schoenberg permanece ampliamente desconocida, Leibowitz comienza a enseñar ese nuevo lenguaje musical a un pequeño grupo de músicos (Pierre Boulez, Michel Philippot, Jeane-Louise Nigg). Es autor del libro *Introduction à la musique des douze sons* (París, 1949), que sirvió de punto de partida para las experiencias seriales que Soto realiza entre 1952 y 1953.

tratando de entender los nuevos sistemas musicales y buscando una estrategia para trasladarlos a las artes visuales.

Cuando entendí la música serial, encontré un mundo fabuloso donde el sonido no era utilizado en función del gusto; el ensamblaje de los valores sonoros estaba perfectamente codificado. Cada valor musical era un número, y utilizando parámetros cuyas medidas no correspondían a las tradicionales, se podía producir una música completamente diferente. Siguiendo ese ejemplo decido codificar los elementos plásticos y restringirme al uso de ocho colores. A cada color le correspondía un número. Yo quería eliminar toda subjetividad ligada al gusto personal, incluyendo al mío. De allí que me restringiera a colores perfectamente definidos. No era un verde oliva con acentos rojizos, ni un rosa oscuro, colores que se prestan a confusión, sino los tres primarios, los tres secundarios, el blanco y el negro (Más tarde introduzco el ultravioleta, que era considerado un color sublime. Por eso preparé un violeta bastante ligero, que introduje en la serie). El blanco era el número 1, el amarillo el 2, el naranja el 3, el rojo el 4, el verde el 5, el azul el 6, el violeta el 7, el ultravioleta el 8, y, finalmente, el negro, el 9. Tras codificarlos, decido permutarlos como se hace con las notas en la música serial. No permutaba colores, sino series numéricas muy sencillas: 4-1, 4-5, 3-7. . . y así sucesivamente.

Cuál no sería mi sorpresa cuando, partiendo de estos elementos básicos y respetando las permutaciones establecidas, pude producir un conjunto de estructuras que funcionaban desde el punto de vista plástico.[52] En algunas de ellas, inclusive, los puntos comenzaban a moverse y a vibrar de una manera impresionista, casi puntillista. Todos esos puntos que descienden a la vertical y vienen además de aquel estudio que hice en *Rotación*, es decir, una proyección del punto hasta donde espacio hubiera. Entonces comprendí que estaba ante un mundo maravilloso, y que era posible codificar los elementos plásticos, como ya lo habían hecho los músicos con el sonido. También seguía preocupado por el problema del movimiento, y por eso introduje algunos elementos que, como en *Rotación*, buscaban sugerir el movimiento de un elemento en el espacio. Eso lo hice en *Estudio para una serie*, de 1952–53 [Fig. 14]. En algunos momentos, entre dos series, ponía una línea de círculos sin color; era solamente una marca que

52. Es importante anotar que, a partir del ejemplo que le ofrecía la música serial, Soto pensó en un método de codificación estricto para el color y la forma, de manera que su distribución sobre el espacio de la tela no respondiera a criterios personales y discrecionales. En este sentido, las estructuras numéricas establecidas se decidían sin saber cuál sería el resultado visual, plástico, de tales permutaciones. De allí la sorpresa que dice haber tenido al descubrir el resultado final. Se trataba en cierta forma de un método de distanciamiento que, por supuesto, solo podía ser eficaz durante un momento. En *Estudio para una serie*, por ejemplo, uno de los números permutados correspondía al color, el otro al número de líneas de círculos.

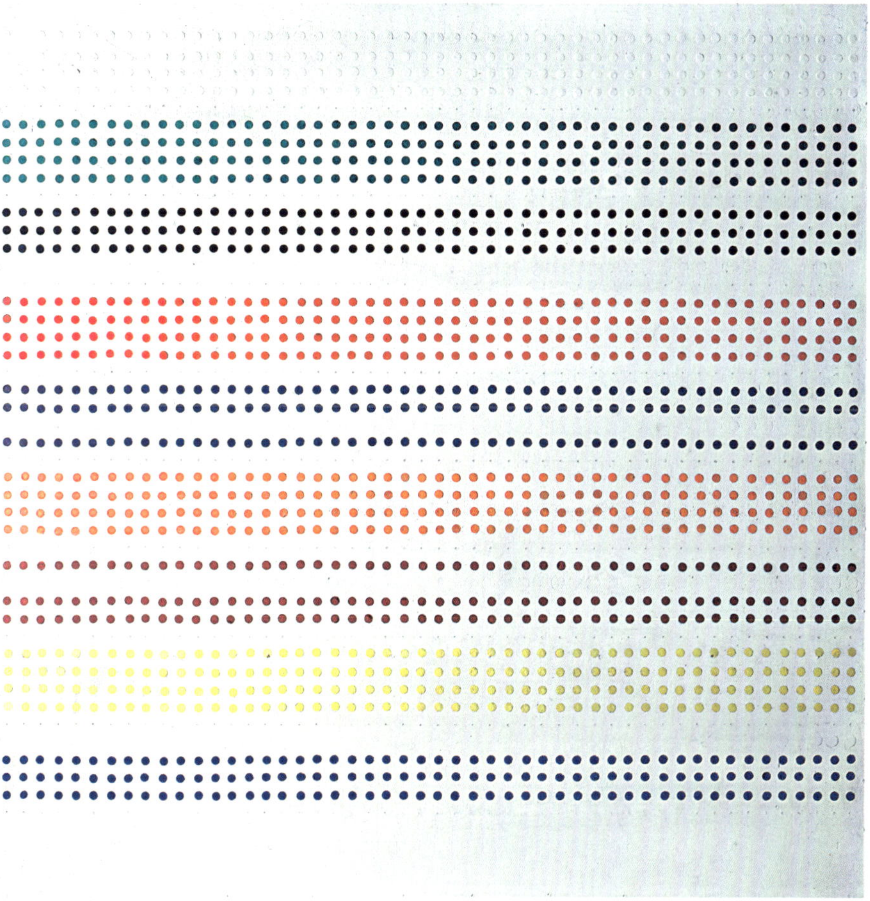

Fig. 14. *Estudio para una serie,* 1952–53.

hacía con un sacabocados. Después indicaba una pequeña línea que, al interior del círculo, parecía girar. . . Unas arriba, otras al lado derecho, la siguiente abajo, de manera que el círculo pareciera girar en el sentido de las agujas del reloj. . .

AJ Conozco esa pieza, pero no recuerdo haber visto las marcas que describe.

JS Lo que pasa es que un día le pedí a Mirtha, la esposa de Carlos Cruz-Diez, que la restaurara para una exposición, y al repintar el fondo blanco se taparon algunas de esas marcas. Si la observas con cuidado todavía puedes verlas en varios puntos.

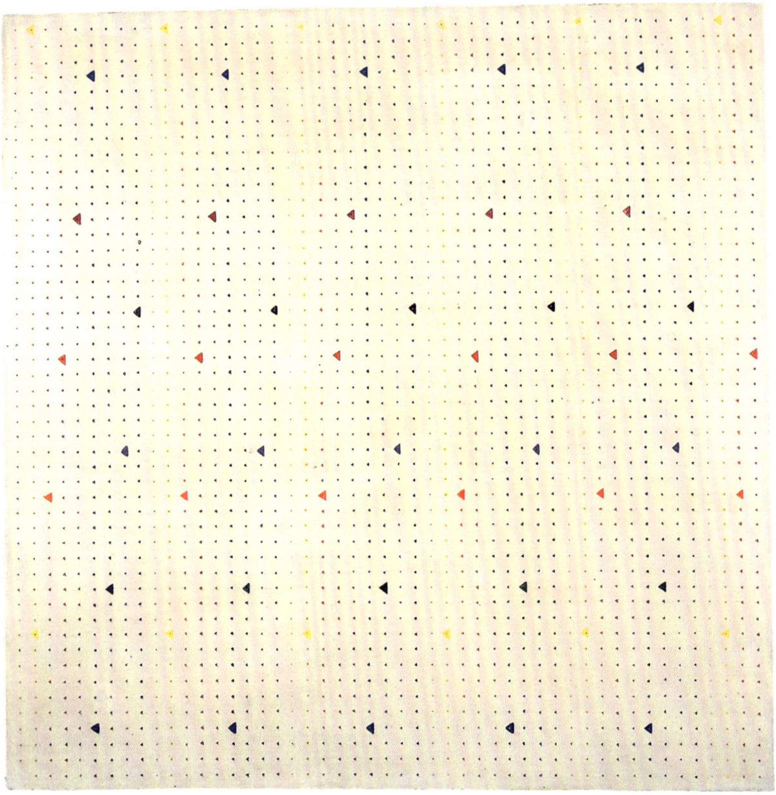

Fig. 15. *Pintura serial,* 1952–53.

AJ La pieza titulada *Pintura serial*, de 1952–53, ha sido reproducida en varios sentidos. ¿Cuando usted la hizo, pensó en darle una orientación precisa? [Fig. 15]

JS Cuando la hice, la pensé con los triángulos orientados hacia la derecha, quizás por eso del sentido que tiene la lectura en el mundo occidental.[53] Pero la verdad es que eso no tenía ninguna importancia para mí. Los triángulos grandes no hacen sino situar la evolución permutable de los nueve colores en su recorrido. Esas dos obras (*Pintura serial* y *Estudio para una serie*) no tienen un arriba y un abajo, posiciones horizontales, verticales o diagonales. Puedes ponerlas en el suelo o en el techo, y su lectura no se modifica, incluso si giramos a su

53. Durante nuestra conversación, Soto indicó que los triángulos mayores estaban originalmente orientados hacia la derecha. Sin embargo, las inscripciones presentes al dorso de la obra, señalando su parte superior, indicarían una orientación de esos triángulos hacia la izquierda. Esta orientación y su coincidencia con la disminución del espesor material de la pintura parecen por lo demás coherentes con la voluntad de pensar lo que Soto llama "la esencia inmaterial del universo".

alrededor. Podrían estar orientadas en cualquier sentido, pero yo necesitaba darle puntos de referencia a la gente para que pudiera entender. Por eso ponía las líneas que indicaban el movimiento, si no la gente no podía entender. Yo necesitaba advertir que funcionaban así. Tal vez eso tiene que ver con mi formación de profesor. No olvides que estudié Pedagogía durante más de cuatro años.

AJ En *Pintura serial* hay además dos hechos curiosos. Por una parte, el espesor material del cuadro disminuye en el sentido indicado por los triángulos grandes, como si quisiera sugerir que la evolución que se describe en él conduce necesariamente hacia su desmaterialización. Por otra, cada triángulo –los grandes y los pequeños– tiene una pequeña perforación en su centro. ¿Qué buscaba, primero, con esa disminución en el espesor de la pintura y su coincidencia con el sentido sugerido por los triángulos, y, a qué preocupaciones correspondían esas perforaciones?

JS Haces una observación bien interesante. Es cierto que si la evolución teórica del cuadro se extiende hasta el muro, terminaría en algún momento por ser inmaterial. Todos esos elementos eran y siguen siendo esenciales en la evolución de mi trabajo. Lo de las perforaciones tiene un origen más circunstancial. En la época, cada vez que enviaba un cuadro mal embalado –por mí por supuesto– y que sufría daños, los organizadores de las exposiciones encontraban más fácil pasarle un rodillo de blanco al cuadro y después repintarlo, que ponerse a restaurarlos. Así que tuve el cuidado de que, por lo menos, el rodillo no llegara a la pequeña perforación.[54]

AJ En su trabajo de esos años hay dos aspectos que me parecen fundamentales y que me gustaría subrayar. Uno de ellos es el deseo de trascender el gusto. Entonces –lo ha dicho en distintas ocasiones– el arte abstracto parecía haber llegado a sus últimas consecuencias. Usted entiende, y de allí la importancia de sus reflexiones, que de continuar trabajando en esa vía, donde el gusto determinaba la construcción de la obra, su trabajo no hubiera pasado de ser una serie de variaciones, más o menos bellas, a la manera de Mondrian. A partir de las experiencias seriales, y especialmente por el abandono casi total de las nociones tradicionales de belleza, gusto y composición, logra encontrar un camino nuevo. La prueba de que esa actitud no era un capricho personal, sino

54. Este curioso método de restauración parece sobre todo indicar el carácter de experimentación banal que se le acordaba entonces a esas piezas y por lo tanto el escaso respeto que se tenía por ellas. Hoy sería sencillamente impensable que los organizadores de un salón repintaran una obra para, supuestamente, restaurarla.

una necesidad de la época, es la impresionante coincidencia entre lo que usted hacía y lo que Pierre Boulez señala sobre su pieza titulada *Structures*, de 1951: "Era para mí un ensayo, eso que llaman la duda, la duda cartesiana; cuestionarlo todo, hacer tabla rasa de la herencia y recomenzar de cero, para ver cómo podía reconstruirse la escritura a partir de un fenómeno que había aniquilado la invención individual".[55] El segundo aspecto es la idea de romper con eso que usted llama el antropocentrismo que ha caracterizado gran parte del arte occidental. El hecho de que estas obras sean estructuras que no tienen un principio ni un fin, sino que podrían continuar infinitamente, hace de ellas el fragmento de una realidad que, en principio, no puede ser comprendida a escala humana.

JS En el fondo, cuando entendí el problema de la abstracción, me dije que era absurdo continuar con un formalismo que no rompía realmente con las estructuras utilizadas por el arte figurativo de todos los tiempos, como lo estaban haciendo muchos artistas de entonces. Y es precisamente por eso que la abstracción que se manejaba a finales de los años cuarenta y principios de los cincuenta no podía avanzar. Lo que se hacía, generalmente, no pasaba de ser una reinterpretación de la estructura geométrica utilizada por los grandes maestros clásicos.

Por ejemplo, te puedo señalar una de las cosas que me fascinaron durante mis estudios en la Escuela de Artes Plásticas y Artes Aplicadas de Caracas, al descubrir la *Venus* de Giorgione. A mí me pareció que aquella figura era algo muy especial y que en el fondo no tenía nada que ver con un desnudo. Cuando me puse a dibujarla, encontré que el cuerpo de la *Venus* estaba compuesto por dos elipses que se entrelazaban a nivel del vientre. La primera se formaba por el torso y la posición de su brazo derecho, mientras la segunda se hacía evidente en la posición particular de sus piernas. Recuerdo que luego, cuando fui a pintar un paisaje, utilicé esa misma estructura para organizar los campos. Ese fue uno de los más bellos que hice en aquellos años. Desde entonces me he dicho siempre que el arte está estructurado de modo tal que no se restringe a la imitación de las formas naturales, y que, inclusive en periodos históricos donde no parecía tener otro objetivo, los grandes artistas utilizaron la naturaleza como un punto de partida desde donde podían construir otra realidad, que es el verdadero sentido del arte. El mejor ejemplo de lo que te estoy diciendo lo encontramos en el Renacimiento.

55. Pierre Boulez, *Par volonté et par hasard*. París: Ed. Du Seuil, trad. Ariel Jiménez, 1975, 70.

Por eso, cuando me puse a analizar la abstracción a principios de los años cincuenta, entendí que no podía avanzar en esa dirección y que así, efectivamente, era una puerta cerrada. Pensaba que al construir mis obras a partir de la triangulación y la geometrización tal y como lo hacían Giorgione y los mejores pintores del Renacimiento, no estaba pensando profundamente el problema de la estructura, sino extrayendo de ellos sus formas básicas de composición, lo cual era casi un plagio. Estábamos usurpándoles a esos grandes artistas su poder de invención, cuando lo que debíamos hacer era inventar la abstracción. Por eso me retiré del amor por Giorgione y por el estudio de la triangulación típica del Renacimiento. Era indispensable encontrar una vía distinta para estructurar la superficie pictórica, de lo contrario, seguiría atado a una tradición de siglos y al antropocentrismo que rechazaba. La figura del hombre no me interesaba, solo me interesaba el hombre como idea, como creador de ideas.[56]

AJ Y es pues en la música donde encuentra esa nueva manera de pensar la estructura.

JS Incluso antes, con las primeras *repeticiones*. En realidad no sé qué intuición tuve para hacer aquellas primeras *repeticiones*. En *Repetición óptica Nº 2* ya existía una intención de romper con la tradición dibujística y con los límites del antropocentrismo. Además, la codificación rigurosa de los elementos pictóricos como yo lo intenté no fue la única salida que se buscó en la época al estancamiento del arte abstracto. También lo hicieron los informalistas del momento. Y yo encontré que esa reacción contra el academicismo abstracto a través de lo informal era bastante interesante, luego entendí que en realidad hacían sensiblemente lo mismo. En verdad, el Informalismo era casi como agrandar segmentos de una pintura clásica para reencontrar el placer del oficio, los empastes a lo Rembrandt, la pincelada y el color, sin romper con las estructuras básicas de la pintura figurativa. Yo entendía la abstracción como idea pura, porque lo abstracto, en la conciencia del hombre, y sobre todo del hombre occidental, no tiene nada que ver con lo representativo. Por principio, tiene que ser estructura pura. Entonces comienzo a buscar con qué actividades podía conseguir una relación que satisficiera mi noción de lo abstracto, y esa relación la encuentro solamente en las matemáticas y en la música. En vista de que no tenía la formación necesaria en el campo de las ciencias, ni tiempo para dedicarme al estudio de las matemáticas durante cinco años, intuí que a través de la música podía encontrar

56. "El pintor sólo es creador cuando las formas de su cuadro no tienen nada que ver con la naturaleza". Kasimir Malevich, *De Cézanne au Suprématisme*. Lausanne, Suiza: L'Age d'Homme, trad. Ariel Jiménez, 1974, 55.

una forma diferente de manejar los elementos pictóricos, una que respondiera mejor al concepto que me hacía de la abstracción y que era la de una manera otra de descifrar el universo.

AJ Sin embargo, las experiencias estrictamente seriales lo ocupan durante muy poco tiempo. Se trató de un ensayo puntual que le ayudó a organizar y controlar los materiales de que disponía, algo así como la organización del espacio de trabajo, de sus herramientas y materiales, pero los retos de la pintura seguían todavía pendientes. Pronto aparecerá la superposición de tramas por planos transparentes y la vibración que resulta de ellas. Usted pasará entonces de una práctica pictórica que sugiere realidades exteriores, como la transparencia aparente del cuadrado o el movimiento de una línea en el espacio, a una que pone

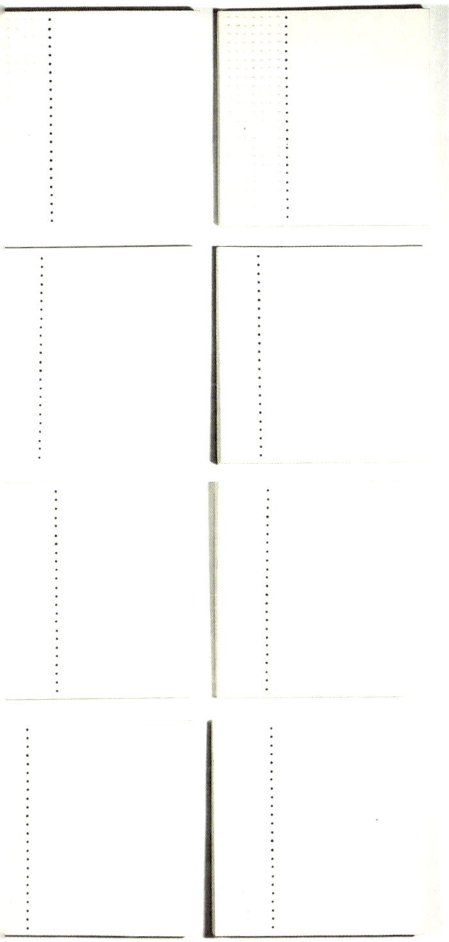

Fig. 16. *Muro blanco,* 1952–53.

en juego fenómenos plásticos y que, en el caso del movimiento, se remite al desplazamiento del espectador.

JS Eso sucede cuando empiezo a sentir la necesidad de introducir el espacio real. El *Muro blanco*, de 1952–53, por ejemplo [Fig. 16], que sigue siendo una construcción serial, puede vincularse con *Rotación*, de 1952. Es la misma idea de un cuadrado que rota en el espacio y que intenté sugerir con la inclinación de los planos hacia abajo, luego hacia arriba, a la izquierda y a la derecha. Lo nuevo es que esta vez ya no está pintado, sino que se da por el espesor mismo del cuadrado. Yo proseguí allí con el objetivo de conseguir una especie de simbiosis entre el muro y los cuadros adosados a él, y por eso coloqué veinticuatro paneles blancos de cincuenta por cincuenta centímetros. Pudieron ser de otro

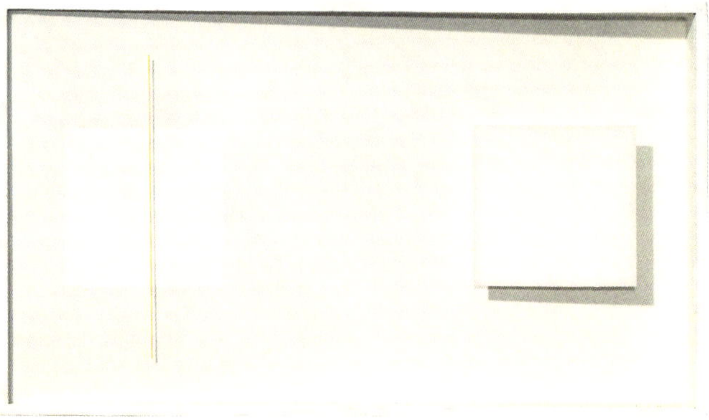

Fig. 17. *Dos cuadrados en el espacio,* 1953.

color, pero el blanco ofrecía menos sugerencias exteriores a la idea, haciéndose más neutral. Cuatro de esos pequeños cuadrados se perdieron en el Museo de Bellas Artes, probablemente en el transporte, cuando hice mi exposición.[57] Entonces traté de reconstruirlos junto a Miguel Arroyo,[58] y recuerdo que nunca estuve satisfecho con la serie que reconstruimos. Algún día, tal vez, podrá reencontrarse la serie original. Todavía tengo la esperanza de que un día sea factible encontrar el resultado primitivo, ya que no se trata de un problema de color. Si volteas las veinticuatro piezas, verás que las cuatro restituidas tienen otro tipo de madera. Sin embargo, no es en esa pieza donde introduzco realmente el espacio, sino en *Dos cuadrados en el espacio*, de 1953 [Fig. 17]. En ella se pueden ver dos cuadrados exactamente iguales, uno que ocupa la parte izquierda del soporte, y otro que está a su derecha sobre un plexiglás transparente, a cierta distancia del fondo. Ante el cuadrado de la izquierda coloqué enseguida una línea vertical destinada a materializar el espacio que se observa entre éste y el plexiglás, mientras el de la derecha crea un cubo virtual al proyectar su sombra sobre el fondo.

AJ Es interesante anotar que en estas piezas, como en las que le seguirán durante casi dos años, la estructura básica es la misma empleada por Malevich en el *Cuadrado blanco sobre blanco*; es decir, dos elementos iguales o equivalentes, uno de los cuales se desplaza con respecto al otro.

57. La exposición titulada *Soto. Estructuras cinéticas*, se inaugura el 30 de junio de 1957 en el Museo de Bellas Artes de Caracas.

58. Miguel Arroyo (1920–2004). Artista plástico, curador y museógrafo, iniciador de la museografía moderna en Venezuela. Director del Museo de Bellas Artes de Caracas entre 1959 y 1976.

Fig. 18. *Desplazamiento de un cuadrado transparente,* 1953–54.

JS Es cierto, yo parto con la intención de dinamizar a Mondrian, pero si se analiza mi producción de esos años, se puede ver que está impregnada del pensamiento de Malevich. Yo quería trabajar el cuadrado como algo inmaterial, por eso pensé en el blanco, o en colores transparentes, incluso en barnices sobre el plexiglás. Traté de construirlo por medio de una repetición de pequeños cuadritos, o por medio de tramas de puntos. En *Desplazamiento de un cuadrado transparente,* de 1953–54, se puede ver claramente esa intención y la base de lo que me llevaría más tarde a la superposición de un plano transparente sobre otro [Fig. 18]. En el fondo, incluso antes de emplear el plexiglás, veía cada uno de esos planos como verdaderas superposiciones. Sobre un cuadrado amarillo se mueven otros dos cuadrados, uno formado por pequeños cuadritos y otro por puntos, lo que los hacía transparentes. Es similar a lo que ocurre en *Desplazamiento de un elemento*

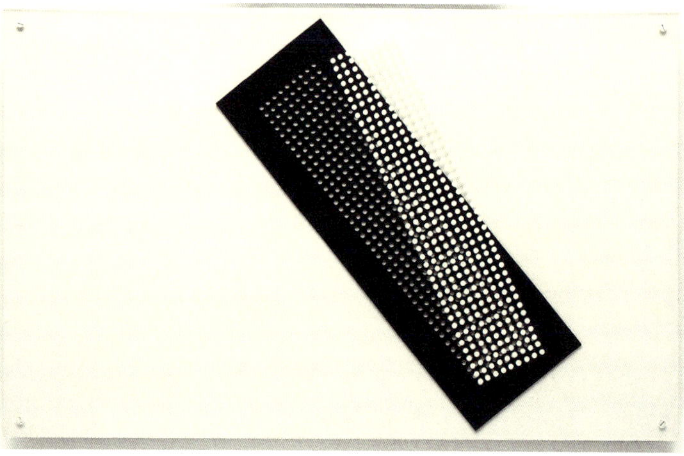

Fig. 19. *Desplazamiento de un elemento luminoso,* 1954.

luminoso, de 1954 [Fig. 19]. Yo había visto a Georges Koskas, cuando creaba superposiciones de puntos blancos sobre puntos negros en el plano. A partir de él se me ocurrió superponer esas tramas de puntos con la ayuda del plexiglás. Recuerdo que estaba un día en el BHV [tienda francesa por departamentos] y recorriendo el departamento de herramientas y equipos eléctricos, me encontré con una rejilla con huecos redondos que utilizaban, si no me equivoco, para colocar piezas de radio o como parrilla de ventilación. Entonces decidí comprarla porque pensé que seguramente podría hacer algo con ella. Empecé copiando todos esos puntos, en blanco, sobre un plexiglás. Luego pinté la rejilla de negro y la coloqué sobre un fondo blanco. La idea era superponer esas dos tramas de puntos desplazándolas ligeramente. De esa superposición y de ese desplazamiento entre dos tramas idénticas aparecieron formas que sugerían la aparición de un tercer valor. Esa pieza me llevó posteriormente a otra donde descubro una situación verdaderamente nueva: *Metamorfosis*, de 1954 [Fig. 20].[59] Superponiendo una trama de puntos sobre una trama de cuadrados pequeños, descubro un fenómeno que me dejó como flotando durante casi una semana: al superponer las tramas aparecían núcleos luminosos que giraban y se movían cuando me desplazaba ante ellos. Cuando Vasarely vio ese cuadro me dijo que lo llamara "Andrómeda", por esas especies de soles que parecían girar. Pero no

59. En conversaciones posteriores Soto parecía dudar sobre la correcta sucesión entre *Desplazamiento de un elemento luminoso* y *Metamorfosis*. Ambas son piezas del mismo año y estudian problemas cercanos. No obstante, la coherencia estructural de *Metamorfosis* y la evidente influencia que tiene en obras posteriores, nos hacen pensar que ella es efectivamente posterior a *Desplazamiento de un elemento luminoso*.

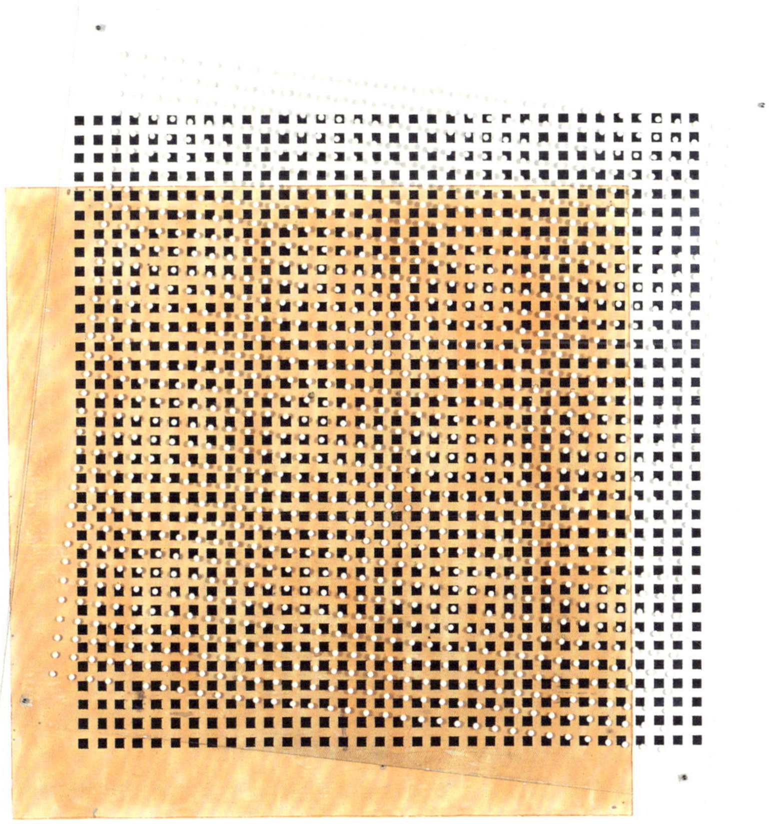

Fig. 20. *Metamorfosis,* 1954.

quise hacerlo, porque eso sugería una base figurativa que no tenía nada que ver con mi trabajo. La llamé *Metamorfosis* porque de la superposición de dos elementos similares surgían esos puntos luminosos e inmateriales. Eran grupos, yo los llamaba grupos, porque aparecían varios núcleos circulares organizados simétricamente.[60]

AJ No deja de ser interesante el hecho de que cuando se produce por primera vez en su trabajo un efecto de movimiento real y de núcleos de luz, usted haya experimentado tanto placer. No puedo dejar de pensar que algún lazo importante lo conectaba con sus lecturas infantiles de Dante, donde Dios era descrito precisamente como círculos de luz, y con el *Cuadrado blanco sobre blanco* de Malevich, esa manera perfecta de atraparla sobre la tela, según sus propias palabras.

JS Quizás y, si te fijas, verás que *Metamorfosis* es una combinación de círculos y cuadrados. . . Cómo uniendo Dante y Malevich. Lo cierto es que observando luego la superposición de los puntos me di cuenta de que estaba pasando algo nuevo; entonces intenté darle animosidad y movimiento a lo que sucedía allí. Finalmente decidí separarlos unos cinco centímetros, introduciendo así el espacio real y consiguiendo un movimiento que aún no alcanzaba en *Metamorfosis*, de donde surge *Puntos blancos sobre puntos negros*, de 1954 [Fig. 21]. Después sigo experimentando y en algunos casos me dedico al estudio del cubo, un poco siguiendo la vía de *Dos cuadrados en el espacio*, de 1953.

Superponiendo cuadrados blancos y negros, otros pintados por medio de un barniz que me permitía darles diversas densidades de transparencia hasta la saturación del blanco, llego a *Cubos sugeridos*, de 1955, que es una pieza donde quise sugerir el cubo a partir de un mínimo de elementos. Enseguida paso a *La cajita de Villanueva*, también de 1955 [Fig. 22].

AJ Que es donde emplea por primera vez la trama de líneas característica de su trabajo posterior.

JS Sí, eso viene tal vez de las primeras *repeticiones*, como aquel cuadro de las erres, donde quería conseguir un estado vibratorio por la repetición de un mismo elemento. En *La cajita de Villanueva* hay un aspecto nuevo, aparte de la vibración,

60. "Sólo cuando el pintor le haga ver al espectador más de lo que hay (físicamente) presentado, podrá producir efectos perceptivos (psicológicos)". Josef Albers. "El Op Art y/o los efectos perceptivos", en *Yale Scientific Magazine*, noviembre de 1965.

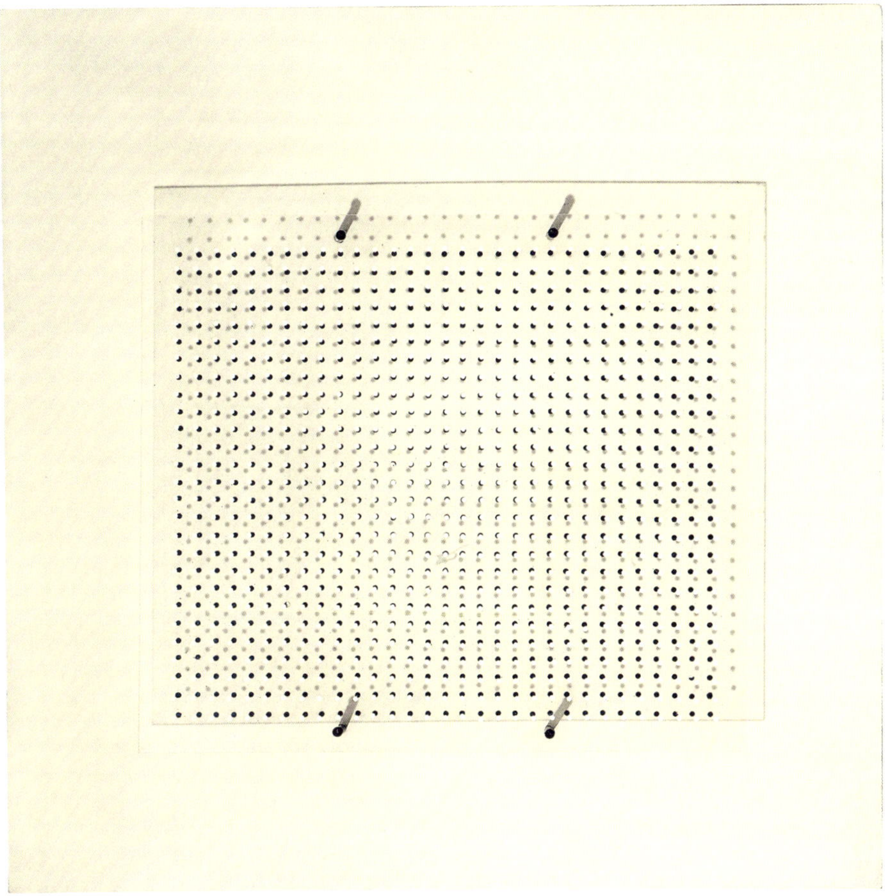

Fig. 21. *Puntos blancos sobre puntos negros,* 1954.

y es que se producía una ambigüedad óptica que hacía difícil determinar dónde se encontraban los cuadrados. De repente te parecía que el cuadrado negro se encontraba en el fondo y a veces te parecía verlo en el primer plano.

AJ Impresiona ver la perfecta coherencia de su proceso, una obra llevando a la otra, una planteando interrogantes que serían resueltas o desarrolladas en la siguiente, con metódica precisión. Casi podríamos imaginarlo a la par del artista que soñó Paul Valéry, trabajando meticulosamente, resolviendo problemas plásticos como un cirujano, con su bata blanca impecable. Para Valéry, y en su caso creo que es igual, el objetivo del artista no es expresar la emoción que siente en el trabajo creador, o ante una experiencia particular, sino en todo caso producirlas en el espectador o, mejor aún, despertar en él la reflexión.

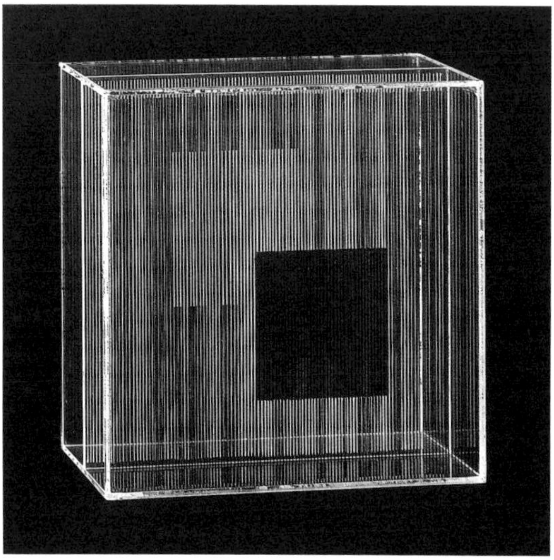

Fig. 22. *La cajita de Villanueva,* 1955.

Ahora, de ese momento se conocen poquísimas piezas, y todas ellas parecen sucederse con una precisión sorprendente. ¿Hizo tan pocas obras entonces o es que muchas se han perdido?

JS No, es así, hice muy pocas. Lo que pasa es que no tenía mucho tiempo para hacer mi trabajo. Recuerda que vivía de mi guitarra, tocando por las noches, de manera que mi tiempo libre era bastante escaso. En ese pequeño margen de disponibilidad trabajaba y realizaba solo las ideas que me parecían fundamentales. Eso fue así por lo menos hasta 1957, cuando de verdad comencé a vender y pude vivir de mi trabajo plástico.

AJ ¿Y cuáles eran sus lecturas y sus preocupaciones intelectuales?

JS La música me había permitido encontrar estructuras independientes del gusto, pero entonces mi gran preocupación era la del espacio-tiempo y las nociones provenientes de la física y las matemáticas. Ahora, como no tenía la menor noción de esas cosas, porque nada más estudié hasta la primaria, y de allí pasé a la Escuela de Artes Plásticas y Artes Aplicadas de Caracas, cada vez que me encontraba con alguien que sabía de eso, le hacía todas las preguntas posibles. Así hice con un amigo mío, Jorge Vicente Ortiz, que era matemático. Con él pasé noches enteras hablando de las nuevas ideas científicas, en las cuales descubro una concepción de la naturaleza bastante alejada de la noción que nos hacíamos sobre ella; sobre la materia, la energía, el espacio y el tiempo.

Más tarde me encuentro con David Medalla,[61] un filipino muy bohemio, y que, según parece, era un genio en matemáticas. Con él hablé mucho sobre mis preocupaciones científicas y un día me regaló un libro donde, me dijo, encontraría todo lo que buscaba. Era *El nuevo espíritu científico* de Gaston Bachelard.

AJ ¿Y siente que esas nociones científicas tuvieron una influencia directa en usted?

JS Absolutamente. . . Desde muy temprano, cuando realizaba mis estudios en Caracas, concebía el arte como una actividad que no se limitaba únicamente a la producción de placer estético, sino que significaba un aporte al pensamiento del hombre, al mismo nivel que la Ciencia o la Filosofía. Siempre he pensado que si en la antigüedad greco-romana y en el Renacimiento, el pensamiento artístico alcanzaba los niveles de la Filosofía y la Ciencia, nosotros debíamos recuperar, en nuestra área de actividades, ese mismo respeto. Por estas razones, la actividad de un artista no era ni es para mí algo impulsivo y destinado a crear eso que llaman un lenguaje personal, reflejo de una personalidad excepcional. Por el contrario, estoy convencido de que en el arte existen problemas que le son propios, que corresponden a un determinado momento histórico, y que es solamente en la medida en que uno pueda encontrarles respuesta que nuestro trabajo adquiere un valor trascendente para la humanidad.

HACIA LA DESMATERIALIZACIÓN DE LOS CUERPOS

AJ El año 1955 es una fecha importante en su historia personal; es el año de la primera exposición histórica del cinetismo en la Galería Denise René, donde comienza realmente su carrera internacional.[62] En lo que toca a su trabajo plástico, es el año de *La cajita de Villanueva*, donde aparece la trama que

61. David Medalla (1942). Artista filipino. En su obra aborda los más diversos medios. Pintor, escultor, performista. Admirador ferviente de Piet Mondrian, fue amigo de Soto en los tempranos años cincuenta y lo ayudó a comprender algunos de los más importantes problemas de la Física moderna.

62. En 1955, la galerista francesa Denise René tuvo la idea de reunir en una misma exposición un conjunto de artistas que, por vías y medios diferentes, buscaban la manera de integrar el tiempo real, y con ello el movimiento, en la obra de arte. La exposición marca el nacimiento oficial del Cinetismo cuyo desarrollo sería considerable en la década siguiente. La orientación de estos artistas era en realidad muy dispar, e iba desde la ironía de un Duchamp que ve en lo óptico una manifestación retiniana y superficial de las artes, hasta un Soto que cree ver en los efectos ópticos una manera de sugerir realidades más profundas a partir de "lo real".

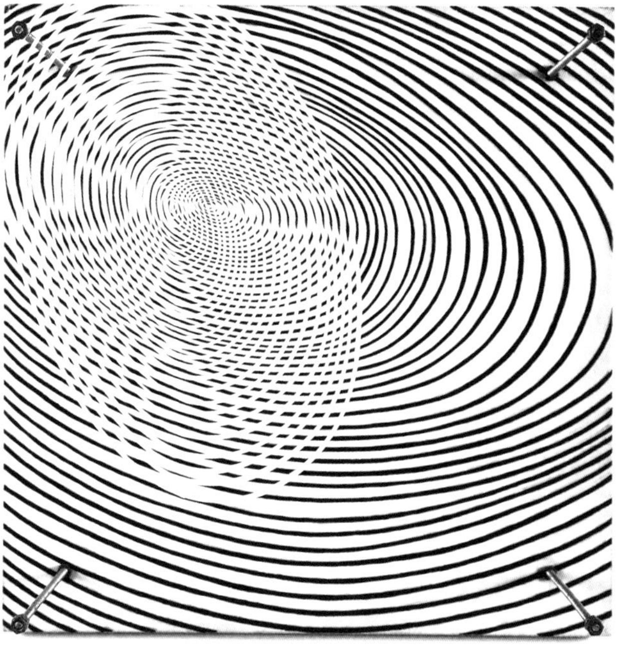

Fig. 23. *Espiral,* 1955.

caracterizará gran parte de su producción posterior, la ambigüedad espacial fruto de la superposición de cubos sobre esa trama, y de la *Espiral*. Un primer periodo de experimentación parece terminar con ello. Se produce entonces en su trabajo un fenómeno similar al pasaje del Cubismo analítico al sintético: una vez resueltas las interrogantes espaciales y estructurales, reaparece el color.

JS *Espiral* nace después de ver la rotativa de Duchamp expuesta en la primera exposición, *Le Mouvement*, organizada por Denise René [Fig. 23]. Yo quise hacer algo similar sin la intervención del motor. Eso lo logré superponiendo dos espirales, una blanca y una negra, solo que la espiral del primer plano gira a la derecha. Eso induce un movimiento óptico producto de nuestro desplazamiento ante ella, casi como si se tratara de un chorro de luz que sale hacia el exterior. En cuanto al color, me dije entonces que si era producto de la luz y yo estaba trabajando con vibraciones luminosas, ¿por qué iba a obviarlo? Entonces introduje el color en su estado vibratorio.

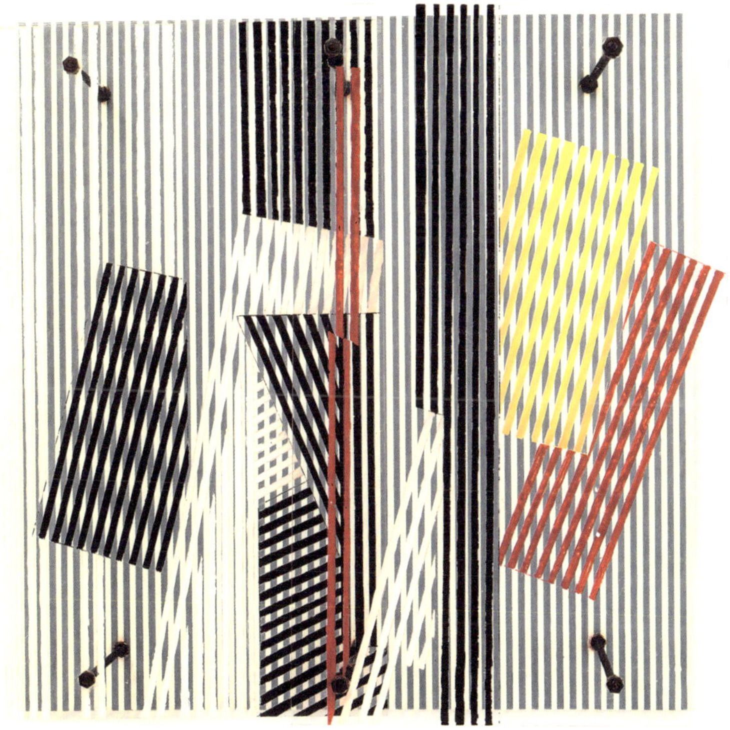

Fig. 24. *Doble transparencia,* 1956.

AJ Era como retomar el impresionismo, esta vez desde la estructura pura, sin la representación del paisaje. Incluso el título de su obra *Luz plateada*, de 1956, retoma el calificativo que utiliza a menudo cuando se refiere al Impresionismo.

JS Es cierto, mi intención era poner al color en estado de movimiento, no como armonía cromática, que es otro de los residuos académicos que huía, al igual que la composición y el equilibrio. Lo que buscaba estaba y está muy lejos de conseguir una bella armonía de colores. Solo quiero conseguir aquellas combinaciones donde el color tenga mayor fuerza vibratoria, y donde la ambigüedad espacial que resulte de sus superposiciones sea evidente [Fig. 24]. Uno de los grandes inconvenientes con el público es que siempre busca la armonía, la belleza de las combinaciones, y eso jamás lo encontrará en mi trabajo.

AJ No obstante, una de sus estructuras cinéticas en plexiglás se titula *Armonía transformable* [Fig. 25].

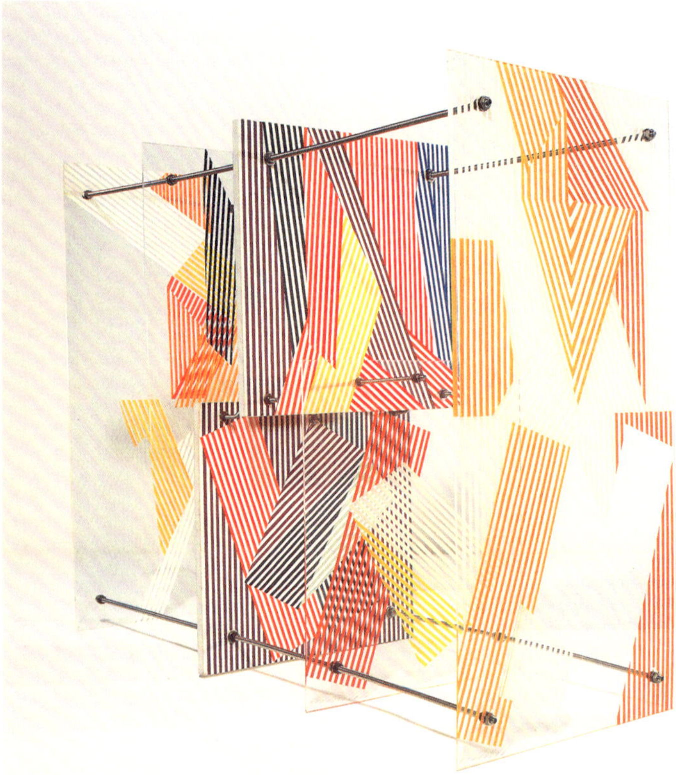

Fig. 25. *Armonía transformable* (vista de lado), 1956.

JS Sí, pero lo hice porque era la única manera de atraer a la gente que no entendía la esencia de la abstracción. Si no buscabas las palabras adecuadas, veían en ellas cualquier cosa menos una obra de arte.

AJ Ahora, en esa *Armonía transformable* sucede también algo importante y que marca una nueva etapa de su trabajo. Su pintura está dejando de ser el plano tradicional donde se proyectaba una "visión". Con ello quiero señalar esa ruptura del plano que servía de fondo, de manera que ya no existe una figura y un fondo, sino una continuidad dinámica que reclama una participación activa del espectador.

JS Claro, y por eso la hice en varios planos. Aunque la ruptura con la relación tradicional figura-fondo ya se daba en *La cajita de Villanueva*. Por otra parte, desde la primera *repetición*, esa que parece un damero, me oponía a esa idea del plano como proyección de una realidad visual.

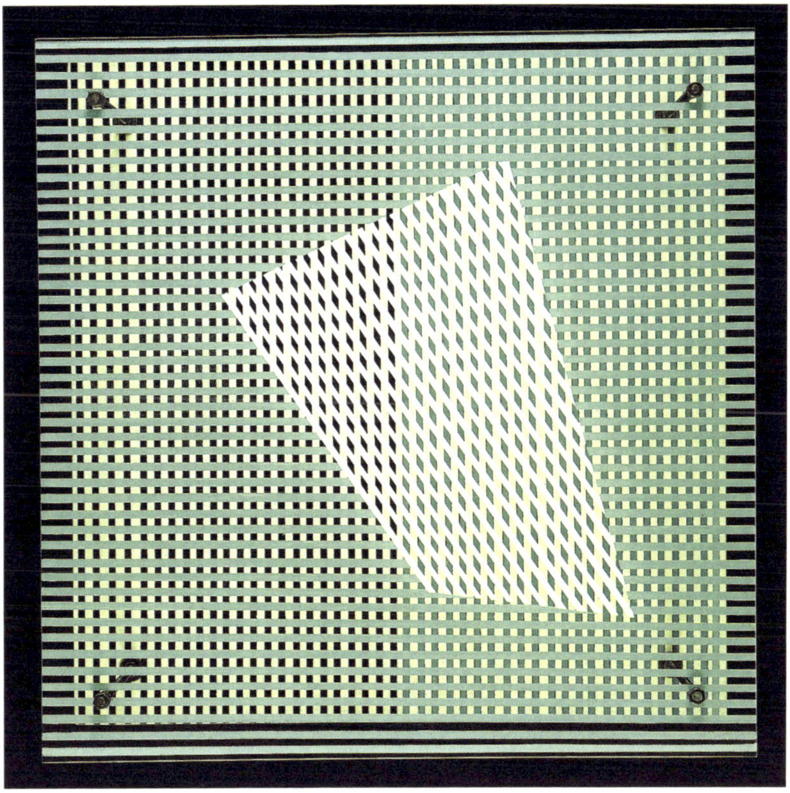

Fig. 26. *Trapecio,* 1957.

AJ En 1957, usted abandona el plexiglás para materializar sus tramas con varillas metálicas soldadas entre sí. Ese mismo año, superpone por primera vez una línea metálica sobre la trama del fondo, abriendo la puerta para las *vibraciones.*

JS Es exacto, y eso ocurre porque quise liberarme del plexiglás. Nunca he querido que se me imponga una idea o una manera de proceder, y cuando siento que eso está pasando reacciono, y es cuando aparecen esos cortes en mi proceso. Con el plexiglás me estaba sucediendo algo similar, se me imponía tan fuertemente que parecía indispensable en mi trabajo y el público comenzaba a verlo como un valor estético, y eso me molestaba, porque a mí me interesaba únicamente como medio para dibujar en el espacio [Fig. 26]. Por eso inventé esa técnica que me permitía superponer las tramas por medio de varillas metálicas soldadas entre sí, sin el aditivo que representaba el plexiglás. Lo curioso es que el resultado de las vibraciones obtenidas daba la misma sensación del plexiglás. Eso lo hice en Venezuela, cuando presenté mi exposición en el Museo de Bellas

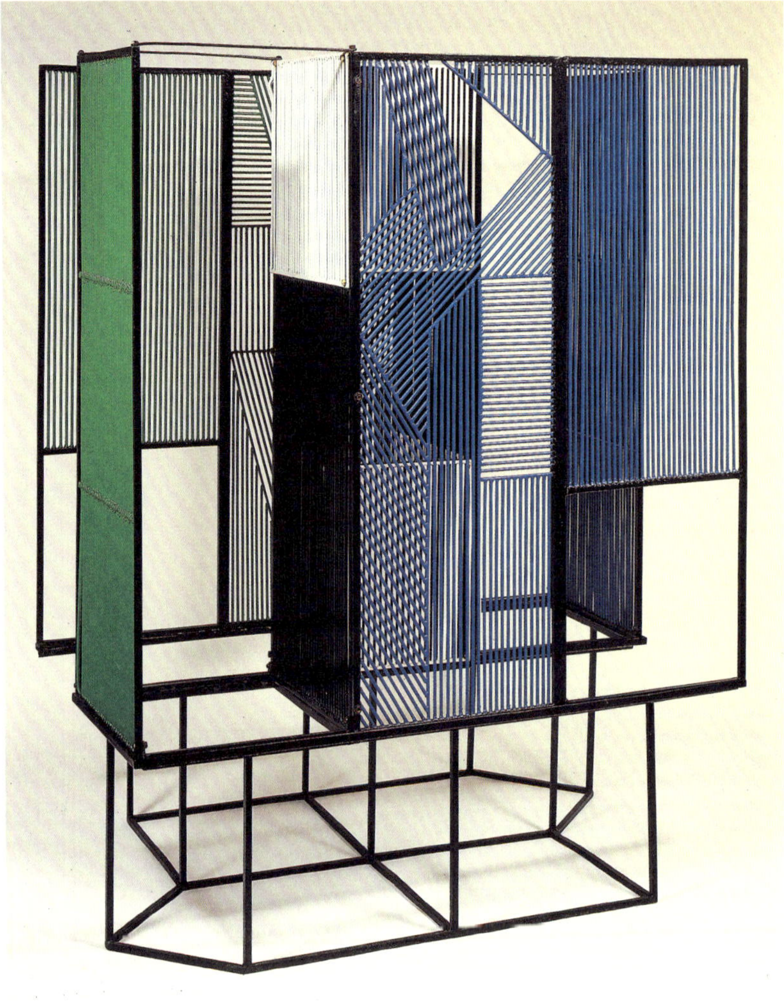

Fig. 27. *Pre-penetrable,* 1957.

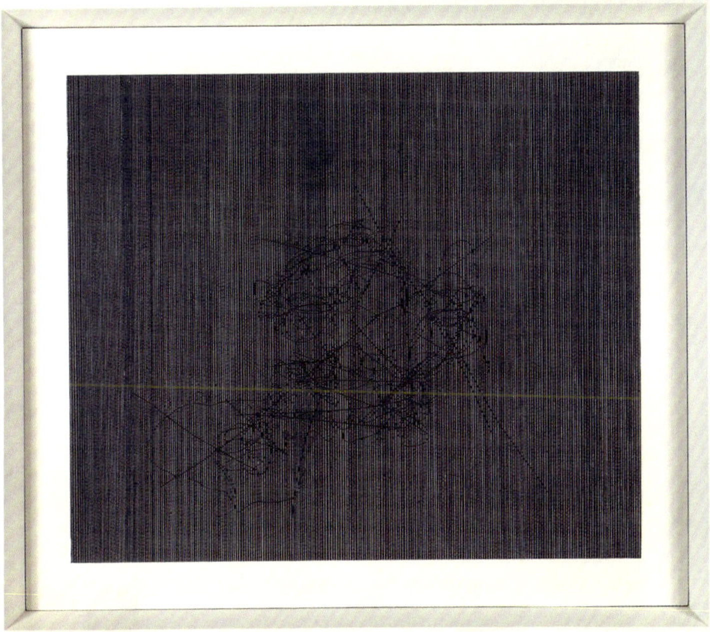

Fig. 28. *Vibración I,* 1958.

Artes. La primera de estas piezas se la regalé a Carlos Raúl Villanueva, porque le encantó. Se la llevó a la universidad y dio una conferencia sobre ella.

AJ Con esas construcciones metálicas está produciéndose además un hecho interesante: son estructuras que, hasta por la técnica empleada, podrían abrirse al espectador, podrían hacerse penetrables, como en efecto sucedería más tarde, hacia 1967.

JS Por supuesto, y eso era en realidad lo que estaba buscando. Una de ellas, *Pre-penetrable* de 1957, que perteneció a Alfredo Boulton[63] y que ahora se conserva en la Colección Patricia Phelps de Cisneros, fue pensada cinco veces más grande [Fig. 27]. Eran maquetas que hacía a esa escala porque me era imposible hacerlas del tamaño previsto. Por eso me divertía tanto ver a los nietos de Boulton jugando dentro de ella.

63. Alfredo Boulton (1908–95). Fotógrafo, crítico e historiador venezolano, autor de *Historia de la pintura en Venezuela* (Caracas: Ediciones Armitano, 1964–72) y de numerosas monografías sobre artistas venezolanos, entre ellas la de Jesús Soto (Caracas: Ediciones Armitano, 1973).

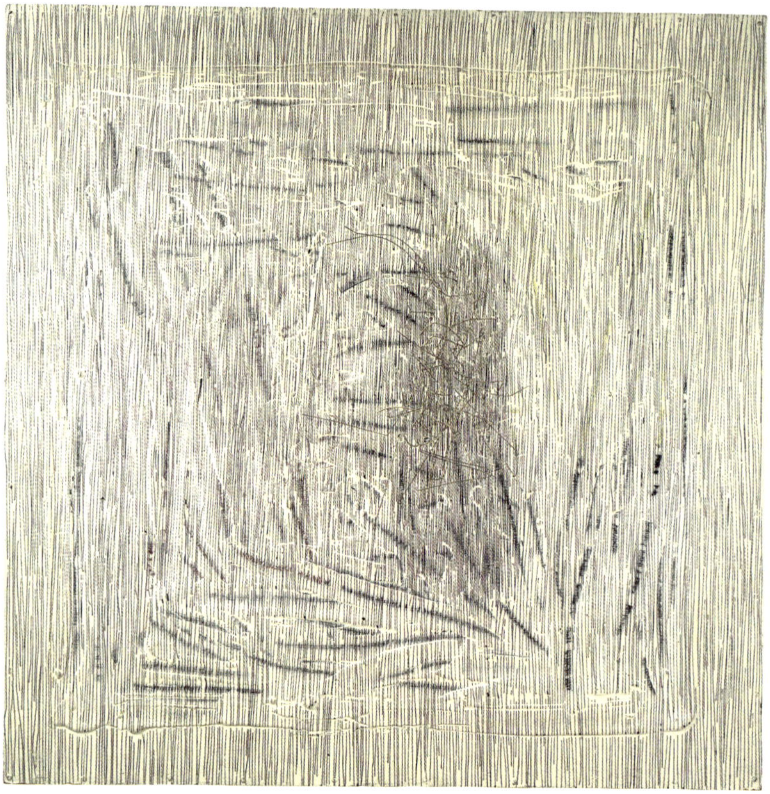

Fig. 29. *Vibración,* 1960.

AJ Inmediatamente después de estas estructuras cinéticas, donde generalmente explota el color con toda su fuerza vibratoria, usted lo abandona progresivamente y se concentra en inquietudes de orden estructural, produciendo piezas a menudo muy sobrias, hasta que en su periodo barroco se reduce prácticamente al blanco y al negro con algunas discretas notas de color [Figs. 28–29]. ¿Cómo se da ese pasaje y por qué?

JS Las estructuras cinéticas en plexiglás se producen en un periodo que dura poco tiempo, cerca de dos años, y donde hice muchísimas piezas. Luego sentí la necesidad de volver a una especie de rigor a partir de los elementos adquiridos. No se trataba de abandonar el color, sino de ponerlo un tanto de lado para resolver otros problemas, como ese que aparece en *Trapecio*, de 1957. Ahí se produce una situación bien extraña; cuando tú te enfrentas a este cuadro sientes como si respirara. Se extiende y se contrae como un acordeón. Es una obra esencial y tal vez algún día estudie a fondo los retos que me plantea [Fig. 26].

AJ Llegamos ahora a un conjunto importante, compuesto por la representación venezolana en el pabellón venezolano en la Exposición Universal de Bruselas en 1958,[64] y el gran mural que hace en los jardines del Instituto Venezolano de Investigaciones Científicas (IVIC), en realidad su primera *escritura*. ¿Qué representan estas piezas en su producción, qué le aportaban?

JS Con ellas puedo realmente dibujar en el espacio, liberado incluso de la obligación de superponer las líneas paralelas. Yo no las llamaba *escrituras*, mi intención era dibujar en el espacio, solo que a la gente le parecían escrituras y me preguntaban lo que podrían significar. . . Después yo comencé a llamarlas así. Allí comienzo nuevamente a utilizar las curvas (Cruz-Diez me hizo observar un día que eran las mismas formas que utilizaba ya en mis paisajes de la escuela y en mis experiencias abstractas de 1950–51). Poco a poco llego a lo que se ha llamado, aunque no me guste el término, el periodo barroco, a finales de los cincuenta. En ese momento viene otro enfrentamiento con la técnica, como había sucedido con el plexiglás. No quería sentirme necesariamente atado a la rigidez de las paralelas.

AJ ¿Este periodo "barroco" nace también como una reacción a la rigidez de la forma, por necesidad de romper con ella?

JS No, no se trata exactamente de una ruptura, puesto que no abandono definitivamente el rigor de la geometría; lo único que quería era demostrarme que mi concepto no dependía de una determinada manera de hacer las cosas. Sentí la necesidad de probarme a mí mismo que podía utilizar cualquier elemento. La idea era tomar objetos anodinos pero fuertemente formales: maderas viejas, alambres, agujas, rejas y tubos, integrarlos a la obra y llevarlos hacia un estado de desintegración a través de la vibración pura. Indudablemente no era nada fácil, y había que hacer un trabajo inmenso para desmaterializar un trozo de madera. En el plano pictórico, de igual modo, introduzco elementos que ya poseía desde la escuela, como las texturas, por ejemplo. Por eso te digo que no se trataba de romper definitivamente con una determinada manera de trabajar, sino de superarla como limitación. Ahora puedo utilizar todos esos elementos con absoluta libertad, pero entonces sentí que era necesario romper con sus

64. Soto realiza, por intermediario del arquitecto Carlos Raúl Villanueva, un importante conjunto de piezas para el pabellón venezolano en la Exposición Universal de Bruselas (1958), entre ellas el llamado *Mural de Bruselas* (hoy en el Museo de Bellas Artes de Caracas), la *Torre de Bruselas* (instalada en el IVIC) y el *Muro de Bruselas* (también en el IVIC), en realidad su primera *escritura*.

ataduras. Y no es porque me lo pidan, o porque algunos quieran que lo haga, sino porque lo necesito en alguna circunstancia específica. Es más, me molesta muchísimo cuando alguien me sugiere que debo hacerlo.

Necesité proceder de ese modo, era imperativo. Tal vez tiene que ver –así lo pienso a veces– con el inmenso salto que tuve que dar para pasar de la pintura paisajística que hacía en Caracas y Maracaibo, porque no tenía ninguna orientación, a la abstracción pura. Cuando descubro el mundo del Constructivismo y de la Bauhaus, me dije que no podía perder mi tiempo esperando concluir el proceso de la abstracción, que mi vida era una sola. Debía lanzarme a la corriente de la abstracción en el punto más alto del momento, tal y como lo encuentro en los años cincuenta, y ver cómo podía hacerlo avanzar. Ahora, es posible que ese salto me haya dejado secuelas, una especie de resentimiento por no haber cumplido con procesos que debieron ser completados. Por eso, quizás, reintroduje en mi trabajo los empastados y los gestos de la pintura. Fue una exigencia interior que resolví en un periodo bastante corto, y lo cumplí con el mayor entusiasmo. Y si otro día se me presenta la necesidad de cumplir con otra negligencia, lo que no está descartado, lo haré con la misma libertad. Lo haré, claro está, dentro de los conceptos que esté manejando, porque cuando hago esas obras barrocas no estaba haciendo paisajes. Mi problema era incorporar cualquier elemento de la vida cotidiana y desmaterializarlo. Y en esto he sido siempre muy honesto conmigo mismo; he actuado de acuerdo a mis necesidades sin tomar en cuenta las exigencias del medio.

AJ Su objetivo era desmaterializar los cuerpos que empleaba, es obvio, y aun así, uno de los conjuntos más característicos y hermosos de ese periodo, los *leños*, le dan una gran importancia a la madera, a la materia que intenta deshacer ópticamente [Figs. 30–31]. ¿Cómo nace esta serie y por qué acordarle tanta importancia a lo que intenta desmaterializar?

JS La serie surge casi por casualidad. Es una época en la que era buen amigo de Jean Tinguely, y a veces nos íbamos a buscar materiales de desecho en unos depósitos, unas especies de chiveras[65] donde vendían materiales de construcción. Ellos recogían los materiales provenientes de casas derruidas. Un día me topé con las vigas de una casa demolida. Eran maderas hermosísimas, que conservaban la huella de todo un trabajo artesanal muy bello. . . Las perforaciones,

65. Chivera es el nombre que se emplea en Venezuela para designar los establecimientos comerciales donde venden repuestos usados para vehículos.

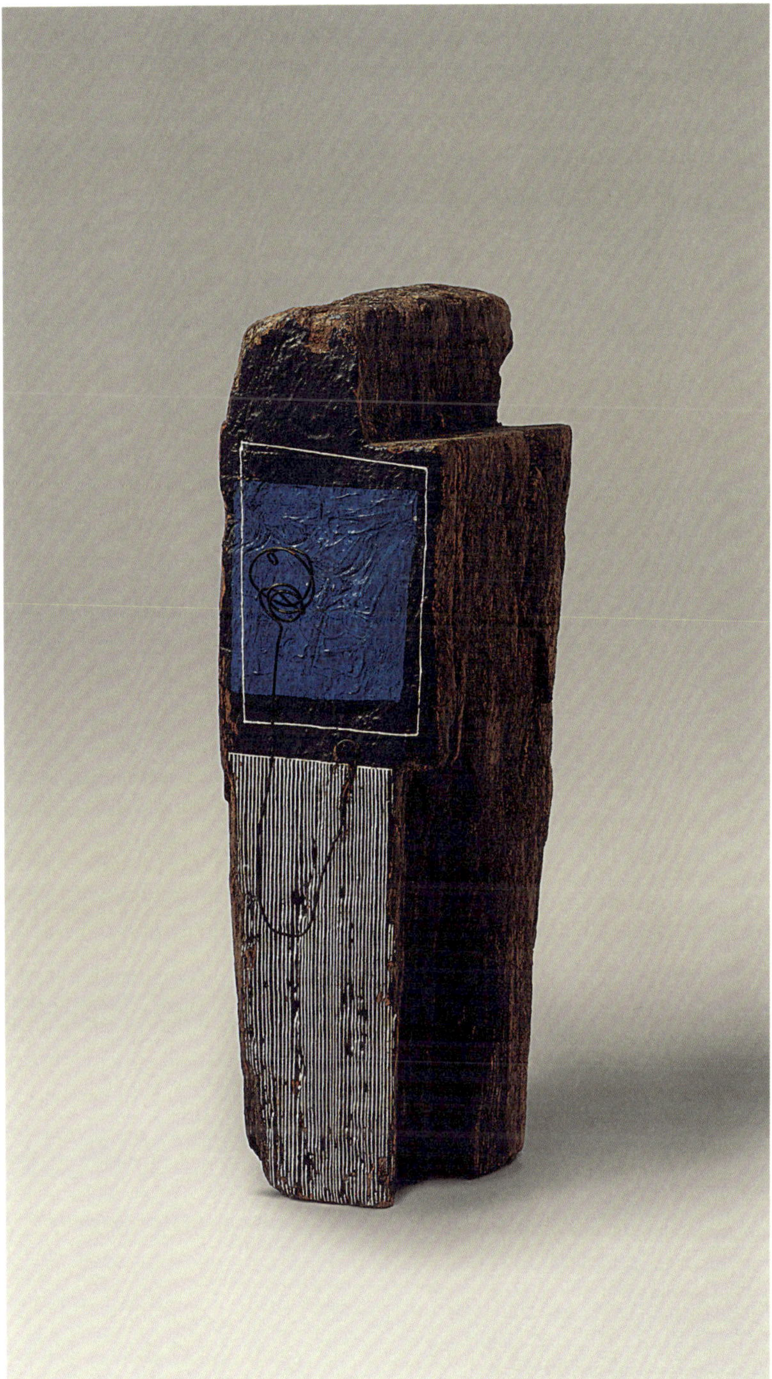

Fig. 30. *Tronco,* 1960.

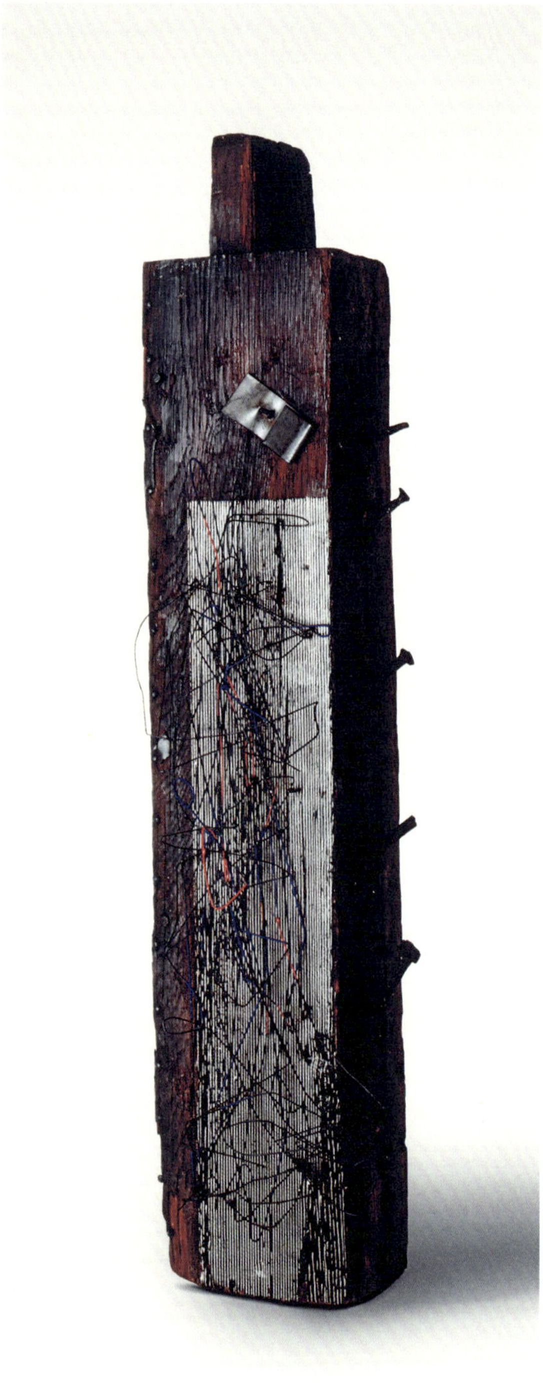

Fig. 31. *Leño,* 1961.

los cortes destinados a encastrar unas en otras, los clavos. . . ¡Eran bellísimas! y como el destino de las maderas era ser quemadas en los hornos de las panaderías (para eso las vendían), me dije que debía hacer algo para rescatar algunas de ellas. Quería salvar esa manufactura artesanal, ese trabajo del hombre. Entonces, como las vendían por kilos, me compré un lote. La serie se detuvo cuando se me acabó el material. Después fui a buscar otro grupo de maderas y ya las habían vendido.

AJ ¿Y las empleaba tal cual las hallaba o las intervenía de alguna manera?

JS Tal cual, ellas quedaban tal como las encontraba, con sus clavos y todas sus características. Lo único que hacía era agregarles una trama para sugerir allí la desmaterialización de un elemento específico. Luego le ponía unas patitas, unos clavos o unos tornillos, pero las maderas quedaban sin intervención alguna.

AJ Es interesante que entre los elementos que se desmaterializan se encuentren a menudo materiales de construcción o herramientas artesanales, como las agujas.

JS Yo quería salvar el trabajo hecho en esas maderas. Con las agujas pasó lo mismo. Un día estaba buscando materiales y me encontré con un paquete de agujas que me parecieron bellísimas. Unas eran grandes, otras pequeñas y rectas, incluso curvas. Ocurrió igual que con las maderas, quise salvarlas haciendo con ellas una obra. También me sucedió algo cercano con una serie de estructuras en metal, las que se ven por ejemplo en *Vibración III*, de 1960–61. Cuando compro mi primer apartamento en París, en la Rue du Temple, teníamos un pequeño depósito en el techo, y como el apartamento le había pertenecido a un artesano que fabricaba pantallas de lámparas, lo encontramos lleno con montones de estructuras metálicas muy bellas. Cuando vi esas estructuras tan hermosas, no quise botarlas todas, sino que conservé un grupo de ellas con el fin de emplearlas en mi trabajo. Eran conos, cubos, círculos tan perfectos que yo era incapaz de hacerlos, así que los integré tal como los encontré. Algunas veces los deformaba un poco, o utilizaba solamente algunos círculos. Esos círculos perfectos que emplee a principios de los sesenta, provienen de ese conjunto.

AJ Muchas de estas obras "barrocas", especialmente las verticales, me parecen tener una relación evidente con el Cubismo sintético [Fig. 32]. Son piezas donde la forma parece deshacerse, y donde pueden verse a menudo fragmentos que, en ciertos casos, parecen acercarse a los desnudos y guitarras pintados por los cubistas. Pienso en particular en una pieza de la colección Patricia Phelps de Cisneros *Vibración III,* de 1960–61, y en *Sin título,* 1962, del Museo de Arte Moderno Jesús Soto,[66] donde esos círculos de los que habla parecen residuos de un cuerpo o de una guitarra [Figs. 33–34].

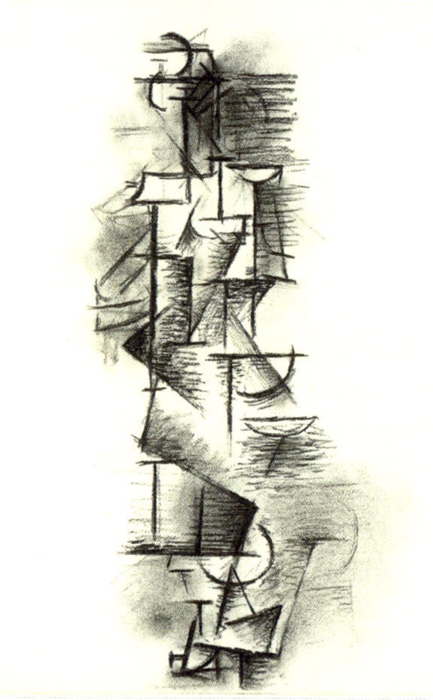

Fig. 32. Pablo Picasso, *Nude woman* [*Mujer desnuda*], 1910.

JS Tal vez, pero no lo hacía con ese fin. Para mí lo importante era llevar a una situación espacio-temporal todas las corrientes que me interesaban: el Tachismo, el Nuevo realismo y otras. Por eso ves todas esas texturas tan evidentes y los materiales de desecho, porque quería darle a esas tendencias una mayor importancia convirtiéndolas en situaciones espacio-temporales. . . Quería hacerlas más eficaces. Por eso oponía texturas nuevo-realistas y al lado las desmaterializaba.

AJ Se trata, en el fondo, de un proceso similar al que lo llevó a dinamizar a Mondrian en 1950.

JS Es exactamente el mismo proceso. . . Yo por lo menos lo intenté, si lo logré o no, quizás se vea en el futuro. Eso fue lo que intenté.

AJ Como sucedió con el mural de 1961, el de la Galería de Arte Nacional. [Fig. 35]

JS Exactamente, solo que ese es un caso especial. Cuando vuelvo a Caracas, en

66. Museo fundado en Ciudad Bolívar, al sur de Venezuela, por Jesús Soto. Fue creado oficialmente en 1969 e inaugurado en 1973. Su edificio, obra del arquitecto Carlos Raúl Villanueva (en su primera etapa), cuenta entre las mejores estructuras museísticas del país. Su colección está conformada por dos conjuntos, uno dedicado a la producción personal de Jesús Soto, y otro a algunos de los mejores creadores de su tiempo, entre ellos los artistas del Nuevo realismo francés (Yves Klein, Daniel Spoerri, Christo, Armand, y otros), y del Grupo Zero, aunado a un pequeño núcleo histórico, donde sobresalen dibujos de Kasimir Malevich, Piet Mondrian y acuarelas de Sonia Delaunay.

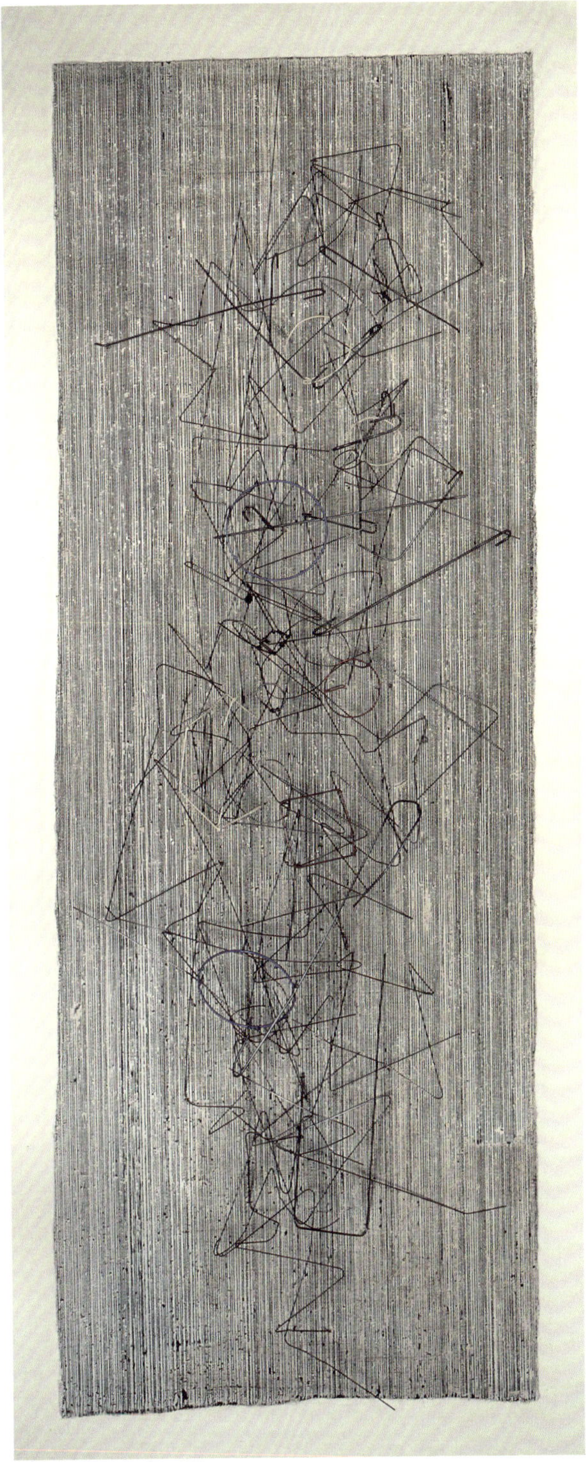

Fig. 33. *Vibración III,* 1960–61.

los años sesenta, *El Techo de la Ballena*[67] estaba activo y entonces un amigo mío, Daniel González,[68] me dice: "Jesús, tengo una idea, cada uno de los artistas hace una obra grande en un solo día, y enseguida las exponemos todas juntas". A mí me gustó su propuesta, porque era una acción que duraba ocho horas. Hans Neumann[69] me prestó un taller y ahí la hice. Por eso ves claramente que el lado izquierdo del mural es una situación típicamente *nuevorealista*, y del lado derecho una situación en movimiento, espacio-temporal. Los materiales del lado izquierdo los conseguí en el taller de Hans Neumann, eran equipos que guardaba ahí, y que eran bastante costosos. . . Recuerdo que Neumann me decía que eso valía unos cinco mil dólares. Y yo le dije que luego la obra se lo devolvería revalorizado. El resto de los materiales, los del lado derecho, los encontré en los basureros. El artista Ángel Hurtado[70] filmó el proceso completo.

AJ Creo que su explicación de ese periodo barroco como producto de las secuelas dejadas por una deuda no cumplida con la pintura es perfectamente coherente. Sin embargo, la experiencia personal se enmarca dentro de un contexto al que no es fácil sustraerse. ¿Existe algún paralelismo entre su mundo barroco, por decirlo de alguna manera, y el Nuevo realismo francés de los sesenta?

JS Conocí a todos esos artistas, fueron mis amigos y exponíamos juntos, porque estábamos tratando de forzar una nueva situación. Pero en el fondo mi actitud era diferente a la suya, lo que se manifiesta más claramente cuando cada uno de nosotros toma su propio camino, después de ese particular momento histórico. Todos ellos fueron estructuralistas muy puros al principio. Lo que sucede es que durante los años sesenta se creyó que el hombre iba a ser prisionero de la mecánica y la tecnología, y a ello se debe en parte toda esa reacción cercana a la rebelión francesa de Mayo del 68.

AJ ¿Tiene ello que ver con el malestar dejado por la Segunda Guerra Mundial?

67. *El Techo de la Ballena:* Movimiento de la vanguardia venezolana, activo entre 1961 y 1968. La agrupación reunió a fotógrafos, escritores, pintores y diseñadores, quienes asumieron una postura crítica ante el poder político, defendiendo, incluso hasta la insurrección armada, los procesos revolucionarios. Con una fuerte influencia del Surrealismo en la literatura y del Informalismo en la pintura, el grupo contó con la militancia de Adriano González León, Salvador Garmendia, Rodolfo Izaguirre, Daniel González, Edmundo Aray y Carlos Contramaestre, entre otros.

68. Daniel González (1934). Pintor, escultor, fotógrafo y diseñador gráfico venezolano, miembro sobresaliente de *El Techo de la Ballena*, agrupación para la que diseñó algunas de sus mejores publicaciones.

69. Hans Neumann (1919–2001). Industrial y coleccionista venezolano de origen checo.

70. Ángel Hurtado (1927). Artista plástico venezolano. Su obra se desarrolla inicialmente dentro del Informalismo abstracto. Es autor de una considerable obra filmográfica sobre el arte venezolano y latinoamericano.

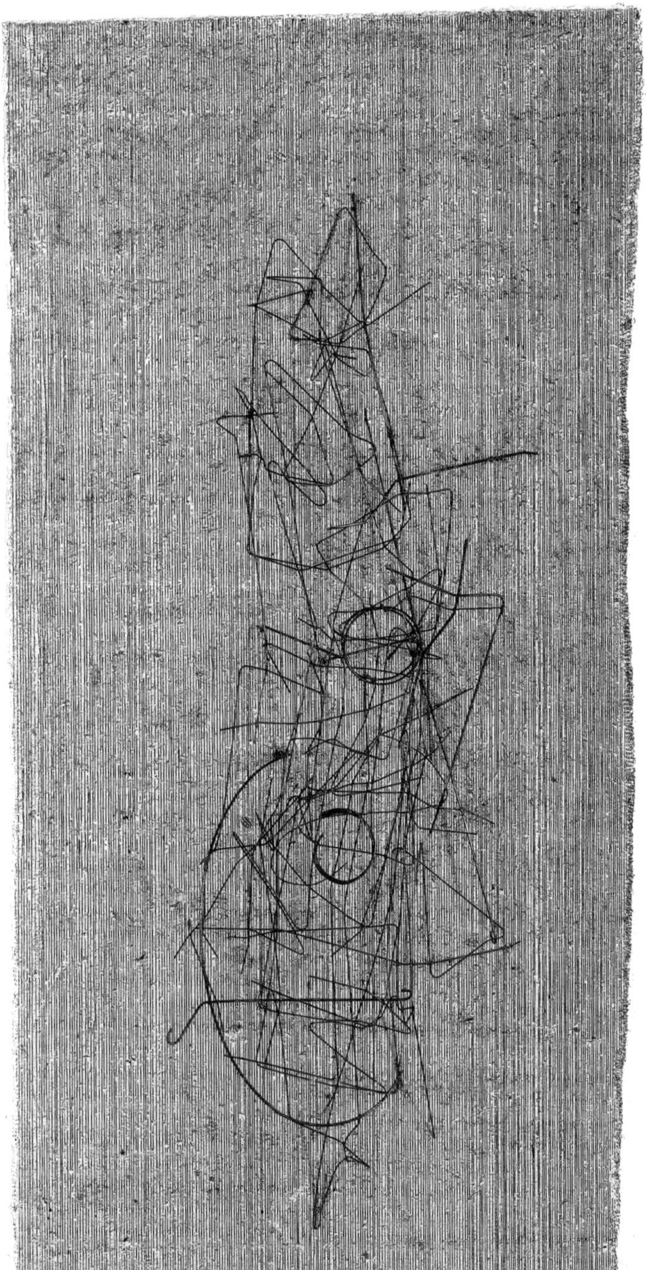

Fig. 34. *Sin título,* 1962.

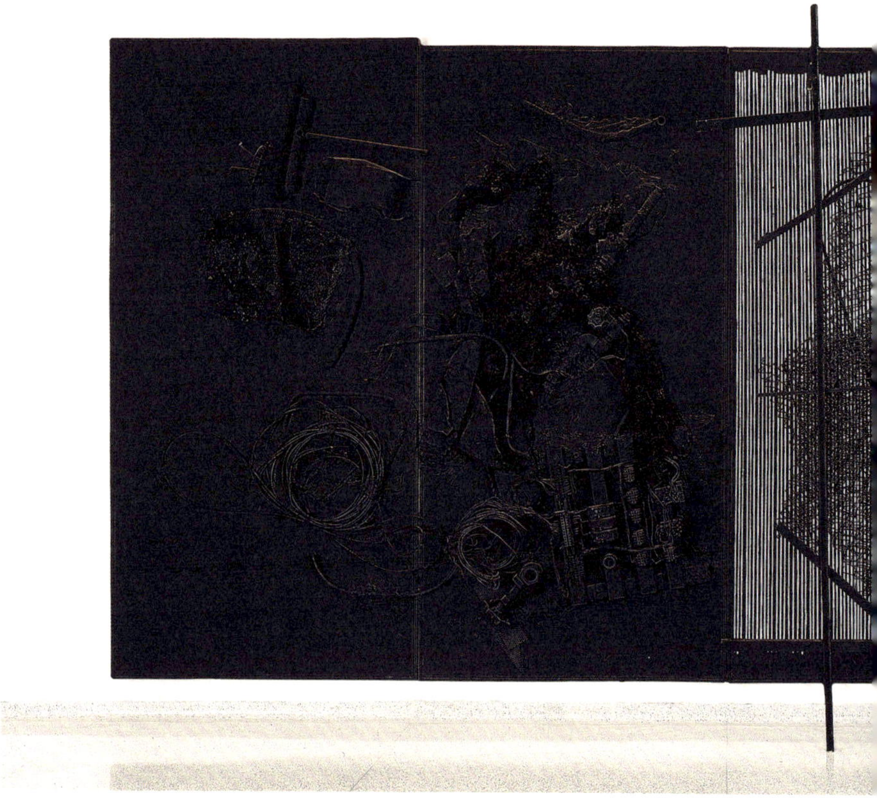

JS No. De la Segunda Guerra Mundial pudo surgir todo ese expresionismo y gestualismo de entonces. En lo que se refiere a los nuevos realistas franceses, y en mi propio caso, se trataba más bien de un comportamiento diferente, no era algo de las tripas.

AJ ¿Y a qué podría atribuir el temor de encerrarse en las estructuras creadas por la tecnología?

JS Bueno, es que la literatura y el cine comenzaron a crear una situación de temor hacia la tecnología y, evidentemente, los artistas son sensibles a esas tensiones sociales. Pero yo era el caso opuesto de Tinguely y en general de los nuevos realistas. Nuestra coincidencia era temporal, más bien de orden formal que de fondo, y por eso nunca pude integrarme completamente a sus ideas. Tinguely, por ejemplo, que era un hombre brillante y culto, surge del perfeccionismo

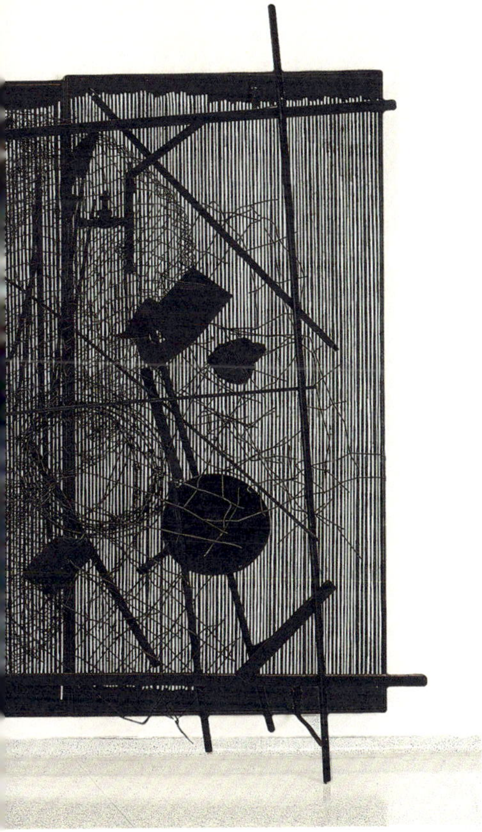

Fig. 35. *Mural,* 1961.

absoluto que es Suiza. Suiza era perfecta en su sistema económico y político. Por eso creo que él reacciona y empieza a burlarse de las máquinas, de los relojes y del perfeccionismo mecánico. Fíjate que son mecanismos absurdos, a medio camino entre la tecnología contemporánea y una especie de mecánica primitiva.

AJ Es una actitud que se intensifica al final de su vida, cuando comienza a introducir en sus maquinarias pedazos de esqueletos, reales o fabricados.

JS Son preocupaciones que responden a otro problema. Él comienza a hacer eso después de su primer infarto. Allí empezó su temor de la muerte.

AJ Sin duda, pero Tinguely hace de ese temor personal un síntoma de nuestra civilización. . .

JS Tal vez, pero tiene que ver con una cultura que ya está cansada de hacerlo bien, y a la cual pertenece Tinguely. El arte se presenta entonces como una especie de antítesis para mover las bases de la cultura, como un llamado a la regeneración. Nosotros, en Venezuela, no tenemos nada hecho; tenemos la naturaleza a nuestro favor, pero estamos empezando a domarla y hasta que no tengamos una estructura social perfectamente formada, no tenemos derecho a destruir. Nosotros no podemos actuar de esa manera, antes debemos construir. Por eso he defendido siempre el concepto de estructura, y quisiera dejarle a mi país por lo menos esa idea. No sé qué valor pueda tener, qué intensidad pueda alcanzar, por lo menos intento dejarla clara y precisa. Quiero estructura para Venezuela y por ende para Latinoamérica. Lo importante, lo que más me preocupa, es dejar en mi campo una noción de lo que este país tiene que ser algún día.

AJ Usted ha manifestado en varias oportunidades su desacuerdo con el término barroco. ¿Por qué cree que no lo define?

JS No, no me define. Yo parto de proposiciones o manifestaciones artísticas contemporáneas a las que quise darle una dimensión espacio temporal, porque pensaba que ellas podían alcanzar una mayor eficacia si las llevábamos al movimiento [Fig. 36].

AJ Sin embargo, la música de Bach lo ha interesado por años.

JS Sí, pero Bach no era un músico barroco, era más bien un estructuralista. Su problema era conseguir el mayor espectáculo con el mínimo de elementos; un trabajo inmenso que no tenía nada que ver con el Barroco.

AJ ¿Y cuál sería en su opinión la esencia del Barroco?

JS El Barroco en cualquier caso buscaba el movimiento.

AJ Una vez cumplida con esa necesidad interior en el periodo llamado barroco, vuelve al control de los elementos plásticos que emplea. Eso sucede hacia 1962. ¿Podría decirme cómo y por qué lo hace?

JS Porque yo creo que el control de los elementos no tiene que ver obligatoriamente con la conducta del artista como persona. Llega un momento en el que necesito reestructurar y entonces trato de evitar toda distracción. El objetivo no es construir una estructura por sí misma, sino conseguir el modo de captar

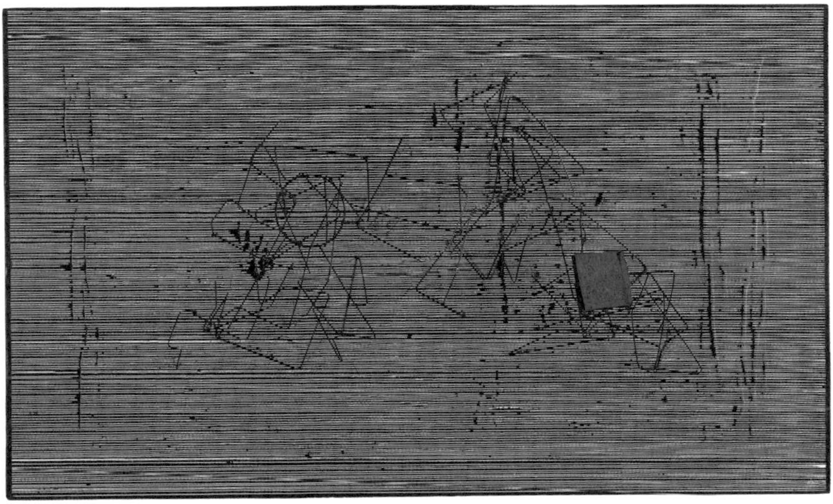

Fig. 36. *Hommage à Yves Klein,* 1961.

valores universales que de otra manera no podrías atrapar. Cuando te metes en un mundo tan vasto como el que estaba manejando en esas obras "barrocas", donde tratas de enfrentarte a valores universales, a esa conciencia universal, que existe, pero que es demasiado grande para la conciencia del hombre, entonces tienes que concentrarte y limitar los medios que empleas. Si no, se te escapan las cosas, te pierdes. Es como si necesitaras crear escaños controlables, antenas que puedan ayudarte a dirigirte mejor en ese mundo. Las posibilidades no se reducen; la ambigüedad espacial, la vibración, la desmaterialización de los cuerpos y todo lo que existía en ese mundo barroco está allí, concentrado. Por ejemplo, fíjate en *Vibration: Cube bleu,* 1962 [Fig. 37]. En ella están presentes el espacio, el movimiento y la desmaterialización de los cuerpos. En las anteriores, el cubo pudo ser una rama o una aguja, aquí se encuentra concentrado en un cubo, en una forma precisa y controlable.

AJ Lo importante, también, de este periodo, es que parece retomar el proceso que se detuvo con las estructuras metálicas 1956–57, para llegar paulatinamente al *Penetrable,* uno de sus aportes más importantes. ¿Podría describirnos el proceso que lo lleva de esas primeras estructuras metálicas que después llamaría *pre-penetrables*, hasta llegar a los *penetrables* que conocemos en la actualidad?

JS Eso fue un proceso muy lento y que parte tal vez, eso me digo ahora, de la fascinación que sentía por lo que pasaba entre las láminas de plexiglás de mis

primeras estructuras cinéticas. Siempre quise meterme dentro de ellas. Más adelante, cuando empiezo a trabajar con las varillas metálicas sobre el fondo tramado, empecé a preguntarme qué pasaría si me metiera dentro de esa vibración. Si comenzaba a superponer las varillas en diversos niveles, como lo hice con el plexiglás veinte años atrás, quizás podría captar nuevos valores. Es lo que intenté en la Bienal de Venecia en 1966, aunque no era verdaderamente un penetrable. Tomé un ángulo y lo cubrí con varillas, tratando de envolver al espectador. Luego, durante los años 1966 y 1967, apareció progresivamente la idea del penetrable por la multiplicación de esas varillas, hasta que llegaron a cubrir todo el espacio y a convertirse en una obra autónoma [Fig. 38].

AJ Si intentáramos hacer una pequeña historia del *penetrable*, creo que el próximo paso tendríamos que ubicarlo en la exposición que Denise René le organiza en 1967, donde las varillas invaden gran parte del espacio, más allá incluso de lo que sucedía en Venecia. ¿Cierto?

JS En realidad se trató de dos exposiciones, una en la galería de la rivera izquierda del Sena, y otra en la galería de la rivera derecha. En la primera expuse mi

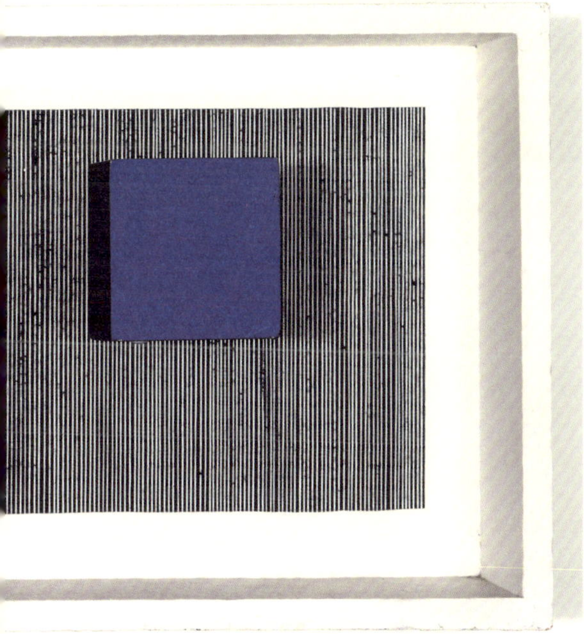

Fig. 37. *Vibration: Cube bleu,* 1962.

primer *penetrable*, aunque no excedía un metro de ancho. Era pequeño, pero las personas podían entrar y se divertían mucho, jugaban adentro. Era un penetrable metálico que iba de techo a piso, con varillas de alambre sin pintura, lo que les daba un color plateado muy bello.[71] Al entrar, como eran varillas metálicas, producían un sonido así. . . [Soto baja la cabeza y hace un gesto con las manos, tratando de describir un sonido envolvente, como el de lluvia].

AJ No deja de ser significativo, a mi entender, que la forma matriz de su primer penetrable sea una cruz negra y ancha, exactamente como la *Cruz negra*, 1915, de Kasimir Malevich. Es como si este primer penetrable nos dijera que al entrar en ese pequeño recinto de luz y sonido, penetrábamos a la vez en el ámbito plástico e histórico definido por Malevich, un ámbito que tiene también una evidente dimensión mística [Fig. 39]. ¿No sugeriría este hecho la posibilidad de una lectura bien particular del *penetrable*, en el sentido de que nos permite

71. Es interesante anotar esa calidad plata de las varillas metálicas. Es el mismo calificativo que Soto emplea para designar la luz de los impresionistas.

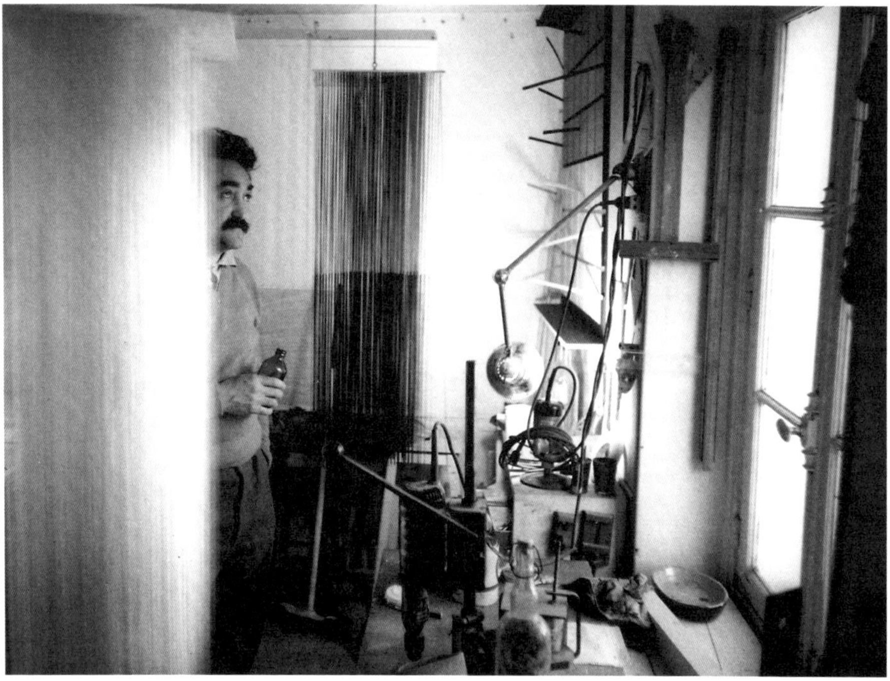

Fig. 38. Jesús Soto en su estudio en París en rue de Turenne, c. 1967.

pensarlo como un dispositivo doblemente redentor, a la vez histórico y, por decirlo de alguna manera, metafísico?

JS Nunca lo pensé de eso modo, aunque me parece una lectura sorprendentemente seductora. En todo caso, lo que buscaba era crear obras verdaderamente envolventes. Yo las llamaba así, "envolventes". Fue Jean Clay quien comenzó a llamarlas *penetrables*; quizás porque le decía que siempre había querido penetrar en ese mundo plástico de mis plexiglases. Y por eso intenté hacer en esa exposición un muro envolvente, una especie de medio óvalo en torno al primer *penetrable*. Recuerdo que el director de la Galería Marlborough vino a ver la exposición, y al ver las varillas que terminaban cerca de la vitrina, me dijo sorprendido: "Parece un sueño".[72]

72. El título que finalmente conservó este tipo de piezas ha inducido tradicionalmente su lectura como una obra penetrable, es decir, como una estructura que se deja penetrar desde afuera por el espectador. Las descripciones de Soto y los términos que empleaba al inicio la presentan como el producto activo de una "pintura" que, por el contrario, busca absorber a su espectador desde adentro. Este simple hecho la inscribe en una amplia familia de obras que, tradicionalmente, ha buscado justamente atraer a su espectador para hacerlo partícipe de lo que sucede en ella, tal y como el mismo Leon Battista Alberti lo describe en su *Tratado de la pintura*, de 1435.

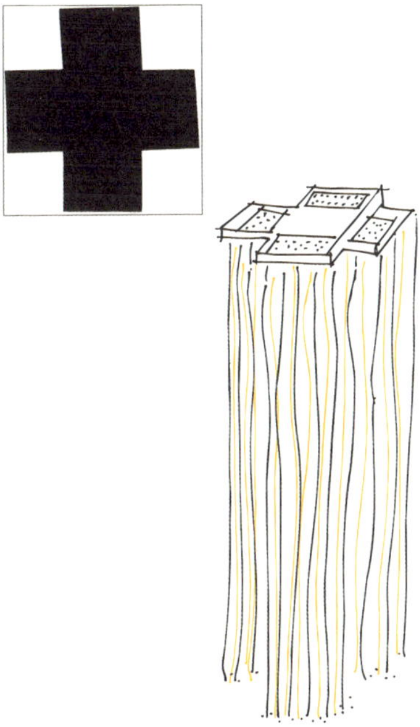

Fig. 39. Esquema de la *Cruz negra,* 1915 de Kasimir Malevich (arriba) y del primer *penetrable,* 1967 de Jesús Soto (abajo).

En la muestra de la rivera derecha, expuse varias piezas: algunos plexiglases y un volumen suspendido que era en realidad la maqueta del gran volumen que mostré en el pabellón venezolano de la Exposición Universal en Montreal. Su soporte era un cuadrado blanco donde se inscribía, en diagonal, una cruz más estrecha que la de Malevich. . . Le gustaba mucho a Villanueva. Esa cruz dibujaba una curva por sus lados. Allí hice además una obra envolvente que partía del techo y cubría uno de los muros de la galería.

Luego de este primer *penetrable,* hice otro de mayor autonomía en la exposición de la Fundación Maeght de Saint Paul de Vence, en 1968. Era un gran cubo virtual con los muros transparentes y rayados. Se entraba en él por una torre penetrable que ocupaba una de las esquinas y, al interior del cubo, se llegaba a un espacio circular formado por las varillas que cubrían las paredes y los ángulos del cubo. Ese círculo estaba descubierto, no tenía techo. Después hice otros *penetrables*, antes del que presenté en mi retrospectiva del Musée d'Art Moderne de la Ville de Paris, en 1969, pero no me acuerdo con precisión de sus características.

AJ ¿Y cuál era su intención? ¿Por qué pensó en una torre de entrada? ¿Por qué dejó el centro descubierto, como una cúpula sin techo?

JS Lo que intenté hacer –eso creo– fue unir la torre de la cruz, la de mi primer *penetrable,* con un espacio envolvente.

AJ ¿Y por qué no hacerlo de la misma altura?

JS Para indicar la entrada. . .

AJ ¿Se ha dado cuenta de que esa estructura es esencialmente la misma de una iglesia barroca, con su entrada claramente marcada y su cúpula interior abierta metafóricamente hacia el cielo?

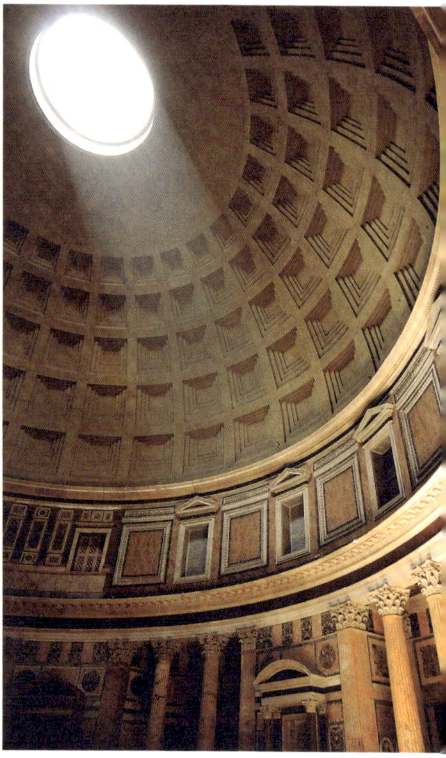
Fig. 40. *Panteón,* Roma.

JS No, no lo pensé de ese modo. Y sin embargo, me recuerda una experiencia que tuve en Roma, durante mi primera exposición en la Galería Marlborough, en los años sesenta. Recuerdo que un amigo mío, Sergio Tosi, me llevó al Panteón romano diciéndome: "Ven conmigo, quiero que conozcas un mundo cercano al tuyo". Cuando entré, me sorprendió ver el espacio de aquel edificio perfecto dominado por esa apertura del techo por donde bajaba un chorro de luz. . . y por donde podía verse el infinito. [Fig. 40]. Es muy parecido a uno de los *penetrables* que hice más tarde, en 1971 [Fig. 41],[73] y donde una serie de varillas penetran un plano abierto en su centro, como un chorro de luz que bajaba del techo, o como el chorro que parecía salir de *Espiral,* de 1955, que salía de la pintura perpendicular a los dos planos de plexiglás. . . . La luz, yo la concibo así, es una especie de intermedio entre la energía y la materia. La energía es lo absolutamente sublime, mientras la luz es ya una primera pérdida de velocidad. . . Es como si la energía fuera haciéndose cada vez menos sublime hasta llegar a la materia, su estado menos sublime. Lo que

73. Soto no afirma que hizo ese penetrable de 1971 pensando expresamente en el Panteón de Agripa, y yo tampoco se lo pregunté en ese momento. En todo caso, la experiencia con el Panteón romano es anterior, lo que permite suponer que efectivamente algo de ella afloró en el penetrable de 1971.

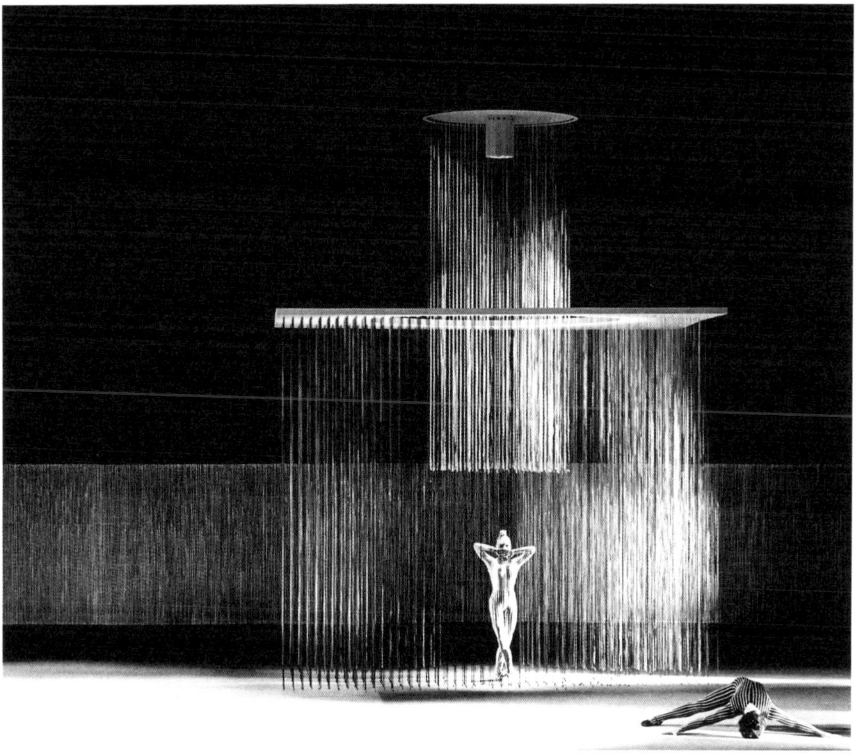

Fig. 41. Escenografía penetrable para *Violostries*, de Bernard Parmegiani. Ballet-théâtre contemporain de Paris, 1971.

no entiendo es por qué lo sublime llega a desublimarse convirtiéndose en materia. . . Incluso así, creo que algún día volverá a su estado originario, sublime. . .

AJ Luis Enrique Pérez Oramas me hizo observar que de los *penetrables* se ha hablado de dos maneras diferentes, o bien insistiendo en la posibilidad de materializar o hacer evidente eso que usted llama "la plenitud del espacio", esa gelatina de la que a menudo me ha hablado; o bien enfatizando su capacidad para desmaterializar ópticamente los cuerpos que penetran en ellos. Ahora, ¿desde su perspectiva, qué es lo más importante en el *penetrable,* esa posibilidad de hacer patente la densidad del espacio, o su capacidad desmaterializadora?

JS Lo importante es demostrar que el espacio es fluido y pleno, porque siempre se le ha considerado, como en el Renacimiento, un sitio donde pueden ponerse cosas, más que como un valor primigenio y universal. A menudo te he dicho que a mí no me importan los elementos, que ellos solo están allí para hacer evidentes las relaciones. Entonces lo que me interesa prioritariamente en el *penetrable* es la densidad del espacio. . . y la gente lo siente así, cuando entra en un *penetrable* siente que ese es otro espacio, y se ponen a jugar, a moverse. Lo discutí mucho con Yves Klein, porque en su pensamiento lo más importante era el vacío. Claro, él lo decía desde la perspectiva de la sabiduría oriental, mientras yo insistía en la densidad del espacio, en su plenitud.

AJ Los *penetrables* son concebidos como estructuras que podrían abarcar la totalidad del espacio. Ahora, ¿si tuviera que realizar un *penetrable* en un espacio irregular, lo haría cubriendo todo el espacio existente?

JS Por supuesto, el *penetrable* no es ni siquiera una obra, es una idea del espacio que puede materializarse en cualquier situación y a cualquier escala. . . De ser posible, podrías incluso cubrir el planeta entero. . . Eso no tiene importancia.

AJ Pese a ello, cuando tiene la oportunidad de hacerlo en un espacio abierto, recurre invariablemente al cubo [Fig. 42].

JS Porque es lo más evidente; si no, el público lo percibe como una escultura o un hecho dibujístico, acordándole a la forma del penetrable un valor estético que no tiene en mi trabajo.

NO HAY ETAPAS DEFINITIVAMENTE CONCLUIDAS

AJ Con la aparición del *penetrable* durante los años sesenta, podríamos decir que se inicia su plena madurez, una etapa durante la cual depura y desarrolla sus conceptos centrales. Sin embargo, dentro de ese periodo de madurez van a nacer las *ambivalencias*, su producción más reciente. Ellas surgen por un proceso de revisión característico de su pensamiento plástico.

JS Después de haber trabajado durante los años sesenta y setenta dentro de una relativa sobriedad en el uso del color, me intereso nuevamente por este elemento desde una perspectiva diferente a la que tuve en 1956–57. Durante esos años me interesé por las posibilidades combinatorias y vibratorias del color, independientemente o contra los conceptos tradicionales de armonía cromática. Mi propósito no era, y nunca lo ha sido, encontrar una bella armonía de colores,

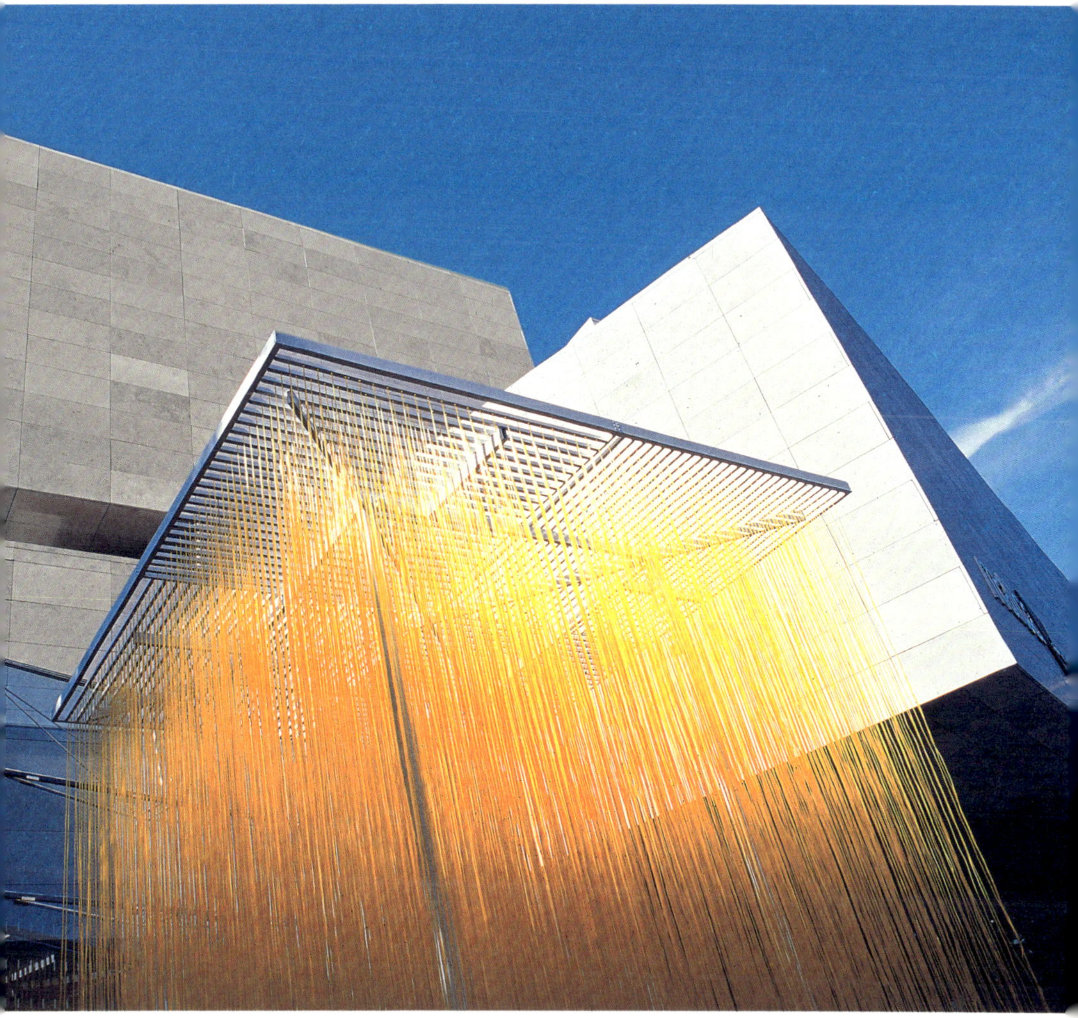

Fig. 42. *Penetrable,* 1992. Instalación temporal, Museo de Arte Latinoamericano de Buenos Aires (MALBA), 2003.

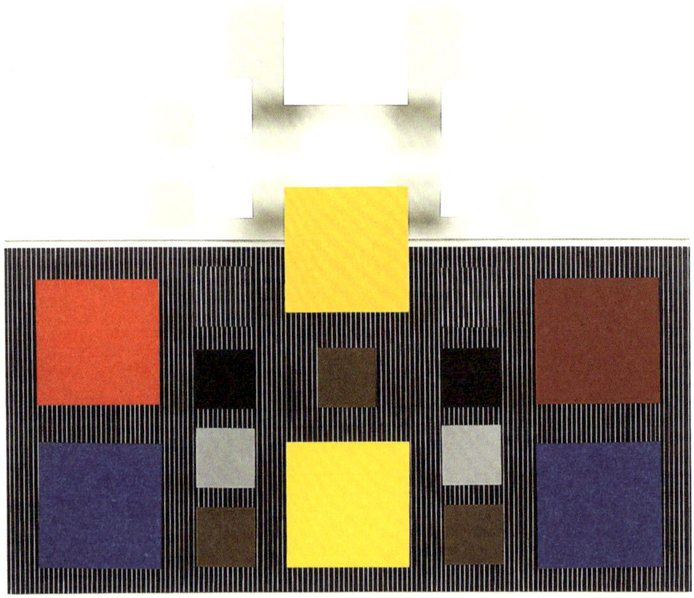

Fig. 43. *Planos ambivalentes,* 1981.

sino ponerlos a funcionar, a combinarse y mezclarse de una manera aleatoria, como si el color formase parte de un magma en medio del cual el hombre encuentra o crea las armonías que le interesan. En el fondo, quería dejarlos coexistir como sucede en la naturaleza, sin ningún concepto preestablecido de la armonía. Todos los colores superpuestos podían crear colores nuevos. Eso fue lo que hice por ejemplo en *Armonía transformable*, de 1956. A finales de los setenta retomo esa preocupación por el color. Jamás he tenido miedo de retomar problemas que puedan mejorarse o que no concluí, ya sea porque me dediqué a inquietudes de otra naturaleza y no pude desarrollarlos, o bien porque no tuve el dominio técnico y conceptual necesario para hacerlos avanzar.

Eso se debe a mi concepción del arte como un conjunto de interrogantes que deben ser resueltas por el artista, problemas que le plantea su tiempo, y no porque al artista le de la gana de hacerlo. La historia del arte lo lleva a uno hacia ese camino, y uno se hace creador en la medida en que logre encontrarles soluciones a esas interrogantes. Los artistas, en general, se preocupan por hacer algo personal, original, mientras yo siempre he pensado que se trata por el contrario de asumir la historia y de hacerla avanzar un poquito, dar un paso suplementario dentro de las problemáticas que ella misma nos plantea.

Las *ambivalencias* son la solución que encontré a un cierto número de planteamientos que se encontraban más o menos implícitos en los grandes pintores occidentales desde finales del siglo XIX, pero que no habían sido desarrollados. A consecuencia de los *fauves*, de individuos como Matisse, Léger, Delaunay, los constructivistas rusos y en general los que intentaron utilizar el color independientemente de la forma y de contenidos extrapictóricos, se manifiesta el poder y la ambigüedad del color, capaz de generar la ilusión de un espacio ópticamente variable, porque algunas manchas parecían avanzar mientras otras parecían retroceder. Más tarde le tocó a los suizos, y a algunos alemanes como Josef Albers, plantear la independencia del color, sin resolver conscientemente lo que he llamado "la ambivalencia espacial del color". Yo sentí entonces que el color estaba necesitando, reclamando, una solución espacio-temporal que bien podía encontrar un lugar dentro de la ambigüedad espacial que a mí me interesaba hacer evidente.

Entonces intenté introducir el color ya no en su estado vibratorio, como lo hice en los años cincuenta, sino el plano de color flotando sobre la superficie del cuadro, para que ellos mismos establecieran una relación cromodinámica. El resultado es una evidente ambigüedad del color en el espacio. Si colocas a un niño ante esas obras, él podrá ver colores que avanzan mientras otros parecen retroceder. Además, esa situación es variable y reversible [Fig. 43]. Ahora, cuando este planteamiento de la ambivalencia cromática en el espacio no me satisfaga ya, me ocuparé de asuntos distintos. Nunca será una ruptura, una negación de los problemas planteados con anterioridad. Para mí no hay etapas definitivamente concluidas y me siento en la total libertad de retomarlas cuando sienta la necesidad de hacerlo.

AJ Sin embargo, hay una diferencia fundamental entre el hecho de retomar problemáticas que no fueron suficientemente desarrolladas y hacerlas avanzar, o encontrar una solución plástica nueva, y lo que siento en algunas piezas recientes, por ejemplo en los *leños* que está rehaciendo ahora [Fig. 44]. ¿Le parece que ellos representan un avance? ¿No indicarían por el contrario la aparición de una posición diferente ante la historia?, ¿no introducirían una cierta intemporalidad de los problemas artísticos?

JS Bueno, lo que pasa es que los hago para los amigos. . . Tengo muchos amigos que se sienten frustrados por no tener una de estas piezas y cuando ellos me consiguen una madera yo les hago un *leño*. . . Es una cuestión de afecto hacia los amigos. . .

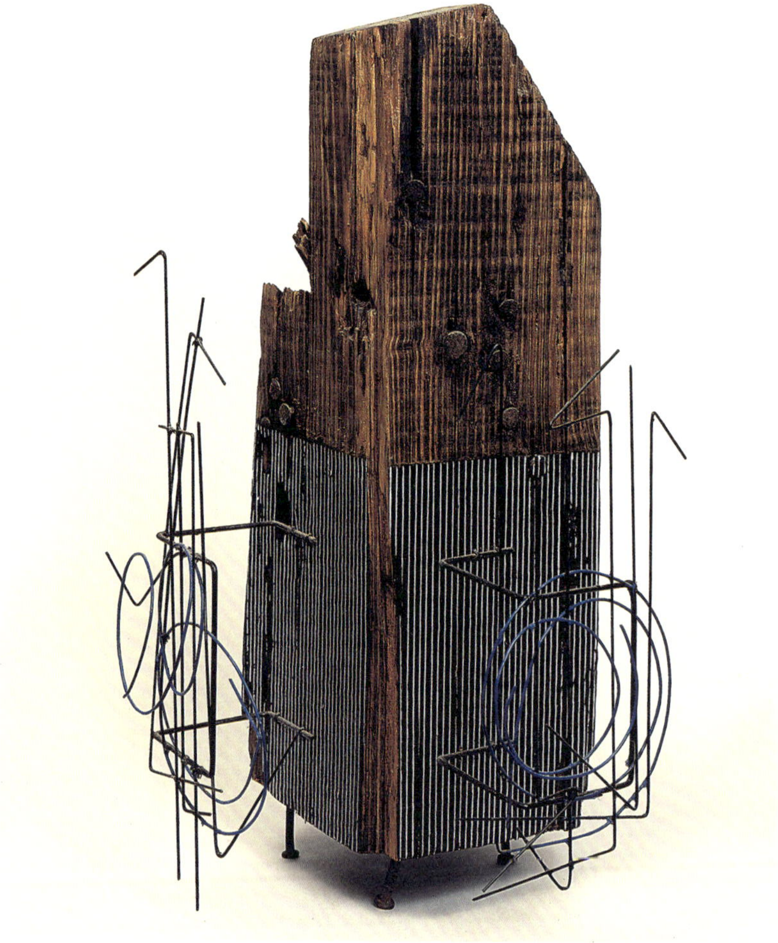

Fig. 44. *Leño,* 2002.

AJ ¿Las considera verdaderas creaciones o un hecho en cierta forma anacrónico?

JS No. Son obras trabajadas como cualquier pieza, y firmadas, solo que recogen, lo que es normal, los aportes de todas las experiencias que he tenido después. No pienso que sean anacrónicas, no creo que se pueda decir eso. . . El arte es un fenómeno intemporal, lo que pasa es que data, pone fechas que le permiten a la historia situarse de acuerdo a periodos, pero la idea impresionista de atomizar la luz sigue siendo válida.

AJ En cierta forma, usted sugiere que la solución plástica encontrada por el artista es fechable y puede ser materia de estudio para los historiadores, mientras los problemas abordados son intemporales.

JS Sí, esos problemas siguen siendo válidos.

AJ ¿Tiene actualmente alguna intuición de lo que podría hacer en el futuro?

JS No sé, no lo sé porque jamás me he planteado lo que voy a hacer mañana. Mi cabeza está llena de muchas posibilidades, lo que es lógico cuando no estás reconstruyendo o estetizando a partir de valores establecidos. Siento que uno tiene un número infinito de ventanas, eternas ventanas, entre las cuales debes escoger por dónde lanzarte. Nunca lo hago preguntándome qué voy a inventar mañana. No veo el arte como una invención gratuita, sino como el desarrollo intelectual del hombre en la historia. No he pasado noches en blanco antes de saber lo que iba a hacer el día siguiente, afortunadamente esos dramas no existen para mí. Si en un momento dado veo la posibilidad de avanzar en un determinado sentido, lo hago, pero nunca me planteo lo que tengo que hacer y, además, no siento ninguna obligación de hacer nada mañana.

ABOUT THE AUTHOR / SOBRE EL AUTOR

Ariel Jiménez is a historian and curator of modern and contemporary art and is Chief Curator of the Colección Patricia Phelps de Cisneros (CPPC). His previous experience includes serving as Director and Chief Curator of the Museo de Arte Moderno Jesús Soto (Ciudad Bolívar), as Director of the Sala Mendoza in Caracas, and as Director of the Department of Education and Audiovisual Media at the Museo de Arte Contemporáneo (Museum of Contemporary Art) in Caracas, Venezuela. He studied art history and archeology at the Sorbonne in Paris, and has curated numerous exhibitions and lectured in both public and private institutions throughout the Americas and Europe. He has published extensively about Venezuelan and Latin American art including: *La primacía del color* (Caracas: Monte Ávila Editores, 1992); *He vivido por los ojos. Correspondencia Alejandro Otero/Alfredo Boulton 1946–1974* (Caracas: Fundación Alberto Vollmer, Inc., and Fundación Museo Alejandro Otero, 2001); *Conversaciones con Jesús Soto* (Caracas: Fundación Cisneros, 2001); *Soto* (Caracas: Fundación Jesús Soto and Fundación Banco de Venezuela, 2007), *Alfredo Boulton and his Contemporaries: Critical Dialogues in Venezuelan Art 1912–1974* (New York: The Museum of Modern Art, 2008) and *Carlos Cruz-Diez in conversation with /en conversación con Ariel Jiménez* (New York: Fundación Cisneros, 2010).

Ariel Jiménez es historiador del arte y curador de arte moderno y contemporáneo. Actualmente se desempeña como el curador jefe de la Colección Patricia Phelps de Cisneros (CPPC). Ha sido director y curador en jefe del Museo de Arte Moderno Jesús Soto (Ciudad Bolívar), director general de la Sala Mendoza, en Caracas y director del Departamento de Educación y Medios Audiovisuales del Museo de Arte Contemporáneo de Caracas. Estudió Historia del Arte y Arqueología en la Université Paris-Sorbonne y ha curado numerosas exposiciones y dado conferencias en instituciones públicas y privadas a lo largo del continente americano y Europa. Entre sus publicaciones sobre arte venezolano y latinamericano destacan: *La primacía del color* (Caracas: Monte Ávila Editores, 1992); *He vivido por los ojos. Correspondencia Alejandro Otero / Alfredo Boulton 1946–1974* (Caracas: Fundación Alberto Vollmer, Inc., y Fundación Museo Alejandro Otero, 2001); *Conversaciones con Jesús Soto* (Caracas: Fundación Cisneros, 2001); *Soto* (Caracas: Fundación Jesús Soto y Fundación Banco de Venezuela, 2001); *Alfredo Boulton and his Contemporaries: Critical Dialogues in Venezuelan Art 1912–1974* (Nueva York: The Museum of Modern Art, 2008) y *Carlos Cruz-Diez in conversation with / en conversación con Ariel Jiménez* (Nueva York: Fundación Cisneros, 2010).

IMAGE CAPTIONS / FICHAS TÉCNICAS

Cover [Portada]: *Penetrable*, 1990. Temporary installation at [Instalación temporal en el] Museum of Fine Arts Houston, 2005. Colección Patricia Phelps de Cisneros

Title page [Portadilla]: Detail / Detalle: *Desplazamiento de un elemento luminoso* [*Displacement of a Luminous Element*], 1954. Colección Patricia Phelps de Cisneros

Contents page [Índice]:
Jesús Soto in his apartment in Paris [en su apartamento de París], 1997
© Ariel Jiménez

Introduction:
Patricia Phelps de Cisneros with [con] Jesús Soto at launch of [en el lanzamiento de] *Conversaciones con Jesús Soto*, February 6, 2002, in [el 6 de febrero de 2002 en] Caracas.

First [primera] (2001) and second [segunda] (2005) editions of [ediciones de] *Conversaciones con Jesús Soto.*

Fig. 1:
Bridge over the Orinoco River [Puente sobre el río Orinoco], Ciudad Bolívar, Venezuela
© Carlos Germán Rojas

Fig. 2:
Jesús Soto as a student in Caracas [Jesús Soto durante sus estudios en Caracas] c. 1943
Courtesy [Cortesía] Hélène Soto

Fig. 3:
Sin título [Untitled], 1948
Oil on board [Óleo sobre madera aglomerada]
84.8 × 71.1 cm ($33\frac{3}{8}$ × 28 inches)
Colección Patricia Phelps de Cisneros

Fig. 4:
Sin título (paisaje) [*Untitled (Landscape)*], 1949
Oil on canvas [Óleo sobre tela]
55 × 48 cm ($21\frac{5}{8}$ × $18\frac{7}{8}$ inches)
Colección Patricia Phelps de Cisneros

Fig. 5:
Jesús Soto playing guitar with his uncle Pedro Soto [tocando guitarra con su tío Pedro Soto], Ciudad Bolívar, 1961
Courtesy [Cortesía] Hélène Soto

Fig. 6:
Kazimir Malevich
Suprematist Composition: White on White [*Composición suprematista: blanco sobre blanco*], 1918
Oil on canvas [Óleo sobre tela]
79.4 × 79.4 cm ($31\frac{1}{4}$ × $31\frac{1}{4}$ inches)
The Museum of Modern Art, New York, Acquisition confirmed in 1999 by agreement with the Estate of Kazimir Malevich and made possible with funds from the Mrs. John Hay Whitney Bequest (by exchange).
Digital Image © The Museum of Modern Art / Licensed by Scala / Art Resource, NY

Fig. 7:
Piet Mondrian
Composition No. II, with Yellow and Blue [*Composición N° II, con amarillo y azul*], 1931
Oil on canvas [Óleo sobre tela]
50.8 × 50.8 cm (20 × 20 inches)
Colección Patricia Phelps de Cisneros
©2011 Mondrian / Holtzman Trust c / o HCR International Washington, DC

Fig. 8:
Composición dinámica [*Dynamic Composition*], 1950–51
Oil on canvas [Óleo sobre tela]
100 × 64 cm ($39\frac{3}{8}$ × $25\frac{3}{16}$ inches)
Fundación Museo de Arte Moderno Jesús Soto, Ciudad Bolívar

Fig. 9:
Repetición óptica N° 2 [*Optical Repetition No. 2*], 1951
Paint on wood [Pintura sobre madera]
189 × 130 × 6.3 cm ($74\frac{3}{8}$ × $51\frac{3}{16}$ × $2\frac{1}{2}$ inches)
Fundación Museo de Arte Moderno Jesús Soto, Ciudad Bolívar

Fig. 10:
Muro óptico [*Optical Wall*], 1951
Paint on wood [Pintura sobre madera]
120 × 370 × 5.10 cm ($47\frac{3}{16}$ × $145\frac{11}{16}$ × 2 inches)
Fundación Museo de Arte Moderno Jesús Soto, Ciudad Bolívar

Fig. 11:
Sin título (Progresión) [*Untitled (Progression)*], 1952
Paint on wood [Pintura sobre madera]
102.1 × 102.1 cm ($40\frac{3}{16}$ × $40\frac{3}{16}$ inches)
Fundación Museo de Arte Moderno Jesús Soto, Ciudad Bolívar

Fig. 12:
Rotación [*Rotation*], 1952
Paint on wood [Pintura sobre madera]
102.1 × 102.1 × 7 arriba × 3 abajo cm ($40\frac{3}{16}$ × $40\frac{3}{16}$ × $2\frac{13}{16}$ top × $1\frac{3}{16}$ bottom inches)
Centre national d'art et de culture Georges Pompidou

Fig. 13:
Sin título (*Maqueta para mural Universidad Central de Venezuela*) [*Untitled* (*Maquette for a Mural at the Universidad Central de Venezuela*)], 1952–53
Gouache on board [Gouache sobre madera aglomerada]
27.6 × 48.3 × 3.5 cm ($10\frac{7}{8}$ × 19 × $1\frac{3}{8}$ inches)
Colección Patricia Phelps de Cisneros

Fig. 14:
Estudio para una serie [*Study for a Series*], 1952–53
Paint on board [Pintura sobre madera aglomerada]
100 × 100 cm ($39\frac{3}{8}$ × $39\frac{3}{8}$ inches)
Fundación Museo de Arte Moderno Jesús Soto, Ciudad Bolívar

Fig. 15:
Pintura serial [*Serial Painting*], 1952–53
Paint on board [Pintura sobre madera aglomerada]
100 × 100 × 7 derecha × 3 izquierda ($39\frac{3}{8}$ × $39\frac{3}{8}$ × $2\frac{13}{16}$ right × $1\frac{3}{16}$ left inches)
Fundación Museo de Arte Moderno Jesús Soto, Ciudad Bolívar

Fig. 16:
Muro blanco [*White Wall*], 1952–53
Oil on paper on wood [Óleo sobre papel sobre madera]
215 × 325 × 5.5 cm ($84\frac{5}{8}$ × 128 × $2\frac{3}{16}$ inches)
Fundación Museo de Arte Moderno Jesús Soto, Ciudad Bolívar

Fig. 17:
Dos cuadrados en el espacio [*Two Squares in Space*], 1953
Paint on acrylic and wood [Pintura sobre acrílico y madera]
30 × 60 × 7.2 cm ($11\frac{13}{16}$ × $23\frac{5}{8}$ × $2\frac{13}{16}$ inches)
Fundación Museo de Arte Moderno Jesús Soto, Ciudad Bolívar

Fig. 18:
Desplazamiento de un cuadrado transparente [*Displacement of a Transparent Square*], 1953–54
Paint on wood [Pintura sobre madera]
100 × 100 cm (39 $\frac{3}{8}$ × 39 $\frac{3}{8}$ inches)
Colección particular [Private Collection]

Fig. 19:
Desplazamiento de un elemento luminoso [*Displacement of a Luminous Element*], 1954
Vinyl dots on acrylic, tempera on board and wood
[Puntos de vinilo sobre acrílico y témpera sobre tabla y madera]
50 × 80 × 3.3 cm ($19\frac{11}{16}$ × $31\frac{1}{2}$ × $1\frac{5}{16}$ inches)
Colección Patricia Phelps de Cisneros

Fig. 20:
Metamorfosis [*Metamorphosis*], 1954
Acrylic, paper, and paint on wood [Acrílico, papel y pintura sobre madera]
100 × 100 × 4 cm ($39\frac{3}{8}$ × $39\frac{3}{8}$ × $1\frac{5}{8}$ inches)
Fundación Museo de Arte Moderno Jesús Soto, Ciudad Bolívar

Fig. 21:
Puntos blancos sobre puntos negros [*White Dots on Black Dots*], 1954
Acrylic, paper, and enamel on wood [Acrílico, papel y esmalte sobre madera]
100 × 100 × 20 cm ($39\frac{3}{8}$ × $39\frac{3}{8}$ × $7\frac{15}{16}$ inches)
Paulina Villanueva, Caracas

Fig. 22:
La cajita de Villanueva [*Villanueva's Little Box*], 1955
Paint on acrylic [Pintura sobre acrílico]
30 × 30 × 15 cm ($11\frac{13}{16}$ × $11\frac{13}{16}$ × $5\frac{15}{16}$ inches)
Carlos Raúl Villanueva, Caracas

Fig. 23:
Espiral [*Spiral*], 1955
Paint on acrylic, metal, and wood [Pintura sobre acrílico, metal y madera]
50 × 50 × 30 cm ($19\frac{11}{16}$ × $19\frac{11}{16}$ × $11\frac{13}{16}$ inches)
Fundación Museo de Arte Moderno Jesús Soto, Ciudad Bolívar

Fig. 24:
Doble transparencia [*Double Transparency*], 1956
Paint on acrylic and wood [Pintura sobre acrílico y madera]
55 × 55 × 32 cm ($21\frac{5}{8}$ × $21\frac{5}{8}$ × $12\frac{5}{8}$ inches)
Colección Patricia Phelps de Cisneros

Fig. 25:
Armonía transformable [*Transformable Harmony*], 1956
Paint on acrylic, metal and board [Pintura sobre acrílico, metal y madera aglomerada]
100 × 40 × 100 cm ($39\frac{3}{8}$ × $15\frac{11}{16}$ × $39\frac{3}{8}$ inches)
Fundación Museo de Arte Moderno Jesús Soto, Ciudad Bolívar

Fig. 26:
Trapecio [*Trapezoid*], 1957
Paint on acrylic and wood [Pintura sobre acrílico y madera]
60 × 60 × 23.5 cm ($23\frac{5}{8}$ × $23\frac{5}{8}$ × $9\frac{5}{16}$ inches)
Fundación Museo de Arte Moderno Jesús Soto, Ciudad Bolívar

Fig. 27:
Pre-penetrable, 1957
Painted iron [Hierro pintado]
165.5 × 126 × 85 cm ($65\frac{3}{16}$ × $49\frac{5}{8}$ × $33\frac{7}{16}$ inches)
Colección Patricia Phelps de Cisneros

Fig. 28:
Vibración I [*Vibration I*], 1958
Paint on wire and plywood [Pintura sobre alambre y contraenchapado]
77 × 89.7 × 28 cm ($30\frac{5}{16}$ × $35\frac{5}{16}$ × 11 inches)
Colección Patricia Phelps de Cisneros

Fig. 29:
Vibración [*Vibration*], 1960
Oil and wire on wood [Óleo y alambre sobre madera]
99.7 × 99.7 × 2.5 cm ($39\frac{1}{4}$ × $39\frac{1}{4}$ × 1 inches)
The Museum of Modern Art, New York
Gift of Patricia Phelps de Cisneros in honor of Luis Enrique Pérez-Oramas

Fig. 30:
Tronco [*Trunk*], 1960
Paint on wood and wire [Pintura sobre madera y alambre]
41.3 × 25 × 14 cm ($16\frac{1}{4}$ × 9 $\frac{1}{2}$ × $5\frac{1}{2}$ inches)
Colección Patricia Phelps de Cisneros

Fig. 31:
Leño [*Log*], 1961
Wood, paint, iron, and wire [Madera, pintura, hierro y alambre]
75 × 21 × 28 cm ($29\frac{1}{2}$ × $8\frac{1}{4}$ × 11 inches)
Colección Patricia Phelps de Cisneros

Fig. 32:
Pablo Picasso
Nude woman [*Mujer desnuda*], 1910
Charcoal on paper [Carboncillo sobre papel]
48.3 × 31.4 cm (19 × $12\frac{3}{8}$ inches)
The Metropolitan Museum of Art, New York
Alfred Stieglitz Collection, 1949.
© The Metropolitan Museum of Art/Art Resource, NY

Fig. 33:
Vibración III [*Vibration III*], 1960–61
Paint, canvas and wire on board [Pintura, tela y alambre sobre madera aglomerada]
150.1 × 60.6 × 19 cm ($59\frac{1}{8}$ × $23\frac{7}{8}$ × $7\frac{1}{2}$ inches)
Colección Patricia Phelps de Cisneros

Fig. 34:
Sin título [*Untitled*], 1962
Paint, metal, and cloth on wood [Pintura, metal y tela sobre madera]
110.5 × 55.8 × 12.5 cm ($43\frac{1}{2}$ × 22 × $4\frac{15}{16}$ inches)
Fundación Museo de Arte Moderno Jesús Soto, Ciudad Bolívar

Fig. 35:
Mural, 1961
Mixed media on wood [Materiales diversos sobre madera]
278 × 492.5 × 62 cm ($109\frac{3}{8}$ × $193\frac{15}{16}$ × $24\frac{3}{8}$ inches)
Fundación Colección Museos Nacionales, Caracas

Fig. 36:
Hommage à Yves Klein [*Homage to Yves Klein*], 1961
Wire, metal sheet, and paint on wood [Alambre, lámina de metal y pintura sobre madera aglomerada]
55 × 95.6 × 4 cm ($21\frac{5}{8}$ × $37\frac{5}{8}$ × $1\frac{9}{16}$ inches)
Colección Patricia Phelps de Cisneros

Fig. 37:
Vibration: Cube bleu [*Vibration: Blue Cube / Vibración: Cubo azul*], 1962
Paint on wood and board [Pintura sobre madera y madera aglomerada]
61 × 25 × 10 cm (24 × $9\frac{7}{8}$ × $3\frac{15}{16}$ inches)
Colección Patricia Phelps de Cisneros

Fig. 38:
Jesús Soto in his Paris studio on rue de Turenne [Jesús Soto en su taller en París en rue de Turenne], c. 1967
Courtesy [Cortesía] Hélène Soto
© André Morain

Fig. 39:
Sketch of [Esquema de] Kazimir Malevich's *Black Cross* [*Cruz negra* de Kasimir Malevich], 1915, and Jesús Soto's first *Penetrable* [y el primer *penetrable* de Jesús Soto], 1967.

Fig. 40:
Pantheon, Rome [Panteón, Roma]
© Tobias Machhaus

Fig. 41:
Escenografía penetrable para *Violostries* (de Bernard Parmegiani) [Penetrable set design for *Violostries* (by Bernard Parmegiani)]
Ballet-théâtre contemporain de Paris, 1971

Fig. 42:
Penetrable, 1990, [Temporary installation / Instalación temporal], Museo de Arte Latinoamericano de Buenos Aires (MALBA), 2003
Painted iron, aluminum, and plastic tubing [Hierro pintado, aluminio y mangueras plásticas]
508 × 508 × 508 cm (200 × 200 × 200 inches)
Colección Patricia Phelps de Cisneros

Fig. 43:
Planos ambivalentes [*Ambivalent Planes*], 1981
Paint on metal and wood [Pintura sobre metal y madera]
100 × 100 × 17 cm (39⅜ × 39⅜ × 6 11/16 inches)
Colección particular [Private Collection]

Fig. 44:
Leño [*Log*], 2002
Paint and metal on wood [Pintura y metal sobre madera]
37.3 × 19.5 × 21 cm (14 11/16 × 7 11/16 × 8 5/16 inches)
Colección particular [Private Collection]

Photography credits / Créditos de fotografía
Rodrigo Benavides, Ariel Jiménez, Tobias Machhaus, André Morain, Mark Morosse, Carlos Germán Rojas, Sucesión Jesús Soto, Sarah Wells

Titles in / Títulos en Conversaciones / Conversations

Carlos Cruz-Diez
in conversation with / en conversación con
Ariel Jiménez ISBN 978-0-9823544-2-1

Tomás Maldonado
in conversation with / en conversación con
María Amalia García ISBN 978-0-9823544-3-8

Jac Leirner
in conversation with / en conversación con
Adele Nelson ISBN-978-0-9823544-4-5

Jesús Soto
in conversation with / en conversación con
Ariel Jiménez ISBN-978-0-9823544-6-9

Forthcoming titles / Próximos títulos

Tania Bruguera
in conversation with / en conversación con
Claire Bishop

Waltercio Caldas
in conversation with / en conversación con
Ariel Jiménez

Luis Camnitzer
in conversation with / en conversación con
Alexander Alberro

Ferreira Gullar
in conversation with / en conversación con
Ariel Jiménez

Alfredo Jaar
in conversation with / en conversación con
Luis Pérez-Oramas

Gyula Kosice
in conversation with / en conversación con
Gabriel Pérez-Barreiro

Julio le Parc
in conversation with / en conversación con
Alexander Alberro

Liliana Porter
in conversation with / en conversación con
Inés Katzenstein

Antonieta Sosa
in conversation with / en conversación con
Ariel Jiménez

FUNDACIÓN CISNEROS
COLECCIÓN PATRICIA PHELPS DE CISNEROS